RULEBREAKERS & GHOST RUNNERS

The British women who asserted their right to run

Katie Holmes

BLOOMSBURY SPORT
LONDON • OXFORD • NEW YORK • NEW DELHI • SYDNEY

BLOOMSBURY SPORT
Bloomsbury Publishing Plc
50 Bedford Square, London, WC1B 3DP, UK
Bloomsbury Publishing Ireland Limited,
29 Earlsfort Terrace, Dublin 2, D02 AY28, Ireland

First published in Great Britain 2026

For legal purposes the Acknowledgements on p. 273 constitute
an extension of this copyright page

A catalogue record for this book is available from the British Library

Library of Congress Cataloguing-in-Publication data has been applied for

ISBN: HB: 978-1-3994-2535-3; ePDF: 978-1-3994-2538-4; eBook 978-1-3994-2533-9

2 4 6 8 10 9 7 5 3 1

Typeset in Bembo Std by Lumina Datamatics Ltd
Printed and bound in Great Britain by Clays Ltd, Elcograf S.p.A

MIX
Paper | Supporting responsible forestry
FSC® C018072

Bloomsbury Publishing Plc makes every effort to ensure that the papers used in the manufacture of our books are natural, recyclable products made from wood grown in well-managed forests. Our manufacturing processes conform to the environmental regulations of the country of origin.

To find out more about our authors and books visit www.bloomsbury.com
and sign up for our newsletters

For product safety related questions contact productsafety@bloomsbury.com

For Mum and Dad

CONTENTS

INTRODUCTION

On Saturday 12 April, 1975, 27-year-old Margaret Ashcroft stood at the start of the Chris Vose 10-mile road race in Warrington, in Northwest England. Wearing her running vest, shorts and trainers, Margaret was there to race. Today, over 50 years later, tens of thousands of women stand at the start of road races in the UK each year. We think nothing of it. We have every right to be there and the idea that someone might stop us from running just because we are women seems far-fetched, ridiculous, unimaginable.

Yet for Margaret being at the start line was an act of defiance. In April 1975, women in the UK were not allowed to race further than four miles on the road, cross country or anywhere. Margaret was a rulebreaker and a 'ghost runner' – a lone woman running without numbers in a men's race.

Running unofficially, Margaret was relying on the race officials turning a blind eye to her presence. They might try to stop her or threaten to report her to the governing body of women's athletics. Her participation could have consequences. The Women's Amateur Athletic Association (WAAA) did not approve of women jumping into races in this way and racing against men was strictly forbidden. The threat of suspension was very real.

One thing Margaret was confident of was that she would finish. A strong cross-country runner, she had won the Cheshire championships. Used to doing 10-mile training runs on a Sunday, Margaret was frustrated that women couldn't race the longer distances. She was ambitious, aiming for under an hour at the Chris Vose 10 – a time still fast enough for a win at 10-mile races today, but fell short of her goal, finishing instead in 62:08, in 120th place, ahead of 42 men.

These details were recorded in a race report in the *Guardian*, which described Margaret as 'an interloper' in the male domain of 10-mile road racing but one of 'a band of pioneers'.[1] An opinion piece in the *Manchester Evening News* was rather more hostile.[2] 'No suffragettes in sport, please', wrote Joe Lancaster, a former marathon runner and the paper's athletics correspondent. He asserted that women's desire to run longer distances was nothing more than 'the latest whim among female athletes' and predicted that once women were running 10 miles they would want to run further. It was the prospect of women finishing 'gruelling' long-distance races in a state of exhaustion that Lancaster found particularly distasteful. If they did so, women would be undermining their femininity: 'While I admit that women can run marathons, they certainly look far more graceful hurdling, high jumping and sprinting.'

What did the woman at the centre of the story have to say about it all? You may well ask. The newspaper articles tell us nothing about what Margaret thought beyond reporting that she said, 'I don't see why women can't race 10 miles,' and that she intended to look for another 10-mile race to run. Sports journalism was an overwhelmingly male preserve. Men's interpretations of what motivated women took up the space. What women themselves thought was of secondary importance.

I, however, have reason to be thankful to the sports reporter at the *Guardian* who picked up on this story. Were it not for his article, I wouldn't have known about Margaret's participation in the race. When I interviewed Margaret in 2024, she was 77 and it was 49 years since she had run the Chris Vose 10. Unsurprisingly, she remembered little about the race, pointing out, 'I never thought anybody would ever ask me about it.'

I took up running in February 2011, aged 47, not out of any burning desire to become a runner but because I had promised to be part of a charity relay team in the Robin Hood Marathon in Nottingham. My older sister Judith had been running for two years by then, but I was mystified by her growing enthusiasm for running. Whenever I encountered runners pounding the pavements, I thought they had an obsessed, driven look. They certainly didn't seem to be enjoying themselves. Having made my promise to the charity, I bought some running shoes, joined a club and ran a five-mile leg of the marathon that September. It took a bit longer than that for the running bug to bite but eventually, of course, it did.

A turning point came when I started attending my local parkrun in 2012. After a few weeks, I realised that people who were running past me were putting in more effort than I was. I made up my mind to try to keep up with them. That day it dawned on me that I could indeed run faster – that there was more than one pace I could run at. And from that moment grew a love of running, which has seen me race not only on the roads but also on the track and cross country – things I'd never done at school.

There are many things that I love about running – being part of a community, time outdoors, the sense of freedom and physical power – but most of all it is the myriad ways in which you can set yourself new challenges. They don't have to be performance driven or about achieving specific times in races. There are all sorts of goals, like running all the cross-country races in your club's leagues one season (not managed that), doing 12 half marathons in 12 months (done that) or doing 500 parkruns (might take another three years).

As I met other women runners, I realised that many of them, like me, only started running in their forties. I was inspired by the women runners in their fifties, sixties and seventies, who made me think that I could keep running for the rest of my life. In 2014, I created the RunYoung50 blog with the aim of interviewing women runners older than me to find out about their experiences and celebrate their achievements. Having turned 50, I was aware that I had reached an age where women are less valued by society and seem to become invisible. They are generally not expected to be physically active, and active older women rarely appear in the media. When they do, the narrative often focuses on them as exceptions to the rule and casts them as 'supergrans'. Exceptional stories can alienate us, as we may feel that we can never aspire to the same level of achievement. For me, 'ordinary' stories hold just as much value and we can learn just as much, if not more, from them.

One of the books I bought as a new runner was a second-hand copy of *The Complete Book of Running for Women* by Claire Kowalchik.[3] The final chapter included a timeline of women's running history and a brief account from Kathrine Switzer about the part she played. Not long afterwards, I listened to interviews with Kathrine and former British marathon record holder Joyce Smith on the *Marathon Talk* podcast. I read Kathrine's book *Marathon Woman* and Jacqueline Hansen's book *A Long Time Coming*, both of which chronicled the fight to get the women's marathon into the Olympic Games.

Kathrine's story is one of the most well known in the history of women's distance running and it was one of the first stories

I heard. In 1967, she was a 20-year-old journalism student at Syracuse University in New York who decided to try to run the Boston Marathon. She was not unprepared. She'd been training for months and had finished a 31-mile training run with her coach, who was going to run the race with her.[4]

She wasn't the first woman to try to enter the Boston Marathon either. Bobbi Gibb had run it the year before, after being refused an entry on the grounds that, 'Women are not physiologically able to run marathon distances.'[5] Kathrine, who entered as part of a university team, filled out the entry form with her initial rather than her first name, and her coach, Arnie Briggs, picked up the team's race packets. Unlike Bobbi the year before, Kathrine had official race numbers, which she wore pinned to the front and back of her sweatshirt.

Kathrine started the race with Briggs, another runner and her boyfriend, Tom Miller. The first few miles passed without incident until the journalists in the press truck caught wind of the fact that there was a woman in the race and began talking to and photographing Kathrine. This alerted race co-director Jock Semple who jumped out of the officials' bus, which was following the runners. Enraged, he ran up behind her and tried to rip the numbers from her sweatshirt. A sequence of photos shows Jock assaulting Kathrine and then being shoved off the course by Miller, a heavily built hammer thrower.

This violent and arresting scene still has the power to shock. It seems to tell us everything we need to know about the exclusion of women from long-distance racing: a man assaults a woman for daring to run in a men's race. It is, however, only one small event in a much larger story – a story which encompasses other races, other countries and other women who were willing to challenge the limits placed upon them.

The story of the development of women's long-distance running in the USA is well documented. Kathrine and two-time marathon world record holder Jacqueline Hansen have both written personal accounts of their campaigns for longer distances for women.[6] Amby Burfoot's *First Ladies of Running* profiles 22 'rebels, rule breakers and visionaries'.[7] More recently, the Starting Line 1928 oral history project has interviewed many of the American pioneers, presenting the interviews as podcast episodes.[8] The Theodore Corbitt Institute for Running History Research publishes lists of the best marathon performances by African American women.[9]

As I found out more about the pioneers of women's long-distance running in the USA, I began to wonder what had happened in the UK. Were British women breaking the rules and running in men's races as well? In *Marathon Woman*, Kathrine mentioned a Scottish woman, Dale Greig, who had run in a men's race in 1964. Who was this woman and why hadn't I heard of her? As I started to look for answers to my questions about British long-distance road-running pioneers, I realised that there were no podcasts or books telling their stories – what they did, how they felt, how long-distance running changed their lives – and nor were they the subject of academic research. As I discovered more about Dale, I felt indignant that this exceptional woman received so little recognition and became determined to find out more about her and share her story. When you read it, you will understand why.

This book is about unearthing the history of Dale and the other British rulebreakers, and weaving together a hidden story using threads of memory from decades ago. These pioneering women have become invisible because as unofficial participants in races their times were not usually recorded or reported. Occasionally, a race organiser would note a woman had taken part or there would be a mention from a local journalist but that was it.

It has been quite a journey for me, as along the way I've gone from being someone writing a blog to becoming a sports historian and a published writer. I've collected and read hundreds of athletics and running magazines; I've catalogued information; I've pored over newspapers and magazines in the British Library, online and in archives in Birmingham, Edinburgh, Paisley and

Leicester; I've tracked people down, met and interviewed dozens of runners, friends of runners and magazine editors; and I've been to conferences, presented at conferences and written articles for magazines. Along the way, I've been helped by dozens of people and some of them have become friends. It has been an enriching experience.

My task was made harder by the gaps in the archives when it comes to women's athletics history. The women and men, all volunteers, who ran the women's clubs and governing bodies probably didn't give much thought to their place in the history of athletics, and therefore didn't ensure that their organisations' activities were documented and preserved. And, traditionally in athletics, it has been men who have kept the performance statistics and records, effectively acting as the gatekeepers who decide what is important and what is not. The Cadbury Research Library at the University of Birmingham houses one of the most extensive collections of athletics literature in the UK, including 27 collections of papers connected with individual athletes, journalists or commentators. All of them are men. Not one woman's papers were deemed worthy of collecting for posterity and the records of the WAAA itself are frustratingly incomplete.

During her PhD research in 1993, when Lynne Robinson (now Duval) visited the offices of Marea Hartman, who had been a driving force in athletics domestically and internationally for over 30 years, it was stuffed to the rafters with folders of minutes, reports, correspondence and programmes from a lifetime of involvement in athletics. It seems that when Marea died just over a year later, no-one stepped forward to save her papers or suggested that they should go to an archive. However, as Lynne notes, it would be wrong to assume that, 'Just because women's experiences have not been recorded there is no story to be discovered.'[10]

These gaps in the official records make gathering the testimony of the women themselves particularly important. The more I looked and the more people I asked, the more rulebreaking

I found. Even so, I've been surprised in the course of my research just how common ghost running was. Nearly every woman I interviewed had one or more stories to tell me, although reliance on memory means that not every event has accurate dates or complete details, and where other sources were available I've drawn on them to fill in the blanks.

There is more to find out about the experiences of women of colour and women with disabilities. I have not covered them to the extent that I would like. And there are more stories to discover and share about the 1940s and 1950s. I still have so many questions and maybe you will have your own as you read these stories.

The women you will meet in this book used their bodies to challenge restrictive rules. Proving they were strong, they asserted their right to be outdoors, to claim some of the public space for themselves. They challenged notions of how women should look, dress and behave, and claimed the right to do things for themselves, rather than always in the service of others.

Many of the women themselves would express it more simply. Like Margaret, they sensed they were better at running over longer distances and they wanted the chance to race them. They wanted the freedom to run in the same way as men did and the opportunity to fulfil their potential as long-distance runners.

We begin with a story of women racing more than 200 years ago, then dive into the beginnings of organised women's athletics in the UK. We go on to meet some of the remarkable, courageous, fearless women rulebreakers. There is Violet Piercy, an extraordinary woman, ahead of her time, who used the media to publicise her road-running exploits in the 1920s and 1930s. Then there is Dale Greig, who undertook cross-country races barefoot over frozen ground and ran with the men in the 1964 Isle of Wight Marathon, two years before Bobbi Gibb ran Boston. And Bridget Cushen, who came to athletics after walking 50 miles overnight on the roads from London to Brighton. There are women who began running as adults thanks to the jogging and fun run craze of the 1970s and Leslie Watson, 'Queen of the

Roads', who ran more marathons than anyone else in the country in the 1980s. Many of the women who ran in the first official long-distance road races in 1975 were rulebreakers too.

These women, acting together and alone, argued with race organisers, got themselves into the papers, stood their ground and broke rules in all sorts of men's road races, including 10-milers, marathons and ultramarathons, as well as cross-country and fell races.

There isn't one heroine in this story. Rather it tells us that we can all play a part in improving sport and making it more equal for women and men. This is as much a story of women using their voices and the power of their bodies as it is about running; of experiencing liberation and empowerment through sport; of providing a role model for others to follow.

We are all running in their footsteps.

1
THE STARTING LINE

'There are many sports which women can and should take part in ... The trouble seems to be that women are too ambitious and anxious to beat men at their own game.'
– Sir William Arbuthnot Lane[1]

One afternoon in October 1733, four young women stood outside the King's Arms on London's Pall Mall. They were there to run in a best-of-three competition from the King's Arms to the Gloucester Tavern in St James's Street and back, a distance of about two and a half miles. The best-of-three format required the runners to compete in up to three heats. In each heat runners who failed to reach a specified point in the course by the time the winner finished would be disqualified. If the same woman won the first two heats, she would be declared the winner. If a different runner won the second heat, there would be a third heat to determine the overall winner. The women had removed as many layers of clothing as they could to make running easier. If they were racing on a common, they might have stripped to their shifts and petticoats, but in a busy city street they chose to remain modestly dressed for fear of unwanted criticism.[2]

The races had been advertised as an entertainment and a good-tempered crowd had gathered, many of them merry from drinking ale and gin at the tavern. Some, no doubt, had placed bets. However, the women weren't running to win a share of the wagers. The prize was a fine linen smock – a valuable item of a quality they could not afford to buy themselves. Hannah Williams, a Hungerford butcher's servant, was the favourite as she had won a best-of-three competition before.

When the sign to start was given, the women set off along Pall Mall, which was crowded with spectators, with more people cheering and shouting from the windows and balconies of every one of the smart houses that lined the street. By the time they reached the turnaround point, Hannah and another, unnamed, woman had a big lead. Hannah reached the King's Arms first with the other runner close behind. The two other competitors were so far back that they were eliminated.

Hannah and her opponent had half an hour to rest, have a drink and have their legs massaged. In the second heat, Hannah was once again victorious, meaning a third heat wasn't required. The two women had run five miles. If Hannah's opponent had won, they would have had to run again to establish the best-of-three winner, covering a distance of seven and half miles.

Hannah was duly presented with the smock to much applause from the increasingly inebriated crowd at the King's Arms, but the losers did not go away empty-handed. The other prizes were a cap, a pair of fine woollen decorated stockings and laced shoes.

Nearly 300 years after this event took place, we know Hannah's name thanks to contemporary newspaper reports and a letter that a well-to-do spectator wrote to a friend. The names of the other women are lost to time and Hannah's name might have been lost to us too were it not for historian (and Olympic 100-metres medalist) Peter Radford, whose extensive research has revealed that Hannah and her rivals were not a novelty. Hundreds of women's races took place in the 18th and into the early 19th century across England, Scotland, Ireland and Wales.[3] The challenging best-of-three format was popular, with women racing over both shorter and longer distances than in the Pall Mall race. Smock racing gave women the chance to demonstrate their athleticism, perform in front of crowds and win valuable prizes. It subverted social conventions, liberating women and, if only temporarily, allowing them to run free. Girls and women of all ages, both unmarried and married, raced. Among them were Black women and Roma women.

Although smock races had largely fallen out of favour by the late 18th century, girls' and women's races continued to form a part of local carnivals and celebrations, and my quick search of the online British Newspaper Archive revealed that 'ladies foot races', usually sprints, were taking place in the UK and Ireland well into the 20th century, for prizes such as 'a gown and tea', money, a silver watch and opera glasses. Women never stopped running; history just forgot about them.

Nearly 200 years after Hannah's victory at Pall Mall, at midday on Saturday 12 February, 1927, dozens of women and men gathered on the concourse of St Pancras Station in London. They were travelling to Luton on the 1.30 p.m. train where the first English women's cross-country championship was due to be held. The event, organised by the recently established Women's

Amateur Athletic Association (WAAA), would take place over fields in the rolling grounds of the Luton Hoo estate, owned by Lady Ludlow. Entrance was by ticket only.[4]

After getting changed in an outbuilding, the 81 runners gathered for the start, which must have been quite late in the afternoon. A photograph in the *Daily Express*, with the caption 'The Amazons who began the race', shows the women standing several rows deep, expectant and enthusiastic, with a few bowler-hatted men behind them. The women wear white tunics which cover their hips, some with a sash belt, black shorts and white ankle socks. Their club badges are sewn on to the tunics and their race numbers are pinned on. Despite the cold, most of the women are wearing short sleeves, but a few wear berets or hats and gloves.

The two-and-a-half-mile course was going to be tough. Some of it was over ploughed fields and the runners would have to climb over fences. The frozen ground was hard and slippery, making falling or twisting an ankle a real risk, but most of the women had raced over similar terrain before, either in club runs or at county championships.

It was an exciting, competitive race with the first four women finishing within two seconds of each other. The winner, in 15 minutes 25 seconds, was 32-year-old Anne Williams from Littlehampton AC, who was just a yard ahead of fellow club member Lillian Styles. Gladys Lane and Violet Hinton of Middlesex Ladies AC finished third and fourth, and their club was awarded the team shield.

Only two of the 81 starters failed to finish, which was a low drop-out rate given the conditions. 'I'll finish if I have to walk,' one determined woman was reported as saying. One competitor withdrew with a foot injury and another stopped after the first lap of the two-lap course. At the finish two women from Ilford AC were so exhausted they lay down on the ground. Having missed the 1.30 p.m. train from St Pancras, they had arrived in Luton late and run straight from the station, making it to the start just in time. Determined to compete in the first 'national', they completed the event, against the advice of the race officials.

At a men's cross-country race, none of these facts would have been deemed out of the ordinary, contentious or newsworthy, but where women were concerned it was an entirely different matter. 'Women hurt in cross-country race' declared the *Westminster Gazette*, adding not one but three subheadings in capitals to make sure its readers got the point: 'Three attended by doctors – Great distress – 2½ mile course too great a strain'. In dramatic tones, the journalist stated that 'there were many casualties', several women collapsed and most of those who finished were 'greatly distressed'. Were the runners really distressed? Or were they just out of breath and tired, as might be expected of anyone who had raced two and a half miles over rough ground? According to the article, this was a matter for doctors to decide and the consensus was that cross-country running was much too strenuous a sport for women. The views of Sir William Arbuthnot Lane, a prominent surgeon and physician, were quoted at length. He considered it absurd for women to compete with men, because, he said, 'Women have a tremendous physical handicap, and consequently there are many sports which men can take part in which should be avoided by women.' He conceded that there were some sports women could play, but concluded, 'The trouble seems to be that women are too ambitious and anxious to beat men at their own game.'

What had happened to make women's racing so scandalous, so contested? What was the 'tremendous physical handicap' that women suffered from? And why were the opinions of medical men given so much weight?

The idea that women were inherently frail and unsuited to vigorous activity evolved in the Victorian period. As Britain became increasingly industrialised, with more of the population living in large towns and cities, the middle classes grew and so did the Victorian ideal of femininity: the middle-class woman's role was to dutifully support her husband in his endeavours, to give birth to and bring up his children, and to create a comfortable and well-ordered home.[5] With these ideals and values informing their thinking, the men who made up the medical establishment in the late 19th century developed a theory of biological determinism – the belief that women are defined by their reproductive system – which constrained women's access to sport and exercise in the Victorian period, and well into the 20th century.

Dr Henry Maudsley's views were typical of many eminent and influential Victorian physicians He contended that, 'Women are marked out by Nature for very different offices in life from those of men, and that the healthy performance of her … special functions renders it improbable that she will succeed, and unwise for her to persevere in running over the same course at the same pace as him.' Completely confident in the infallibility of his opinion, Maudsley stated that it was 'the plain statement of physiological fact.'[6] Women's lives, their very beings, were ruled by their gynaecological functions and woe betide the woman who attempted to enter the public spheres of higher education, work, politics or sport.

Doctors contended that all aspects of girls' and women's lives should be regulated in such a way as to ensure optimum fitness for motherhood. The menstrual cycle was poorly understood, and menstruation was medicalised and seen as an illness. Doctors generally thought that the loss of blood during menstruation weakened girls' and women's constitution and so during their periods, girls and women were thought to be physically and mentally weak. As a consequence, it was believed to be important to avoid both physical and intellectual exertion when menstruating. Some doctors asserted that 'overstimulation' of the female brain could lead to 'stunted growth, nervousness, headaches, hysteria and insanity' – an argument that was also used to keep women out of higher education.[7]

Another widely accepted idea – the theory of finite vitality – was that all human beings only had a certain amount of energy available to them across their whole lives. If too much energy was expended in youth, the individual would become weak and ill later in life. As girls and women bore the 'burden' of menstruation and childbirth, it was especially important for them to preserve their store of energy and not waste it on sports or on excessive studying. If they undertook vigorous physical activity or used their brains too much, they would not be optimally fit for motherhood and would produce weak, sickly children.

Victorian male doctors like Maudsley represented their theories of female health as objective fact, but in fact they were subjective, influenced by sexual ideology, class prejudice and racism. They believed a woman's role was to be a wife and mother, and her place was in the home, not out playing sport. These doctors were mostly preoccupied with the health of the upper- and middle-class women who made up their patients. They gave scant thought to working-class women, who were generally thought to have stronger constitutions and therefore the safeguards against over-strain did not need to be applied to them. There were eugenicist fears that if upper- and middle-class women did not safeguard their reproductive health, they would produce defective children and the 'British race', by which, of course, they meant the white British, would deteriorate. These children would lack the physical strength, good health and character needed to secure the future of the British Empire.

Although ideas about the benefits of exercise for girls and women began to gain ground from the 1860s, even the educationalists and female doctors, such as Dr Elizabeth Garrett Anderson, who promoted exercise still adhered to the view that its main purpose was to ensure health and fitness for motherhood. Doctors assumed the authority to say what it was suitable for women to do. Moderation was the watchword and endurance activities, such as running, were viewed as inherently harmful and to be discouraged. Victorian medical myths cast a very long shadow over the development of women's sports, and particularly of athletics for women.

Another development which limited women's participation in athletics was the codification of the sport, which began with the founding of an Amateur Athletic Club for men in 1865.[8] The creation of rules for many sports, including athletics, arose from the playing of games in Victorian British boys' public schools. The 'cult of athleticism' associated with sport was a fundamental expression of masculinity. The values and behaviours underpinning sport, such as fair play, courage, aggression and competitiveness, were defined as inherently male.[9] Inevitably, this meant there would always be less space for women in sport, women's sport would be seen as secondary and inferior to men's, and women who ventured into the field of 'men's sports' would be characterised as 'masculinised'. In the 1880s and 1890s amateurism became the cornerstone of a new model of sport, and athletics in particular, in an attempt to curb professionalism and commercialisation, which could taint sporting values.[10] Consequently, until athletics began to relax its rules in the 1980s, athletes could not make money from their sport and, most of the time, needed to cover the costs of competing themselves.

We should not be surprised that when the men's Amateur Athletic Association (AAA), the governing body for athletics in England, was established in 1880, no thought was given to women's involvement in the sport. While the popularity of athletics for men and boys grew rapidly, girls' and women's involvement in athletics remained peripheral until 1921, when an invitation from abroad provided the impetus for the creation of a national organisation for women's athletics.

By the 1920s, women's golf, hockey and lacrosse were already well established with their own independent associations, formed in 1893, 1895 and 1912 respectively, and women had been competing at the Wimbledon Lawn Tennis Championships since 1884. By contrast, women's athletics, as an organised sport, was still in its infancy. Whereas hockey, lacrosse and cricket had been developed and championed by educationalists in girls' public schools, and at the first women's colleges at Oxford and Cambridge, athletics events, such as sprints and throws, were more likely to be a fun part of annual sports days than organised competition.

In *Athletics of To-day for Women*, published in 1930, respected athletics writer and coach Frederick AM Webster observed that World War I created opportunities for women to participate in sport, whether working in the services or in munitions factories: '… the girls who served … learned the love of sport, which builds up abounding health and beautiful bodies.'[11] For example, a women's sprint race was occasionally put on alongside men's events at meetings organised by AAA-affiliated clubs or at the extremely popular charity sports meetings that raised funds for wounded soldiers, such as the Aircraft Workers' Sports and the Australian Auxiliary Sports events, both held in the summer of 1917.[12]

Their wartime experiences proved liberating for many of the women who entered the workforce in their hundreds of thousands, taking on roles previously assigned to men and earning their own money. Women gained confidence and their expectations changed. In the post-war period, there were new forms of leisure and entertainment for those who could afford to enjoy them, from going to the pictures to see the latest Mary Pickford movie to spectating at speedway, an exciting new sport introduced from Australia. Certain social conventions were relaxed and sport began to open up to women.

The athletic exploits of 15-year-old Elaine Burton from Leeds, as reported in northern newspapers, show that there were still sprint races for women at some men's athletics meetings after the war. On 24 May, 1919, Empire Day, Elaine won a North of England Ladies' 100-yards championship race in 13 seconds. The papers began to describe her as 'the world's champion runner' and in August she lowered her sprint time to 12 and three tenths of a second, reducing it again to 12 seconds by May 1920.[13] Large companies, such as the Post Office, Lyons and Selfridges, had their own sports grounds and put on athletics events for their female employees, and a few universities organised athletics competitions for female students. At the Aberdeen University Sports in the summer of 1919, there was a 220-yards race, high jump and long jump competitions, and, rather oddly, a sack race for women.[14]

While in the early 1920s, Bristol, Birmingham, Manchester and Edinburgh universities all set up clubs or organised competitions.[15]

It was an invitation from France – where women's athletics had its own governing body, the French Women's Sports Federation – that sparked the creation of Britain's first governing body for women's athletics.[16] The Federation had begun to organise national cross-country as well as track and field competitions for women in 1918, starting with France's first-ever women's cross-country race in April that year. Its president was the formidable Alice Milliat, a highly regarded administrator and a vocal campaigner for better recognition of women's sport. By 1921 Alice had already begun fighting a long battle to get women's athletics included in the Olympic Games.[17]

Born Alice Million in 1884 in Nantes, Alice discovered her passion for sport at age 20 when she spent some time working as a teacher in London. Here, she experienced English sporting events, saw how girls were taught sport at school and acquired an enduring passion for rowing. In 1904, Alice married a Frenchman, Joseph Milliat, in London, but was widowed after just four years. After further travel abroad, she returned to France and devoted herself to women's sport, while working variously as a translator, accountant and sales representative.

In 1919, on behalf of the Federation, Alice had written to Baron Pierre de Coubertin, founder of the modern Olympic Games and president of the International Olympic Committee, to ask for women's athletics to be included in the Olympic programme. Coubertin brushed aside the request, reiterating his view that women had no place at the Games. Alice began to form a network of contacts with athletics organisations in other countries. This no doubt proved useful when the International Sporting Club of Monaco and the daily newspaper *L'Écho des Sports* decided to organise an international women's athletics competition, to be held in Monte Carlo at the end of March 1921.

Webster records that the invitation for Britain to send a team to Monte Carlo ended up with Joe Palmer, a well-known athletics official. Unfazed by the fact that there was no British women's athletics team, Palmer and Major WB Marchant, the newly appointed director of physical education at Regent Street Polytechnic in London, set about putting one together from women who attended physical education classes at the Regent Street and Woolwich polytechnics. The polytechnic colleges specialised in technical education, and ran day and evening classes for people without the means to go to university. They also had sports facilities and were home to many sports clubs.

In the first week of January, after finishing work at a Lyons Corner House Café, 27-year-old Mary Lines made her way to the Regent Street Polytechnic for the first women's gymnastics drill class of the new year. To the great surprise of Mary and her friends, they were told that there was a chance for some of them to go to Monte Carlo to take part in a gymnastics competition against women from other European countries. Fairly soon they heard that there would be athletics and basketball competitions, too. Basketball had been introduced to Britain from America in the 1890s and had soon become a popular game for girls and women.[18] The polytechnics probably had women's basketball clubs, but they didn't have women's athletics clubs. Palmer had just a few weeks to train the team. Could any of the women run, jump or hurdle? Webster reports that at the first Saturday-afternoon session at Paddington Recreation Ground, they could do all these things 'after a fashion', but it took a month for them to get the hang of sprint starts and passing the relay baton. Hurdling was practised 'over a pole perched upon two sticks'. They didn't even have time to practise the throwing events. It was a different picture for the more experienced basketball team who were 'getting into really great shape'. On 21 March a reporter from the *London Evening News* was at Victoria Station to see the team set off for Monte Carlo by train. There was much excitement and high spirits among the 'pretty girl athletes', who were accompanied by Miss Julia Andrew, who worked as a coach at both polytechnics.[19] The seven-strong athletics team was captained by Mary, the oldest member of the team. The competition was dubbed the 'Olympiade' and 'Women's Olympics' by the press.

In the athletics, the British women competed against teams from France, Italy, Switzerland and Norway. Mary was the standout performer, winning the 60 metres and the 250 metres with world bests. She also won the long jump, finished second in the 800 metres and ran on the winning British relay teams in the 8 × 100 metres and 4 × 75 metres. To top all that, she played on the victorious British basketball team, which beat the French Fémina-Sport team 8–7 on the final day of the competition. I wonder if the elite athletes of today, who specialise in just one or two events for most of their careers, would be envious of the opportunities athletes like Mary had to compete in several disciplines. On the way home, elated by their victories, the young women decided to form their own club and the London Olympiades Athletic Club (LOAC) was born. It was the first athletic club exclusively for women to be formed in Britain.

Seven months later, on 30 October, British athletics and football teams competed in an international women's match against France at the Pershing Stadium in Paris. Mary set world bests of 11.8 seconds in the 100 yards and 43.8 seconds in the 300 metres, and was part of the winning British relay team. The decision to mix imperial and metric distances may seem odd, but as British athletes were training and racing over imperial distances, and French athletes over metric distances, it was probably adopted to be fair to both teams. The British team won the athletics match, but the footballers had to be content with a 0–0 draw. The next day at a meeting in Paris with representatives from France, England, Italy, Spain, Czechoslovakia and the USA, Alice created the International Women's Sports Federation (FSFI), which was the international governing body for women's athletics until 1936.[20]

The new opportunities for international competition for women meant there was a need for England to get organised and set up a governing body for women's athletics. In October

1922, the WAAA was founded with Marchant as treasurer and Mary as one of the committee members.

The WAAA was the first, largest and most influential of the British women's governing bodies. Initially covering only England, its remit later extended to Wales as well. The Scottish WAAA was formed in 1930, and the Northern Irish and Welsh associations in 1951. The original plan had been that the WAAA would become an affiliated body of the men's AAA, but the men eventually decided they didn't want to be responsible for women's athletics and the WAAA went its own way. Looking back in 1989, Vera Searle, who had been a leading athlete in the 1920s, said, 'The men didn't want anything to do with us. They were afraid of a lot of fierce women interfering!'[21]

However, from its inception, and throughout its existence, the WAAA relied on the support of men. It was founded from a standing start. Team sports, such as hockey, lacrosse and cricket, which had been played in girls' schools, had women coaches and a competition structure. Women's athletics had neither. Men's knowledge and experience were needed to get women's athletics off the ground and to help set up and run women's athletics clubs. Men's clubs also controlled the athletics tracks and facilities. Women needed to negotiate access and men were important allies in achieving this. Male support was also important in facing the criticism of women's athletics from the press, the public and the powerful male athletics establishment.

From the start the WAAA was concerned with protecting girls and women in athletics. This is reflected in one of the association's aims: 'The assurance that women should compete only in suitable surroundings and desirable conditions.' The association was particularly concerned to avoid exploitation by the press, which was reflected in its insistence on suitably modest clothing. The kit stipulated by the WAAA for athletes in 1922 was: '... closefitting black knickers reaching to not more than 4 inches from ground when kneeling, a loose white tunic of stout material belted, with elbow sleeves, reaching to 10–12 inches below waist.'[22] Vera Searle, who began competing under her maiden name of Palmer in 1923, remarked good-humouredly many years later: 'Obviously I would have been faster had I not had to race with so much spare [material] in the shorts flapping in the breeze – but this was our regulation racing dress then.' Athletes from other countries, such as Japan, were less encumbered.[23] The WAAA also advised its athletes to bring a warm coat and two pairs of 'running pumps'. These would probably have been the flat, thin-soled leather lace-up shoes which we see athletes wearing in newspaper coverage of national and international athletics competitions at the time. Stockings were optional, but some parents insisted on them. The mother of Muriel Gunn, the 1920s long jump star, refused at first to let her compete in bare legs, seeing it as immodest and inappropriate for a young woman.

The continuing power of the Victorian idea of female frailty was reflected in the cautious approach of the WAAA when considering which events were suitable for women. As sports historian Lynne Robinson noted in her PhD thesis,[24] particularly in the early years the WAAA was 'very conscious of the contemporary debate about the effect of sports on female athletes' and 'always careful not to be seen as putting their athletes at physical risk.'

Trial events were held to assess the risks associated with the introduction of new disciplines. Robinson gives an example from 1923 when the association was considering whether it should introduce the pole vault and 'hop-step and jump' (triple jump). The WAAA commissioned two doctors and a male coach, who studied an athlete as she attempted the events. Their subsequent report led to a unanimous decision that, 'Both events were entirely unfit for women and should not be allowed.' This decision had a long-lasting impact. It would be more than 60 years before the pole vault and the triple jump were added to the national track and field championships.

In its early years, the WAAA subscribed to the finite vitality view that people have a limited amount of energy to use over their lifespan, so the association supported limited distances and lighter throwing weights for girls and women. The furthest women athletes ran in international competition was 1000 metres and the longest track race in the WAAA Championships in the 1920s was the half mile or 880 yards, although cross-country races were up to three miles.

Following the formation of the International Women's Sports Federation (FSFI) in October 1921, Alice Milliat renewed her request for women's athletics to be added to the Olympic Games. Coubertin's refusal led Alice and the FSFI to develop an ambitious plan – a separate Women's Olympic Games based on the model of the official games. The first women's Olympic Games, featuring only athletics events, were held at the Pershing Stadium in Paris on 20 August, 1922, with seven track and six field events. Women from five nations – France, Great Britain, USA, Czechoslovakia and Switzerland – competed in front of thousands of spectators, with the British team winning the trophy provided by the French government. Mary won the 300 metres and the long jump, and during the 4 × 110 yards relay, which Great Britain won, she was timed setting a 100-metres world record of 12.8 seconds. Again, there was a mix of imperial and metric distances, accommodating the British and American athletes who trained and raced over imperial distances.

The games were a great success, but there was no way the patriarchal International Olympic Committee was going to allow women to use the term 'Olympic'. Following a stiffly worded objection, the FSFI agreed to rename their event the Women's World Games and three more editions were held, in Gothenburg in 1926, in Prague in 1930 and in London in 1934.

Alice, elected president of the FSFI in 1922, continued to lobby tirelessly for women's athletics in the Olympics. At the 1924 Paris Olympic Games, women competed in swimming, diving, fencing and tennis, but athletics was not on the programme. Eventually, after years of negotiation, the international governing body, the IAAF (now World Athletics), agreed to add women's athletics to the Olympic programme at the 1928 Amsterdam Games, but not the 10 events that Alice and the FSFI wanted.[25] Instead they were offered only five: 100 metres, 800 metres, 4 × 100 metres relay, high jump and discus. The Olympic Games used metric measurements for track and field from the start, obliging British and North American athletes (as well as athletes from countries that made up the British Empire) to adapt to racing over metric distances.

Women from seven countries won medals in Amsterdam, but none went to British athletes. Believing that the IAAF and International Olympic Committee were attempting to dissolve the FSFI and convinced that women's athletics should be separately organised, the WAAA decided to boycott the Games. As sports historian Jean Williams points out, this is the only gender-based boycott in Olympic history.[26]

At the Amsterdam Olympic Games, on 2 August, 1928, nine women – three from Germany, two from Canada and one each from Poland, Sweden, USA and Japan – lined up for the final of the 800 metres. It was a competitive race until the last half lap where Lina Radke, the world record holder, opened up her lead to win decisively in a new world record time of two minutes, 16.8 seconds. It was a milestone event in women's athletics – the first women's 800 metres at the Olympic Games and evidence that women could excel at the distance. The first three women all finished within the previous record time.

Surely this was something to be celebrated? Instead, it became a very different sort of milestone; a controversial and damaging one in the development of women's athletics. How could this happen? Some male journalists invented a dramatic, sensational story about the finish. According to several reports published in British and American newspapers, several of the exhausted women had collapsed, falling to the ground, distressed, sobbing and fainting from the exertion. The *Daily Express* questioned whether girls should take part in 'such strenuous events' and said that six of the 'girls' had collapsed after the race, with one 'weeping bitterly' and in pain, and unable to get up for a quarter of an hour. The reporter from the American magazine *Harper's* came up with the most notorious comment: 'Eleven wretched women, five of whom dropped out before they finished, while five collapsed after reaching the tape,' he wrote.[27]

Not all the reports were so hysterical. The sober *Scotsman* printed a measured account of the race, describing Radke's performance as 'a splendid run' and noting that she finished with 'plenty of strength in hand', and calling second-placed Hitomi of Japan's performance 'a great display of pluck'.[28] Many of the other British papers carried positive reports, but the damage was done. The myth of women collapsing after the race took hold, to the extent that it is still sometimes re-told today. Its potency was two-fold. It reflected continuing concerns over female frailty – the Victorian medical myth that endurance sport would damage women's fertility – and it served the misogynistic purposes of the men who controlled international athletics and wanted to keep women out of the sport. The International Olympic Committee hadn't wanted the women's events in the first place and was only too willing to eliminate the 800 metres from the women's programme. It would be 32 years before it was re-introduced.

Interestingly, the WAAA more or less ignored this decision. The 880 yards remained on its championship programme and in 1936 the mile was added, with women continuing to run in challenging cross-country races of up to three miles. Meanwhile, in the USA, women did not run the 800 metres again until the late 1950s when it was announced that it would be included at the 1960 Rome Olympics.[29]

Although the 'plucky' cross-country runners at that first national championship in 1927 were not universally condemned, early athletes were typically both enthusiastically celebrated for their performances and heavily criticised for challenging social norms. Continued criticism, the myth of 1928 and the lingering fear of potential harms to women were to be limiting factors on the development of women's athletics for decades. It would be a very long time before women were officially allowed to race long distances on the roads, but in 1926 one woman was willing to break with convention and run a marathon. That woman was Violet Piercy.

2

VIOLET PIERCY
LONDON TO WINDSOR IN RECORD TIME (FOR A LADY)

'I did it to show the women are quite as able as men to accomplish feats of endurance.'
—Violet Piercy[1]

On 6 August, 1926 at around 9.40 p.m., a 20-year-old woman wearing a red two-piece bathing suit, goggles and a pink cap emerged from the rough waves of the English Channel on to a pebbled beach near Kingsdown, a few miles north of Dover. The frenzied cheers and enthusiastic applause of thousands of well-wishers rang in her ears. American Gertrude Ederle had become the first woman to swim across the English Channel.

Since Captain Matthew Webb had made the first crossing 51 years earlier, the challenge had captured the public imagination. Dozens of men and a few women had attempted it, some of them on several occasions, and all but five men had failed, falling victim to strong tides, poor weather and cold water. Ederle was the sixth person to succeed and also the fastest to date, beating the time set by Argentinian Enrique Tirabocchi in 1923 by almost two hours.[2]

The day after the swim, Ederle was filmed opening some of the 200 telegrams which had arrived overnight.[3] She looks relaxed, laughing and joking with her companions and none the worse for wear despite her considerable feat of endurance. 'I just went along fine all the time. I never felt the least bit bad until last night when I lay in bed,' she told the press.

Ederle's swim was daring, hazardous and ambitious, but in 1926 she wasn't the only woman in Britain taking risks in pursuit of sporting glory. Experienced 'motor ace' Violet Cordery raced in both mixed and women's races at the upper-class Brooklands circuit in Weybridge, Surrey. In March 1926 she led a team that set a long-distance motoring record of 15,000 miles at Milan's Monza track and in May she competed, along with a few other women, in motor races on the beach at Skegness, watched by thousands of spectators.[4]

The twenties were a dizzying decade of crazes, from sweepstakes to sunbathing and 'shingled' (bobbed) hair. It seemed as if a new fad was proclaimed every week. There was a great demand for novelties in everything, from fashion to food. This commercialisation of popular culture extended to sports, which became an integral part of the developing mass entertainment industry.[5] Travelling was easier, and sporting events and spectacles such as the Skegness beach races drew crowds of thousands. From 1920, when the first wireless broadcast was made in the UK, radio took off in a big way and by 1926 nearly a third of homes had a wireless. Families could listen to dramatic reports of sports events in far-flung places that they would never be able to attend. The immediacy of radio turned sportsmen and women into national and international celebrities overnight.[6]

Ederle's achievement may well have been the impetus for the extraordinary exploits of long-distance runner, Violet Piercy. Some commentators grumbled that the first woman to cross the English Channel was American and, just a few weeks later, Violet, eager to show that British women were just as capable of feats of endurance, announced to the press that she was to run a marathon.[7] On the day after completing the distance, she said, 'I did it because I wanted to show the Americans what we can do … and to prove that Englishwomen are some good, after all.'

In 1926, the marathon was still a relatively new athletic event and it was raced exclusively by men. The marathon had been revived in 1896 and featured in the first Olympic Games in Athens that year, when competitors ran around 25 miles. It was not until the 1908 London Olympics that the modern-day marathon distance of 26 miles, 385 yards was first run. In 1921, it was adopted as the standard distance by the international governing body, the International Amateur Athletic Federation (IAAF).[8]

The marathon became a regular fixture of men's athletics in Britain thanks to the Polytechnic Harriers Marathon or Poly. Established the year after the London Olympics and starting from the same spot as the Olympic marathon, Windsor Castle, the Poly was sponsored by the *Sporting Life* newspaper, which awarded a massive silver trophy worth £500. For several decades it was the principal British marathon race, attracting a top-class field of domestic and international competitors.

Violet was a member of London Olympiades Athletic Club, but club training didn't include long-distance running, so how did Violet prepare for her attempt on the marathon? We know she ran many laps of the athletics track where the Olympiades club sessions were held. There were also short weekly cross-country runs during the winter. She ran twice a week and gradually increased the length of her runs until she was covering almost the full marathon distance. She also skipped to keep fit.

Violet's marathon took place on Sunday 3 October, but because she was not permitted to take part in a men's race, it was a solo run. Crime novelist and sports historian Peter Lovesey carried out extensive research into Violet's runs and personal life, and he determined that the 'marathon' she ran that day was about 20 miles rather than the now standard distance.[9] However, as any distance of 20 miles or more was generally described as a 'marathon' at the time, it's not surprising that both Violet and the press reported it as such.

Violet started at Windsor Castle, 25 miles west of London, the starting point of the Poly marathon. She set off at 4.20 p.m., heading east through the countryside to Hounslow, a distance of about 10 miles, arriving at 5.40 p.m. as it was getting dark. For the rest of the time, she was running through a more built-up, suburban environment. It seems strange that Violet chose to start so late in the day, but this may have been in the hope of avoiding the heavy traffic which clogged the suburban streets: double-decker buses, lorries, delivery vans, motorcars, cabs and the occasional horse-drawn vehicle, as well as cyclists and pedestrians.

Having completed the first half at about an 8-minute-mile pace, from Hounslow Violet slowed to a 14-minute-mile pace. She was mainly jogging in the road, accompanied by friends in two cars, perhaps teammates from London Olympiades. As there were no traffic lights or pedestrian crossings, progress was slow, and it took her a while to negotiate the junctions, roundabouts and crossroads. Gas and electric streetlamps cast a dim glow and Violet had to watch her step. Her only sustenance during the run was a glass of water and some sugar lumps provided by the friends who were accompanying her.

It took Violet another two hours and 20 minutes to cover the remaining 10 miles to her finishing point at Battersea Town Hall in Southwest London. She reached the imposing Victorian edifice at 8 p.m. Her time for the 20-mile marathon was 3:40:22

and Violet became an overnight sensation. London press agencies picked up the story, which appeared not only in British newspapers but also in papers in the USA, Australia and New Zealand, along with photos of Violet in her running kit. But who was this vocal proponent of marathon running and expert self-publicist, defying convention to pursue her ambitions?

Violet Piercy was born on Christmas Eve 1889, the daughter of George Piercy, aged 68, and his third wife, Louisa Sophia Piercy, aged 38. Her brother, Norman, was a year older. The Piercys lived in a modest semi-detached house near the railway line in Croydon, a London commuter town. George owned land and houses in the area and was 'of independent means', an indication that this was a comfortable middle-class existence.

Family life was shattered when George died just two weeks after Violet's birth and Louisa was left with two children under three. It is likely that the family lived off the income from rents generated from the properties and land in George's estate. When Violet was seven, the family suffered another tragic loss. Norman died, leaving her an only child.

Louisa was able to afford to send Violet to an independent, fee-paying girls day school in Croydon. Here, Violet received an education deemed suitable for middle-class girls who were destined for marriage, not employment or careers. Games would have included calisthenics or gymnastics and team sports, such as cricket and hockey. Team games like cricket were judged appropriate for girls as they would develop their character and prepare them for the physical demands of motherhood.[10]

Over time, the Piercy family's wealth dwindled, though. By 1901, they no longer had a live-in servant and Louisa had taken in a lodger to generate extra income. Family life unravelled further in 1902 when Louisa appeared in court twice accused of persecuting a neighbour. Her bizarre behaviour included dressing up as a 'black ghost' and throwing stones at the neighbour's window. The court cases were widely reported in the local and national press. How humiliating this must have been for 12-year-old Violet. Violet's character as an adult suggests that this was a transformative experience. She was self-reliant with a certain degree of toughness, which enabled her to flout gender norms. But she was also described as a loner.

Not much is known about Violet's life, but after leaving school she probably found work in one of the jobs suitable for middle-class girls, such as clerical work or typing. These were not well paid and did not offer women independence. Women's pay was lower than men's in all types of employment. A female clerk might be paid a third less than a man doing the same work. There was an assumption that women were economically dependent on men. They did not need to be paid as much as men because they did not need to support a family.[11]

When World War I broke out in 1914, Violet, aged 24, may have become involved in the war effort. As hundreds of thousands of men left to fight on the Western Front in France and Belgium, women were needed in ever larger numbers to work in industry, in munitions factories, on farms, as nurses, in the civil service and in their own uniformed services. A single woman was expected to continue living with and looking after her parents until either she married or they died. This is what Violet did until Louisa's death in 1916. After this, she may have lived with relatives as was customary for single middle-class women.

Between 1914 and 1918, 750,000 British men were killed in the war – 9% of all men under 45. Social historian Virginia Nicholson describes Violet's generation, the women born between 1885 and 1905, as women 'who unquestioningly believed marriage to be their birthright, only to have it snatched from them by four of the bloodiest years in human history.'[12] Many saw their sweethearts or fiancés leave for the Front, never to return. A higher proportion of officers were killed than soldiers in the lower ranks. As officers were mainly drawn from the upper and middle classes, young women from those classes were disproportionately affected by the casualties. The first post-war census, in 1921, revealed that in Violet's age group, 25 to 34, there were 239,000 more unmarried women than unmarried men. Ten years later, around half of these women, including Violet, would still be single.[13]

Marriage was a way of acquiring social status and ensuring financial security. It was much harder for Violet to make her way as a single woman. While we know almost nothing about any romantic attachments she may have had, there is a suggestion that in her early forties Violet had not given up on the idea of marriage. In a court case in 1932, it was mentioned that Violet, now 42, had sued a Mr Percy for assault and obtaining money from her under promise of marriage. However, being single gave Violet the liberty to pursue her own ambitions in a way that would have been impossible had she married.

There is no record of what Violet was wearing for her 1926 marathon but a 1927 Pathé newsreel, filmed a few weeks after the first national cross-country championship, shows her training in the same kit as the cross-country runners: a white jumper with long sleeves, collar and the London Olympiades badge on the front, and black shorts.[14] Tall, slim Violet also wears a dark woollen hat over her bobbed hair, white ankle socks and dark leather shoes with a strap and low heel. Violet wore this style of shoe for all her road runs. While it might seem highly impractical for running, there was not much choice of footwear for athletes in the 1920s and there were, of course, no road running shoes for women. Most running shoes were leather. Specialised track shoes had removable iron spikes. Cross-country shoes were either leather or canvas with rubber soles or spikes for grip. Men running on the roads would have worn either flat leather or canvas shoes. Perhaps we should not be surprised that Violet just chose to run in the most comfortable pair of shoes she had.

The run was celebrated as a sensational spectacle and some commentators were positive, citing it as evidence of what women could achieve. In its two-page 'Women in Sport' spread, the weekly magazine *The Illustrated Sporting and Dramatic News* congratulated Violet Piercy and motorist Violet Cordery, linking what they had accomplished to Gertrude Ederle's swim, saying that they 'bring women's record of achievements to a pretty high total this year.'[15]

But there was also criticism. The *Westminster Gazette* reported on the run, calling it a 'remarkable feat', but the same edition carried a censorious editorial, expressing the hope that Violet's run would be a one-off and that 'no other girl will be so foolish as to imitate her.' It conceded that women did have some athletic ability but insisted that, 'There are obvious considerations which suggest that girls and women should be discouraged from attempting feats of endurance, which place a great strain not merely on the heart, the lungs and the muscles, but on the entire system.' In conclusion, it pronounced that women should be banned from endurance sports.[16] There was no need for the editorial to be explicit about the 'obvious considerations', as readers would have known this was a reference to the potential harm to women's reproductive health.

The writer expressed a concern that marathon running could be fatal, saying that the Italian runner Dorando Pietri had nearly died competing in the marathon at the 1908 Olympic Games. Pietri was in first place when he collapsed several times towards the end of the race. Having been helped across the finish line, he was disqualified. Why this risk was acceptable for men but not for women was not explained, but women were clearly considered to be the weaker sex, they were therefore presumably more likely to succumb to the adverse physical effects. *All Sports Weekly* put its opposition more succinctly: 'thousands who have an open mind on the value of athletics will join the objectors. The marathon should be cut out by the women.'[17]

The Women's Amateur Athletic Association (WAAA) was more circumspect in its comments to the press. Major WB Marchant, who had been one of the coaches of the 1921 Monte Carlo team and was now the WAAA honorary secretary, commented that it was a remarkable feat for a woman but noted that the association's rules did not permit races over 1000 metres. The longest distance in the WAAA track championships was 880 yards, but British athletes sometimes ran the slightly longer distance of 1000 metres in continental matches. As Violet's run had been a personal endeavour and she had not been in an official race, he said she would not be censured by the association – it was outside their remit. However, by 1928, as reported by a *Daily Mirror* journalist, the WAAA, under its new honorary secretary, Mrs Goold, was 'directly opposed to road racing, and to events of inordinate distance anywhere.'[18]

The 1926 marathon run marked the start of 10 years of long-distance running for Violet. But it was more than that. Her feats were accompanied by what we might now term a media campaign. Violet took every opportunity to promote long-distance running for women and displayed an aptitude for getting media coverage which many of today's running influencers might envy.

Just five days after her run, Violet gave a 10-minute talk on BBC Radio entitled 'My Run from Windsor'. The full text has been lost, but a short excerpt was published in a newspaper, the *Essex Newsman*:

> We are only at the beginning of a new epoch of women athletes ... I feel sure that the cult of athletics among women can do nothing but good, and will tend towards producing a race of women capable of and suited to motherhood ... At the basis of all athletics is rhythm, co-ordinated movement and clean living, and the parents who encourage their sons and daughters to take up athletics will help them to become good citizens.[19]

Violet was adept at making her case. By referring to athletics as ideal preparation for motherhood, she implicitly refuted the argument that it was harmful. Her assertion that athletics was all about rhythm was also intentional, as steady, rhythmic exercise was precisely the type of activity recommended by doctors for girls.

In another publicity coup, in April 1927 Violet appeared in a Pathé newsreel shown in cinemas. The silent film was entitled

'The Runner: Miss Violet Piercey, the long-distance Record Holder' and was two minutes long.[20] The first slide poses the question: 'Anyone here like to run 26½ mile, nonstop?' It then states that 'this lady did – from London to Windsor in record time (for a lady)'. Violet is shown training, running on a road through a London park, accompanied by a car and three male cyclists. The next segment shows her at an athletics track, skipping and running, wearing the heeled shoes which seem to have become her trademark. The text says that she skips for fitness, and runs to get faster and beat her record. A slow-motion film of Violet running is intended to reveal her superior running form.

Violet's celebrity led to Pathé featuring her in another, more curious, newsreel in 1930.[21] It was a novelty item about a butcher who was using a tame sheep to promote his business. Violet, in her customary running kit, is shown outside the butcher's shop feeding the sheep, then running with it on a lead on the road and on the pavement. The sheep is somewhat uncooperative, but Violet is smiling and seems to be having fun.

After another well-publicised solo run, this time 10 miles, in July 1927, Violet shared her views in the *Westminster Gazette* in an article entitled 'How to be Slim'.[22] The 1920s saw the start of the modern preoccupation with slimness for women, as fashions changed to become more revealing of the female form. Violet may have been one of the first people to connect running with losing weight and she repeats her assertion that running is healthy. By linking running to a more socially acceptable activity, dancing, she seeks to give it legitimacy and respectability: 'Running is about the healthiest form of exercise a woman can have, especially in these days of the 'slimming' craze. A girl will cheerfully run – for that is what it amounts to – miles and miles in dance halls and yet shrinks from the idea of running on a road, which is far healthier and quite as effective.'

Following a further marathon run in 1928, Violet addressed head on the alleged masculinising effect on women of too much sport in another statement to the press.[23] Lots of 'nice girls' are athletes, she says, explaining that women can be sporty without being unfeminine and unattractive. It doesn't make them 'rough and ungracious'. Instead of spending their time 'powdering our noses in musty boudoirs', women like 'as much fresh air as we can get.' Violet acknowledges the powerful hold of conventional ideas about the activities suitable for women by asserting that athletes can still be good housewives and mothers. To say otherwise is 'sheer bunkum', she declares. And no woman need be afraid of taking up long-distance running as it does not jar the muscles: 'If you develop a correct style it is not difficult to travel long distances without experiencing sheer fatigue.'

Violet's celebrity led to some new and intriguing invitations to race. As women couldn't compete against men, this meant that her races had to be solo runs against the clock. On August Bank Holiday Monday 1927, she stepped on to the rain-drenched cinder track at Stamford Bridge stadium in West London. It was 4.15 p.m., towards the end of the day at the British Games, a men's athletic meeting. Despite the poor weather, there were still thousands of spectators watching from the large stand on the east side of the track. Earlier in the day, the men had set out on a thirteen-and-a-half-mile road race, but Violet was the only runner in her 10-mile event. Starting with a lap of the track so that the crowd could see her, she ran out of the stadium on the roads for nearly five miles of the Poly marathon route, accompanied by a cyclist, before turning round and returning to the stadium for a final lap of the track.

Although Violet was no doubt cheered at the start and end of her run, it must have been a lonely nine and a half miles out on the roads. How did she pace herself when she had no-one to run against? Her time of 1:13 meant she was running a 7:18 per mile pace. Perhaps she could have run faster with competition, but for Violet this wasn't the point. Her motivation was to be present and to show that women could run long distance.

As sometimes happened at day-long men's meetings, on this occasion there were a few women's exhibition events in the programme, including a relay, a 440-yard race, and javelin and long jump competitions. Violet's invitation came because of her celebrity. The organisers reckoned her presence would add to the meeting's crowd appeal, but they had no real interest in promoting women's road running. This was a novelty, a spectacle, a one-off. Nevertheless, it meant that a road-running woman received press attention again and helped to keep Violet's one-woman campaign alive.

Violet continued to promote the idea of women running marathons, with three more solo runs, each more or less following the Poly marathon course from Windsor. In May 1928, the heat forced her to give up after 20 miles. In May 1933, aged 43, Violet ran again, this time with the backing of *Sporting Life*, the sponsors of the Poly marathon. Charles Packford from the paper acted as referee and timekeeper. Violet was described as 'running through thousands of cheering people' on the route and a suitably grand finish on the stage of the Shepherd's Bush Empire music hall was arranged.

Her final marathon run took place in 1936 on the day of the men's Poly, Saturday 13 June, and over the same measured course. She started shortly before the 78 male runners and finished in 4:25 or 4:30 – accounts vary. Today, Violet is recognised by World Athletics, the international governing body, as a marathon world record holder. Since 1987, World Athletics has published a world records progression list. Many experts have contributed historical records data, including Peter Lovesey, who provided data about Violet's performances, which led to her inclusion in the progression list.[24]

In March 1935, Violet once again demonstrated her flair for publicity when she announced a spectacular challenge – a five-and-a-quarter-mile run from Highgate Hill in North London to the Monument, a well-known landmark in the City of London. Upon arrival, she planned to run up the Monument's 311 narrow, dizzying, spiral steps. Huge crowds of spectators turned up to watch on Saturday 30 March and, true to her word, once Violet reached the Monument she ran to the top without stopping. Her total time was 46 minutes, 15 seconds. Violet had to contend with heavy traffic and a cold headwind, but she said, 'I did it to show the women are quite as able as men to accomplish feats of endurance.'[25] To show how fit she felt, she said she'd be happy to sprint up the stairs again. Thankfully, no-one asked her to. She told the press she had trained by running up escalators on the London Underground. One can only imagine what the reaction of commuters must have been.

In the 1930s, the WAAA's stern opposition to women's road racing of any kind relaxed. Women were permitted to race short distances on the roads, but the long distances Violet attempted remained prohibited. In 1933, the WAAA held its first national road walking championship, over a distance of approximately three miles. And in October 1935, Ilford AC, a mixed club, organised a women's road relay race at Chigwell Row in Essex. The race, six laps of one and three-quarter miles, attracted top teams from the Southeast and became a popular annual fixture. According to the London newspapers, it was the first British women's road relay.[26]

After leaving London Olympiades, Violet joined Mitcham Athletic Club, a mixed club, which viewed the arrival of 'the noted marathon runner' as quite a coup, stating, 'Miss Piercey is in a class of her own where long-distance running is concerned and this should prove to be a big asset in building up this side of the women's section.' Men and women trained separately, but occasionally there were social runs with other clubs. For example, on Saturday 13 October, 1934, both the men's and ladies' sections enjoyed a cross-country run with Horsham Athletic Club, followed by a tea and a get-together. The men covered three miles and the women two.

On the following Saturday, 20 October, under the auspices of the club, the ever-enterprising Violet somehow managed to organise a women's three-mile road race at Mitcham – a highly unusual event. Knowing Violet's go-ahead spirit, it's possible that she turned an informal social run into a race by contacting the press and announcing it. She certainly talked up the race, saying it would attract 'well over 50 women athletes from all the leading clubs'. Her focus was on making the race happen and getting press coverage. She was not one to get bogged down in going to committee meetings, following rules and getting race permits.

While it may not have attracted 50 athletes, newspaper photographs show 15 women wearing race numbers at the start. The winner, in 18 minutes, 45 seconds, was Peggy Camfield of Mitcham AC, followed by her sister Gwen, a top cross-country runner. There's a lovely photo of a smiling Peggy being held aloft by jubilant fellow athletes after the race. The papers declared the event to be 'the first women's road race in this country'. However, the jubilation may have been somewhat tarnished when it subsequently transpired that the race was not official. Neither the regional men's AAA nor the WAAA had given approval. There had only been verbal permission for the race to go ahead and no permit had been granted.[27] This could have led to repercussions, such as suspension from competition for Violet and the women who competed. However, it may be that the governing bodies decided to limit their actions to reprimanding Mitcham AC. Violet remained a member of the club.

After her 1936 marathon, Violet contacted newspapers in 1937 and 1938 announcing her intention to set records at shorter distances but no record of these runs taking place has been found. After this, Violet seems to have disappeared from the public eye. Why did a woman who had used the press so effectively cease to appear in the papers? The press may, in all likelihood, have lost interest in Violet's exploits when World War II disrupted daily life. And Violet may have been more preoccupied with the war effort than with athletics.

We don't know what Violet was doing during the war, no records exist that we can trace, but she was next mentioned in a snippet in a gossip column in the *Sheffield Weekly Telegraph* in 1950. Describing her as a marathon runner, and mentioning her run to the top of the Monument in 1935, it stated that she was 'still as fit as ever, though shy of giving her age.' She was 60. What happened to Violet after this is unclear. Records show that she was still living in Southwest London, not far from Mitcham, in 1958. After that, despite detailed research by Peter Lovesey, there is nothing. Although he did discover a death registered in April 1972 when Violet would have been 82, which may have been her.

An elderly woman of no fixed address was admitted to University College Hospital in London and died of a brain haemorrhage, hypertension and a kidney-related infection. There was uncertainty about the patient's surname and it was recorded as 'Pearson otherwise Piercy otherwise Pierce'. Her occupation was given as cleaner for the Greater London Council. No-one came forward to organise the woman's funeral or to claim her estate, which was worth £2500. It seems likely that this woman, dying alone, homeless and unknown, was indeed Britain's first female marathon runner, Violet Piercy.

Violet was written out of history because, as Peter Lovesey observes, she didn't fit into the traditional athletics narrative. Her marathon runs weren't officially recognised at the time and therefore weren't included in early athletics histories, which were ordered according to the standard programme of track and field events. Her achievements were of no real interest to the WAAA, so they had no reason to celebrate or remember her. The disruption of World War II changed the news agenda – there was a new focus and Violet and her exploits were forgotten. As well as being a rulebreaker, Violet was a visionary. In 1934, she predicted that in the future long-distance running by women would no longer be a novelty, an oddity, a matter for censure. Looking back, we know that she was right, but it took strength of character, courage and conviction to say it then.

I haven't found any evidence of Violet's example inspiring other women to run long distance themselves and, so many decades later, I may never find any, as this testimony is most likely to come from interviews or personal accounts rather than newspapers or archives. However, this doesn't mean she had no lasting impact. People went to watch her in their thousands, they heard her on the radio, saw her in news clips and read about her in the press. She accomplished her aim of proving that 'women could stick the distance' and opened people's eyes to what was possible.

What happened next? During the war there were very few men's road races and it took a while for men's athletics clubs to rebuild themselves afterwards.[28] Women's clubs continued to put on road relays. I have discovered that Birmingham Atalanta Ladies Athletic Club organised their first road relay in 1941 and it continued until at least 1948, and other clubs started road relays after the war. After a break in national competition since 1939, the WAAA quickly organised its first post-war track and field championships in August 1945 and its first cross-country championship, over two and a half miles, in March 1946. (The Scottish governing body took longer to recover, holding its first post-war track and field championships in 1949 and cross-country championship in March 1951.) The 1948 London Olympic Games gave athletics a huge boost, with crowds of over 80,000 drawn to Wembley Stadium each day. Women's athletics was in the limelight thanks to the four gold medals won by superstar Dutch athlete, Fanny Blankers-Koen, with three British women taking silver behind her. Meanwhile, the most popular format for women's road racing was still relays. In 1963, the WAAA held the first national road relay championship. But what of longer distances? I'm not aware of any women rulebreaking by running in men's road races until the 1960s. However, one example from cross country shows that some women were quite willing to race against men if the opportunity arose.

Elizabeth (Liz) Brade-Birks joined the Women's Royal Naval Service (WRNS) in 1954, aged 18, to train as a radio mechanic. At school she had played hockey, netball, rounders and tennis, and had gymnastics and swimming lessons. Athletics wasn't taught. When I interviewed Liz in 2020, she told me that she did, however, run three-quarters of a mile to the station every morning to get the train to school, always cutting it fine. Liz was keen on playing in the WRNS hockey and cricket teams, but in 1955 was required to compete at the naval base's sports day and ran in her first ever race, 100 yards. After her potential was spotted, she was recruited to the athletics team and ran sprints in inter-services and Navy championships. In 1957 she met her future husband, Trevor Joyce, who was in the Navy at the same base. He got permission from the physical training instructors for her to run in the men's monthly cross-country training run, which was between three and six miles. As Liz put it, 'I ran myself into the men's team. They chose from the frontrunners in the men's run.' There was no women's team for her to join as they didn't run cross country.

She went on to run with the men's cross-country team in services competitions. Everything was fine until one day in 1959 when the team was competing at an event that included a team from Southampton University. Unfortunately word got back to the WAAA that Liz was competing in men's races and she was told in no uncertain terms that she was never to run with men again.[29] She and Trevor married shortly afterwards and she left the WRNS, as most women did on marriage. By then, she'd been competing for Gosport AC for two years and was one of Britain's best milers and cross-country runners. In 1961, she ran the world best time for the mile that year at the Southern area championships: 4:58.5. In the 1960s, more British women began to push against the limitations placed on them as athletes by running in men's races. Foremost among them was a remarkable Scottish woman, Dale Greig.

3

DALE GREIG

MUCH MORE THAN A FOOTNOTE

'Women are always being kept down.
They have to fight all the time for equality.'
– Dale Greig[1]

On a sunny afternoon on Saturday 23 May, 1964, a young Scottish woman, Dale Greig, lined up to run a marathon at the coastal resort of Ryde on the Isle of Wight. She was the sole woman in a field of 67 men. Dale had experience of the marathon's notoriously hilly course, having run parts of it with men from Ryde Harriers on previous holidays to the island, and in March 1963 she'd run the whole route the day after taking part in the English national cross-country championships. Dale knew she'd done the miles of training needed to take on the gruelling course, recognised as 'one of the toughest in Great Britain,'[2] but even so she was feeling nervous.

Despite the ban on women running road races longer than four miles, Dale wasn't worried about the race officials trying to stop her. Ryde Harriers, the organisers, had agreed to let her run on the proviso that she started four minutes ahead of the men. They hoped this measure would enable them to avoid censure from the Amateur Athletic Association (AAA), which had issued the permit for the race. They could argue that Dale was not part of the official race at all and was instead taking part in a time trial.

However, Dale was feeling a little uneasy at the press attention she'd received. Shy and modest, she hated being the centre of attention. Local papers had carried stories about her before, but this time a national newspaper had come calling. That morning, a journalist from the *Daily Express* had insisted on interviewing her. She'd talked to him in the garden of the home of Bill Ross, a Ryde Harriers member and a friend. After that, the journalist had wanted to take pictures of her running. Dale had got changed into her running kit: a plain, square-necked, sleeveless top, cotton shorts and plimsolls. She and Bill had gone out on to the well-manicured suburban streets near his home, where she had obliged the journalist by being photographed running up and down a short hill, both on her own and with Bill. There had been more questions from reporters once she got to the starting line on the esplanade.

It all felt a bit awkward and uncomfortable, but firm in her conviction that women were capable of running the marathon distance, Dale had taken this chance to say so. Going further, she had boldly declared that her aim was to beat the time that an American woman, Merry Lepper, had run six months before when she had crashed the Western Hemisphere Marathon in Culver City, California. Merry had finished in 3:37 over a flat course. Of course, Merry's time wasn't official as the international governing body, the International Amateur Athletic Federation (IAAF), didn't recognise the women's marathon. The longest recognised distances for women's records were 800 metres and its imperial near-equivalent, 880 yards. However, athletics enthusiasts kept a record of these unofficial performances.

Dale calmed her nerves by chatting to Bill, who was also competing, and her mother, Anna, who gave her some words of encouragement. As usual, there was quite a crowd at the start, and as she set off at four minutes to two, a few voices called out, 'You show 'em, girl' and 'Good luck, Dale'. After running through the spectator-lined streets of Ryde, she was out on the country roads. She enjoyed the first two miles on her own before the leaders in the men's race passed her. Eventually Bill, who was 56, caught up with her and they ran together for some of the race. By the time they reached the 10-mile point, low cloud had blown over, making it oppressively humid.[3]

Keen to avoid any criticism should Dale become unwell from the exertion of the marathon, the race director had decided it would be prudent to have an ambulance following her round. 'Ridiculous!', Dale thought. She was confident she was going to finish, but making a fuss was not in her nature and she decided it would be better to go along with it. Feeling comfortable despite the heat and the hills, Dale's average pace was under eight-minute miles.

After 22 miles, Dale slowed down, but she was not about to drop out. In fact, she passed some of the male runners in those last few miles. Afterwards, she told the papers that the men looked embarrassed. A couple who had given up and were sitting by the side of the road decided to start running again when they saw her.[4] At last, the runners re-entered Ryde and Dale ran along the esplanade with crowds of locals and holidaymakers to her left and the Solent to her right. It was a strange experience to hear so much cheering as she approached the finish. As she crossed over, her mother, who had followed the race in a car, appeared and gave her a big hug. A wave of relief and exhaustion washed over Dale. Her time of 3:27:25 would have earned her 35th place had her participation been official instead of a time trial. There were 49 male finishers.

As she drank water from a paper cup, a clutch of journalists surrounded her asking questions. How did you manage to finish when some of the men have given up? What are you going to do next? Will you do another marathon? Dale found it rather tiresome and was glad when she managed to get away from them, excusing herself by saying she was tired. In fact, she was elated, delighted to have run faster than Merry Lepper. She had set a new mark for women.

Far from exhausted, after a bath and some tea, Dale went to the evening social dance and prize-giving at the Royal York Hotel, staying until midnight. The next morning there was just enough time for a dip in the cool waters of the Solent before she and her mother began the long journey back to Paisley.

Dale may have underestimated the impact her run would have. By the time she and her mother got back home to the modest maisonette they shared at 56 Tannahill Road, Paisley, her name had appeared in dozens of newspaper articles. She probably saw the Saturday evening editions of the local papers at the dance. 'Tough girl Dale shocks the men' proclaimed the *Sunday People*, which went on to say that Dale had run 'to prove that women are tougher than men think.'

Dale's sister Cynthia, at home in Scotland, only found out that Dale had run in the race when she saw an article and photo in the *Sunday Express* headed, 'Dale – Marathon girl No 1'. The coverage swelled on Monday when the dailies carried the story. Most headlines focused on the novelty of the event: 'Dale's run has men in a spin,' 'Men given marathon surprise' and 'Woman shocks.'[5] The more sober *Scotsman's* headline was 'Athletics history by Scots girl – runs full marathon'. Dale had made it clear that by participating she was making a point about women's exclusion from road races. The press coverage was mainly positive, but the *Daily Mirror's* Sportlight column was dismissive:

> TALKING POINT: Should women be encouraged to run the marathon course of 26 miles 385 yards? DALE GREIG, a 27-year-old secretary from Paisley, covered that distance on Saturday in 3hr. 27m. 45s. and aims to challenge an American girl who, three months ago, did it in 3hr. 35m. The idea does not intrigue us. Forget it, Dale![6]

Was Dale going to challenge Merry Lepper to a race? It was widely reported that she intended to. Whether this was true or not, she was clearly stung by the *Daily Mirror's* tone and dashed off a letter to them straightaway. On 28 May the Sportlight column reported that the paper had received a note from her saying, 'Forget it … I'm challenging no-one.'

The men's governing body for the Isle of Wight, the Southern Counties AAA, were quick to send their own letter, reprimanding Ryde Harriers and stating that 'In athletics women are not allowed to compete with men, and we feel that in the future all possible steps should be taken to prevent a repetition of this, particularly as the resulting publicity is not good for the sport.'

The *Daily Express* contacted Marea Hartman, honorary secretary of the WAAA, for her opinion, but far from supporting Dale's fantastic achievement she made it very clear that there were no plans to change the limits in place for women: 'We have no races over 4½ miles. It's felt these distances are too much for women … As for women running against men – No. The discrepancy in ability is too great.'[7]

In spite of all this Dale remained proud of her achievement. When I visited her relatives, Rosemary and Niki Kidd, in 2023, four years after Dale's death, they showed me a scrapbook containing newspaper articles about the race carefully cut out and stuck down either by Dale or her mother. Other items that

Dale kept show that she was particularly delighted to receive acknowledgement from her peers. Among her papers is a letter from the far more forward-thinking Scottish Marathon Club, congratulating her on her 'splendid performance' and offering her an honorary membership. Founded in 1944, the club had never admitted a woman. Indeed, for more than a decade Dale was its only female member.

One might expect that unassuming, reserved Dale would have decided to avoid the spotlight, but she had a spark of fire and a strength of conviction that made her determined to speak up for women. A month after the marathon, in an interview with a local paper, Dale mentioned the four-mile limit for women and lamented the lack of competition in Scotland and internationally.[8] In August 1964, a profile of Dale in the *Daily Record* with the headline 'Dale fights 4-mile limit' described her as angry at the outmoded athletics rules: 'We are not allowed to run more than HALF-A-MILE in the Olympics. Officials think that far enough for us. It is a Victorian idea which still sticks. I run 5 to 6 miles a day in training.'[9] Asked if she would run a marathon again, she replied, 'If it was made an official race for women I would certainly have a crack at it again.'

How did Dale come to be standing on that start line 350 miles away from her home in Paisley? And in an era when no-one thought of women as long-distance athletes, what made her decide to regularly run 10, 20, even 30 miles, on the roads?

At 6:30 a.m. on 15 May, 1937, twin girls were born at Brabloch Nursing Home in Paisley. Delighted at the safe arrival of the girls, Bob and Anna Greig, who had married in 1932 and were in their thirties, decided to call one daughter Dale after the doctor who had delivered the twins, Dr John Dale.[10] They named the other Cynthia.

At that time Paisley was the world capital of thread making. The Coats company's Ferguslie thread mill and the Anchor thread mill employed tens of thousands of men and women, as well as teenage boys and girls. Bob was a foreman at Ferguslie and Anna worked there before their marriage, too. The family were tenants in a flat at 78 Maxwellton Road, a property adjoining the Ferguslie mill site and built by the Coats company.

Dale and Cynthia grew up accustomed to the busy life of the street with workers and delivery vans coming and going, and the noise of the mill machinery an ever-present background to their lives. Happily, the Greigs survived the war unscathed, despite a bomb falling just 200 metres from their home when the Luftwaffe blitzed Clydeside in 1941. But tragedy struck little more than a year after the war ended. On the evening of Sunday 29 December, 1946, Bob Greig died suddenly at home. He was 49. The doctor who certified his death, recording the probable cause as a cerebral haemorrhage, was Dr Dale who had delivered the twins nine years before. Anna was with Bob when he died, and Dale and Cynthia probably witnessed his death, too. This traumatic event must have strengthened the bonds between Dale, Cynthia and Anna, and they remained close throughout their lives, with Anna and Dale living together until Anna's death in 1984.

In 1954 when Dale and Cynthia turned 17, the family was living at 56 Tannahill Road and Anna was working as a telephonist. She was ambitious for her daughters. They both attended the John Neilson Institution, a well-regarded, mixed, selective school, which stood on a hill overlooking the town centre. A rather imposing Italianate building with a central dome, known locally as 'the porridge bowl', it was here that Dale's love of sport developed. She was in the hockey XI and a team photograph from 1955, her last year at school, shows her standing confident and smiling in a white blouse, striped tie, below-the-knee dark skirt, dark knee-high socks and leather boots. She was the school champion at sprinting and high jump, and competed for the Renfrewshire youth team in the latter. Judged good enough to compete in adult races, despite still being a teenager, she was the Renfrewshire senior 880-yards champion, although she wouldn't have been allowed to race that far at school.

Dale was involved in other school activities, too. She was a member of the debating society and worked on the school magazine, *The Neilsonian*. The school prided itself on producing good citizens distinguished by 'their standard of conduct, sense of duty and spirit of service'.[11] These values informed Dale's choices and aspirations. From the age of 16, she taught Sunday School at Paisley Abbey Church and deciding a career as a teacher was a natural next step.

I asked the University of Glasgow about Dale's time there and received scans of various papers, including her application forms, from the archives department. Her first application to university, in 1954, aged 17, reveals that the seeds had already been sown for a lifelong dedication to increasing opportunities for girls and women in athletics. She wrote in her application that she was very interested in athletics and that for the past year she had been helping to set up a 'ladies' section' at Paisley Harriers, one of the two men's clubs in the town.

In 1954, Dale decided to stay at school for another year to improve her grades in her higher exams. In the summer of 1955, *The Neilsonian* featured a list of mottos from each of the girls who were about to leave. Dale's was: 'Woman is woman's natural ally.' It was particularly apt as just a few years later Dale would work with other women to create a new women's athletics organisation. To bring about change in athletics in patriarchal, conservative Scotland, women would need to work together.

After reapplying to the University of Glasgow in the autumn of 1955, aged 18, Dale began her first year of an arts degree, taking classes in Latin, history and geology. Cynthia, meanwhile, had begun working for BBC Scotland; in 1961 she married Alexander Kidd, a road runner.

In her first year at university, Dale competed for the university women's team, winning the 440 yards at the Scottish Inter-Universities Championships. A week later, she was second in the 880 yards at the Scottish National Championships. Abruptly, Dale then left the path she had chosen for herself. She would never become a teacher, nor would she graduate from university.

She left at the end of her first year, having uncharacteristically failed some exams and missed others. Whatever the reason was for this change of direction, without it Dale might never have undertaken her rulebreaking runs or achieved all that she did for women's athletics in Scotland.

Soon after the university year finished, Dale found a secretarial job with an employer who shared her passion for athletics, the publisher and printer Walter Ross, at his offices at 69 St Vincent Street in the heart of Glasgow's business district. Walter, 36 and married to Winifred, was an athletics enthusiast. As well as providing printing services to many athletics organisations, he sold books and athletics shoes from his business premises. With all these connections and comings and goings, Walter had his finger on the pulse of what was happening in athletics in Scotland, the UK and wider afield, and soon Dale did, too.

In 1946, Walter had started *The Scots Athlete*, the first magazine devoted to Scottish athletics. The magazine gave scant attention to women's athletics until Dale began working for him, but her influence can be seen straightaway in the new Women's Notes page in the October 1956 issue. Now more than two pages of the 20-page publication were devoted to women's performances. Dale's regular column was all the more unusual given that writing about athletics was a male preserve. None of the other regular articles in *The Scots Athlete* were written by women and the most popular athletics publication in the UK, *Athletics Weekly*, only featured female contributors once in a blue moon.

In Women's Notes, Dale always gave fulsome praise to other athletes for their achievements, only ever mentioning her own in passing. Having been beaten by eight seconds at the 1958 Scottish women's cross-country championship, she wrote in the June issue:

> Ina Mae Mooney (Jordanhill TC), at her first attempt for National Cross-Country honours, ran with excellent judgement to take the lead half a mile from home and emerge

> a decisive winner by some 40 yards from D. Greig ... with Helen Cherry ... finishing as last year a very close third.[12]

Her dry sense of humour comes across in her comments on the course which sounds rather challenging by today's standards: 'Springburn Harriers laid out a nice two-mile country course of varied going, marred slightly perhaps by rather many barbed wire fences.'[13] Dale went on to criticise the lack of opportunities for Scottish female athletes. The 1958 annual cross-country match with England, which she would have been selected for, having finished second in the Scottish championship, had been cancelled due to lack of funds. And Dale and other athletes who weren't sprinters would have no opportunity to represent Scotland at the forthcoming British Empire Games (now known as the Commonwealth Games) in Cardiff in July 1958. The male athletes would have eight running races, the longest being the marathon. In contrast, the female athletes would have to be content with two sprints: 100 yards and 220 yards. For Dale this was both personal and political. She was speaking up for herself and for all the women who were denied the chance to compete for their country.

Not only colleagues, Walter and Dale were also great friends. It was through Walter that Dale formed ties with the Isle of Wight. Bill Ross was Walter's older brother. Walter and Winifred would visit Bill and his family every year for the week of the marathon. Dale started to accompany them on these trips. Bill's son Malcolm, who kept in touch with Dale and visited her in her later years, recalls that Dale and Walter were both great readers of books on the history of politics, internationalism and pioneers from the past, and 'very independently left wing in their outlook'.[14] Walter's death in 1993 at the age of 74 was a profound loss for Dale.

Dale's attempt to establish a ladies' section at Paisley Harriers failed and shortly after leaving university she joined Bellahouston Harriers, a mixed Glasgow club, but there wasn't much on offer for women.[15] Self-reliant, Dale decided that the best way to get a women's athletics club in Paisley was to set one up herself. In

1959 she founded Tannahill Harriers, the town's first women's club, and affiliated it to the Scottish Women's Amateur Athletic Association (SWAAA). No doubt she chose 'Harriers' for the name because this traditionally denoted a cross-country club. The club's one-page constitution, found among her papers, shows that Dale recruited a committee from among her friends in athletics – Walter Ross was president – and appointed herself secretary and treasurer.

Most clubs didn't have their own facilities, instead they met at public tracks or sports grounds. We don't know if Dale's club had formal training sessions, but although she recruited a few other athletes, including Pat (Patricia) McCluskey and Katrine McNicol, as they were both from Greenock on the south bank of the Clyde, 18 miles away, it seems unlikely that they all trained together in Paisley. In 1960, Dale, Katrine and 19-year-old Pat made up the Tannahill team that won the team competition in the Scottish national cross-country championships, with Dale first and Pat second. However, for most of the 15 years that Dale kept the club going, she was the only member. This meant she had to meet all the costs, such as affiliation and entry fees, herself, but it also gave her the freedom to decide which races she wanted to enter and she didn't have to wait to be selected by a club official.

A long article about Pat published in the *Greenock Telegraph* in December 1960 described how she had struggled to carry on with athletics after leaving school at 17 in 1957. She wanted to join one of the harriers clubs in Greenock but was told, 'We are strictly for men only'. The men's clubs didn't want to be bothered with setting up a women's section, because, they said, it was 'impossible'.[16] Pat began to feel she was wasting her time. Eventually a male friend offered to train her and one of the men's clubs let her train with them at track sessions. After Tannahill Harriers' win at the Scottish cross-country championship in March 1960, struck by the fact that two-thirds of the winning team were from Greenock, Pat redoubled her efforts to start a club for girls in her hometown. Her vision was to provide young girls with something she'd struggled to find for herself – the opportunity to continue in, or take up, athletics after leaving school. For three years Pat persisted when others might have given up. Eventually Rankin Park Community Centre in Greenock agreed she could set up a girls' club there and the Rankin Park Ladies' Amateur Athletic Club and Harriers was born. Starting in April 1960, with an all-female committee, by the end of the year, 40 girls and young women were meeting regularly for training and taking part in events. Pat continued competing at track and cross country, and in 1961 she and Dale reversed their positions in the national championships with Pat taking the win and Dale finishing second.[17]

Dale loved cross country. She felt at home running across rough ground, climbing over fences and scrambling through ditches of ice-cold water, and was not afraid of mud, snow or rain. Cross-country racing was meant to be tough – its purpose was to build strength and endurance for track. When I interviewed Doreen King, who was friends with Dale in the 1960s, she recalled that Dale often ran barefoot if a race was over fields and encouraged her to do likewise. In March 1968, *The Scotsman's* report on the three-and-a-half-mile national championship race in Musselburgh noted that both Doreen and Dale had run without anything on their feet. It clearly didn't put them at a disadvantage as Dale won and Doreen was second.[18] I've seen athletes lose their shoes in knee-deep mud in cross-country races, but it's hard to imagine runners today choosing to run barefoot.

Although Dale did win bronze medals in the mile race at the Scottish national track and field championships in 1958, 1959, 1960 and 1966, cross country was where she excelled. Her first Scottish cross-country championship was the 1957 race, where she finished fifth, earning selection for the annual match race against England. But Dale could see that women's cross country was languishing in Scotland. In 1959, when she finished third at the championships, only 12 women started. Whereas the men had races most weekends, there weren't enough women's races. Consequently, the standard of performance wasn't very high and nowhere near as good as in England, where there were county and area races, as well as the national championships, which regularly attracted more than 80 athletes.

Frustrated at this situation and keen to improve things, in 1960 Dale led an initiative to create a new association for Scottish women's cross country. From Dale's papers and documents in the SWAAA archive, it's clear that even though she was still only 22, Dale was willing to represent the new association. In a letter to the SWAAA honorary secretary, she explained that its aims were 'to encourage more interest … by promoting more races and more activity in the winter months.'[19] The SWAAA committee was receptive to the idea – they were well aware of the problems, having faced some criticism in the press.[20] Nevertheless, the establishment of the Scottish Women's Cross Country Union is testament to Dale's diplomacy and negotiation skills. There were many issues to be ironed out: the financing of the new organisation, its membership, its area of activity and, most importantly, its relationship to the SWAAA.

The Scottish Women's Cross Country Union adopted a badge with a thistle atop a barred gate and the blue and white saltire (Scottish flag) as the background. The minutes of the 1961 SWAAA annual general meeting acknowledged both Dale's leadership and the positive impact of the new cross country union: 'Much progress had been made in their first year and individual performances were high.'[21]

Dale served as honorary secretary of the union from 1960 to 1966 and remained involved until its demise in 1993, when all the men's and women's governing bodies were compelled to amalgamate into a new organisation, the Scottish Athletics Federation. Over the four decades of the union's existence, many of Scotland's best cross-country runners served on its committee, including Pat McCluskey and two runners who we will meet later in this chapter, Palm Gunstone and Aileen Lusk.

Dale finished in the top three in the Scottish cross-country championships for 11 consecutive years from 1958 to 1968, winning the title four times, and also travelled to England to compete in the English championships, where her highest finish was sixth in 1964.

In 1966 the Scottish Women's Cross Country Union found itself at the centre of controversy after its cross-country championship went ahead on a day when other sporting fixtures, such as football matches, had been cancelled. The races were held on 19 February at Bellshill, near Glasgow, in wintry conditions – six inches of snow and icy ground. Echoing the critical coverage of the 1950s, some Scottish newspapers carried sensationalist pieces claiming that girls had been forced to drop out and the story was picked up by the *Daily Express*. An article entitled 'Too cold for soccer – but not the girls' featured a photograph of a teenage girl who appeared to have collapsed and another of a woman being helped to her feet.[22]

Contrary to the melodramatic impression given by the paper, just three of the 106 girls and women in the races had dropped out. The journalist interviewed Dale, who had come second in the senior race, and she was adamant that the conditions were safe, insisting that if the circumstances were the same next year they would run the championships again. She told the reporter, 'You just take the weather in your stride. It's part of the sport … Only fog cancels cross-country.' Dale pointed out that many women wanted to race 10 or 15 miles, rather than being limited to a maximum of four as they were at the time. However, the journalist's line of questioning irritated her so much that she was goaded into making some of her most outspoken statements to date: 'Women are always being kept down. They have to fight all the time for equality … There should be no restriction. I would like to see women training twice a day, running 100 miles a week, as far as the toughest man.' This, she said, could lead to a tremendous improvement in British women's athletics. The idea of women running 100 miles a week must have seemed extraordinary, ridiculous even, to the *Daily Express*' readers. The journalist acknowledged Dale's authority to speak on the matter, but described her views as 'spartan'. Concerns over women's suitability for endurance sport were ever-present.

But what did the girls themselves think? The *Daily Record* carried an article headed, '"Amazons" in the blizzard', in which three teenagers from Muirkirk in Ayrshire countered the criticism, saying they were used to running in cold, snowy conditions.[23] One of them was 13-year-old Janette Lowe, the collapsed runner pictured in the *Daily Express*. She explained, 'I injured my ankle in training on Wednesday. But this was my first big race and I would not have missed it for anything … I was not exhausted. I fell because I twisted my ankle.' Her mother said the race was a 'great experience' for Janet. Unconcerned about the conditions, she said, 'I don't think it is cruel to ask girls to run in the snow.'

In 1968, 10 years after her article about the lack of international competition for women in *The Scots Athlete*, Dale got the chance to represent her country in an official international race. She and Doreen King were among six women selected for the Scottish team for the second International Cross-Country Union Championships. Women had finally got an international championship the previous year, 64 years after the first men's championship was held in 1903. In 1968 the men's international championship took place in Tunisia – the women's in Blackburn. Less exciting perhaps, but the UK was an obvious location, because there was only one overseas women's team competing against England, Scotland, Wales and the Republic of Ireland – the USA. Doreen was the first Scot in the international, finishing 12th, with Dale 14th. Together with Margaret MacSherry and Leslie Watson they won the bronze team medal.[24]

Palm Lindsay had been unable to get to the controversial 1966 championships from her home in Dundee due to snow-blocked roads. Born in Dundee in 1946, much of Palm's family life revolved around athletics and Dundee Hawkhill Harriers, the 'Hawks', one of Scotland's oldest and most successful clubs. Her father George, a teacher, had joined the club in the 1920s and one of his brothers was a member too. Dundee Hawkhill has the distinction of being the first harriers club in Scotland to admit women, establishing its women's section in 1928, two years before the SWAAA was formed, and Palm's mother Margaret was one of its earliest members. She features, along with her sister, in a women's section photo from 1931–32 and – amazingly – she is sitting among 40 other women, a large number at a time when women's athletics was just getting started. One of Margaret's brothers also competed for the club.[25]

As the daughter of an athletics pioneer, it's hardly surprising that as soon as she was old enough, at the age of 13, Palm joined the Hawks. She did well on the track, progressing to 1500 metres and the 3000 metres when it was introduced, and winning district championships. In cross country, she won the hotly contested club championships three times in the 1960s and again in 1973/74 and competed in the Scottish nationals. Palm was part of a strong Hawks cross-country team that won the national championships for three consecutive years, 1970-1972. She represented Scotland at three World Cross Country Championships, in Belgium in 1973, in Italy in 1974, and in Morocco in 1975. In 1974 Palm's mother, Margaret Lindsay, was the president of the Scottish Women's Cross Country Union and acted as team manager at the championships in Monza. Palm's husband Doug was in the men's team, making it something of a family trip.

Palm's parents were both involved in officiating and Margaret was president of the club for a few years. When the Commonwealth Games came to Edinburgh in 1970 they served as athletics judges and Palm took holiday from her job as a secretary at Dundee University to volunteer in the communications team at the Meadowbank stadium, answering the phone when judges called up with queries.

Palm was seventeen when she first met Dale at the Musselburgh Round the Bridges road races in November 1963. The women's one-and-a-half mile race was her first race away from home. She remembers Dale encouraging all the runners and says that, 'It was after that I fell in love with road running but there were no other road races for us to compete in.' She competed against Dale in cross-country races, but really got to know her as a friend when Dale persuaded her to become honorary secretary of the Scottish Women's Cross Country Union in 1969. I met Palm in May 2023, when we were both involved in filming a feature about Dale for the TV programme *Great British Railway Journeys* at Pollok Country Park in Glasgow. After our interviews had been filmed, we went for lunch and Palm shared some of her memories of Dale with me.

Dale's leadership and determined spirit, as well as her complete lack of regard for appearances are evident in a story Palm told me about the 1971 English national cross-country championships. Dale, Pat Spence (née McCluskey) and Palm had travelled to Wolverhampton together and after the race they all had trains to catch. Pat and Dale were returning to Glasgow and Palm was going to visit her fiancé, Doug Gunstone, in London. They didn't have much time and Dale said they would need to run fast and get a move on after the race. It was four miles to the station! Palm recalls, 'We were covered in mud, grabbed our clothes and bags from under a tree and took off, running like mad,' with Dale leading the way.

As they neared the station they collided with a huge crowd of Liverpool FC football fans. Dale shouted, 'Just keep going!' but Palm lost sight of her and Pat. Palm finally made it through the throngs, arriving at the station just in time to see Dale and Pat sprinting up their platform, chasing a departing train. Dale grabbed hold of the last carriage door and jumped on, closely followed by Pat. 'I couldn't believe they made it', Palm says. It's remarkable that the three of them had the energy to run four miles to the station immediately after finishing a tough race. The fact that they made it was down to Dale. As Palm points out, this was at a time when it wasn't common to see women running and they must have made quite an impression dashing through the crowd 'in t-shirts and shorts, carrying a motley array of clothing, and splattered in mud.'

Perhaps it was the new mood of optimism that characterised the 1960s which encouraged women in several countries to challenge their exclusion from long-distance road racing. Just two months after Dale's Isle of Wight marathon in May 1964, Mildred Sampson, a member of Owairaka Amateur Athletics Club in Auckland, New Zealand, set a world best, 3:19:33, in a time trial organised by her club.

Bobbi Gibb's participation in the Boston Marathon in April 1966 was widely reported and marked the start of a loosely organised movement in the USA with at least 18 American and three Canadian women and girls running unofficially in marathons between 1966 and 1969.[26] In May 1967, a 13-year-old Canadian, Maureen Wilton, improved on Mildred Sampson's world best time when she ran 3:15:22 as an unofficial competitor at a race at York University in Toronto, Ontario.

In West Germany, in September 1967, Dr Ernst van Aaken, a medical doctor who believed that children and women were natural endurance runners, invited two female members of his athletics club, OSC Waldniel, to take part in a marathon. After starting 30 minutes behind the men, 27-year-old Anni Pede, a mother of two, finished in a new world best time of 3:07:26 while 19-year-old Monika Boers crossed the line in 3:19:36.[27]

Remarkably, when the inaugural Black Forest (Schwarzwald) Marathon took place in Southwest Germany in 1968, 51 women competed. It was a 'people's race' – open to runners who weren't part of an athletics club – and had a generous cut-off time of 10 hours, allowing fast walkers to participate. When the race organiser submitted the permit request to the athletics governing body, he conveniently 'forgot' to include the section that described women's participation in the race.[28] Women who might be interested were contacted and five countries were represented: Germany, France, Austria, Switzerland and the USA. German Marthel von der Berge won the women's race in 4:19:57. Women took part in 1969 and 1970, too, with the governing body apparently turning a blind eye. In 1971, the organisers included the women's race in their permit request for the first time, and it was approved, a year before the Boston Marathon officially admitted women.

Dale trained as if she had long-distance races to enter. Running brought her enjoyment, solitude and liberation from society's expectations of activities suitable for women. Although she would have been aware of what was happening in other countries, there were no female examples for her to follow in the UK. At a time when it was rare to see people out running, she would go for long runs of 20 miles or more, sometimes accompanied by Walter Ross or another friend, but often on her own. *The Scotsman* article published after the Isle of Wight Marathon conveyed just how unusual Dale's dedication to running was, stating that, 'Running is Miss Greig's life. It is her work as well as her full-time hobby.' Explaining that Dale regularly ran 14 miles home from work in Glasgow, it went on, 'On one such training spin she was stopped twice by policemen, slightly disconcerted to see a lady in a running kit cantering along the road on her own.'[29]

Doreen King, born in 1945, first met Dale in the early 1960s after Dale came to her club, Bellahouston Harriers, one evening. Watching the track races at the 1960 Rome Olympic Games on TV got 15-year-old Doreen interested in athletics and, after joining the Harriers, she quickly fell in love with running, especially the longer distance cross-country races.[30] I interviewed Doreen in 2025 after Palm had introduced us. Doreen described how Dale, eight years her senior, had become a role model for her. Dale was the person you would refer to for everything. She said, for example, that Dale posted out a weekly bulletin with women's race results and information about upcoming fixtures. Doreen described Dale as, 'the glue that kept it all going in those days,' adding, 'She did so much behind the scenes, writing to us with whatever's going on and keeping everyone in touch.' In the winter, there were cross-country races nearly every weekend and a small, dedicated group of women would turn up to each one, prompted by Dale's reminders.

From 1964, Doreen competed several times in a groundbreaking two-mile track race that Dale organised annually at Seedhill in Paisley. In the early 1960s, two miles, the imperial equivalent of 3000 metres, wasn't an official track distance for women, either in the UK or internationally. The Seedhill race may well have been the only track race at that distance in the world for women.

After leaving school, Doreen got a job in an office in Glasgow city centre. Running was an outlet for her, a release from the boredom of secretarial work. She went running every lunchtime at Dawsholm Park, where she would often meet Dale and run laps with her. They encountered a few male runners, but no other women. Doreen ran in the evenings as well, sometimes with a club and sometimes on her own. She told me that while she always felt safe, other people saw runners, particularly women, as an oddity: 'Sometimes men would shout at me … because it wasn't the norm then to see women out running in shorts. You felt you were doing something quite different from anybody else.' She remembers that in the 1960s there was no sportswear for women athletes. 'I sent away for a tracksuit that I found advertised in a newspaper – a baggy cotton unisex garment. My auntie made me a pair of shorts in the club colours and I just wore any short sleeve tops I had.'

Dale's Isle of Wight Marathon run inspired Doreen to become a ghost runner herself. In either 1965 or 1966 – she is unsure of the year – she ran in the Scottish Marathon in Glasgow. Despite not having done any special training for the race, she had no difficulty keeping up with the men. She puts this down to her fitness at the time. Doreen waited until the men set off and joined in at the back. No-one tried to stop her. 'It was fine. Nobody objected, because I was just running it. They couldn't really stop me running in the road,' she recalls.

Highland games take place across Scotland in the summer months and are associated in many people's minds with traditional Highland sports like the tug-o-war, hammer throw and tossing the caber. They often include races. In Dale's time, the women's races were usually sprints, but Doreen remembers that Dale persuaded the organisers of several games to put on longer races for women – the mile or half mile. In the summer, Dale, Doreen and the other cross-country women would travel to different games together, winning prizes in the races.

The men's races were often long-distance events on the road or hills, and on at least one occasion Dale managed to break free of the women's programme and compete unofficially against the men. In July 1969, at the Kinlochleven Games in the Highlands, Dale ran in the Mamore Hill Race, an arduous 14-mile route. There were 33 runners and Dale's time of 2:24:04, 37 minutes behind the winner, Don Ritchie, led to her being given the ladies' award for the best performance at the Games.[31] In *Voices from the Hills*, Steve Chilton's book about pioneering women fell and mountain runners, Christine Menhennet recalls that 16 years later, in 1985, race officials still didn't want to let her run in the Mamore Hill Race as they didn't have a permit for women. They only gave in when she, too, stood her ground and insisted she was going to run whatever they said.

Dale could be very persuasive. In the 1970s, other race organisers agreed to let her run unofficially in men's races. In 1971, she celebrated her 34th birthday, on 15 May, by running the Isle of Wight Marathon for a second time. A local paper reported that Dale's training had been curtailed due to a burst blood vessel in her foot.[32] The injury started to bother her five miles into the race, but she wasn't about to give up: 'She began limping, but every time first-aid men offered help, she replied: "Just a few more miles." Her left shoe was smothered in blood at the finish.' However, Dale was a little disappointed to finish in 3:52:15, a slower time than in 1964.

On Spring Bank Holiday Monday, 31 May, 1971, Dale was among the 26 starters at the Isle of Man 40, a race of nearly 40 miles over the winding, hilly roads of the famous motorbike Tourist Trophy circuit. This was another rulebreaking run. The certificate awarded to her by the organisers, Manx Amateur Athletic Association, records her time – 6:48:00.[33] The *Paisley Daily Express* reported that the Mayor of Douglas presented her with 'a handsome trophy' in recognition of her achievement. It would be 1982 before another woman, Anne Gomer, ran in the race, this time officially.

On Saturday 4 September, 1971, Dale was in Fort William in the Highlands for the Ben Nevis Race, a 13-mile race up and down Britain's highest mountain. It was a big event for the small town, attracting around 200 men from Scottish and English clubs, and the Armed Forces. As its population swelled with visiting runners, one journalist described the atmosphere in the town as 'electric', and the race was the main topic of conversation in shops and pubs for days beforehand.[34]

Surprisingly, Dale wasn't the first woman to run the Ben Nevis race. In 1955, 16-year-old Kathleen Connochie, daughter of the race's medical adviser, ran it, having trained with one of the men on the Ben Nevis Race Association's committee. In the teeth of opposition from the men's governing body, the Scottish Amateur Athletic Association (SAAA), the race committee allowed her to start two minutes after the men and her time was recorded.[35] Kathleen never ran the race again, but remained associated with it all her life and was there to greet Dale when she finished. The *Aberdeen Press and Journal* reported that Dale was made to start 15 minutes before the men. She had hoped to beat Kathleen's time of 3:02, but finished just over a minute slower, hampered by foot problems again. The paper described her as limping in 'with her shoes soaked in blood from blisters' – further evidence of Dale's steely determination.[36]

Four years after Dale's run, in 1975, Joan Glass attempted to enter the Ben Nevis race. In Steve Chilton's *Voices from the Hills*, she explains what happened: 'My entry was refused because it was a men's race and they returned my entry fee. However, we persisted because there was a ladies' record and we pointed this out. We asked it if I could have a go at beating that time.'[37] Grudgingly, the committee eventually agreed to let Joan run the course and to time her, but she was told she had to start one minute after the men. Without Kathleen's and Dale's examples, Joan's run probably wouldn't have been allowed. Joan and other women participated in this unofficial way until the first official women's race was organised in 1980, although unfortunately it was cancelled due to adverse weather conditions. The Fell Runners Association was formed in 1970 as an organisation for men and in the 1970s and early 1980s women faced and fought many barriers to be accepted as fell runners.

Dale's longest rulebreaking run was the UK's most famous ultra, the 53-mile London to Brighton road race, which had started in 1951 as part of the Festival of Britain. The Road Runners Club (RRC) was founded the following year to continue the race as an annual event and to promote men's long-distance running. All the top long-distance men joined the club, but women couldn't join. For the first 17 years of the RRC's existence there were no female members, but in 1969 its council decided to recognise the role women played in organising club events by permitting them to join as 'lady associate members'. The lady associates weren't given any say in how the organisation was run. They weren't given voting rights. Their role was to facilitate men's sport and they had to pay a five shillings subscription fee for the privilege.

Running London to Brighton had been a notion for Dale since the 1950s, when she'd met Arthur Newton, a renowned ultra-distance runner, at Walter Ross' home. In the 1920s, Newton had set a record for the fastest run from London to Brighton, which was a popular challenge route for walkers, runners, cyclists and motorists. In 1972, a rumour that an Australian woman intended to take part in the race spurred Dale on to her own unofficial attempt. She wanted to be the first woman to run it.[38]

When preparing for ultra races Dale would build up her long run to be close to the race distance. Setting off early in the morning, she ran westwards from Paisley, carrying her tracksuit and often her swimming costume, via Bridge of Weir to Largs, a seaside resort on the Firth of Clyde, a distance of 26 miles. Sometimes she would hire a towel and go for a swim in the outdoor pool or stop for a cup of tea and a scone in a café. Anna sometimes travelled by train to meet her there. Dale might return home by train or, if she wanted to run further, follow the coastal route northwards towards Wemyss Bay, Inverkip and Gourock. Running all the way to Gourock added 15 miles to the route. The seaside towns all had stations so she could easily catch a train back to Paisley from any of them.

On Sunday 1 October, 1972, to the 7 a.m. chimes of Big Ben, 59 men set off from Westminster Bridge to run the 53 miles to Brighton. Dale wasn't with them. She had agreed with the RRC that she would set off an hour before the men. At the 14-mile point at Coulsdon, the leading men were startled to find there was a woman in their race.[39] Astonishingly, she had nothing to eat before, or during, the race, having eaten her last meal the evening before. Dale was running with Walter Ross and Malcolm Ross, Walter's nephew, supported Dale, driving to places along the route to give her fruit drinks – her only sustenance. Dale reached the finish line at Brighton Aquarium in 8:30:04, equivalent to a pace of 9:38 per mile and 'a very creditable performance' according to the report in the club newsletter. Dale and her supporters went to the traditional tea party at the Old Ship Hotel where the Mayor of Brighton presented trophies, medals and certificates to the male runners. As there wasn't an official women's race, Dale's reward was a big cheer when her performance was mentioned. This may well have meant more to her than a trophy.

Once again, Dale's run was covered in the press. In the Monday edition of *The Times*, Dale was the lone woman featured on a page devoted to men's athletics, football, golf, cricket and equestrianism. At the bottom of a report on the race, a brief description of Dale's participation appeared under the title 'Brighton belle'. The *Liverpool Daily Post* reported that after crossing the line, Dale expressed her ambition for women's running: 'I'm hoping that in a year or so there might be a women's race over this distance. There are quite a lot of people interested all over the world.'[40] Despite Dale's hopes, it was going to take another eight years and more rulebreaking before the RRC would officially admit women to the race.

Dale supported other women to run long distance. In May 1972, four women from Rankin Park Ladies Harriers undertook a 50-mile sponsored relay: Pat Spence, Rita Docherty, Phyllis Docherty and Caroline Lafferty.[41] Club founder Pat was the first to run and Dale set off with her in heavy rain, accompanying her for the first eight miles of her 14-mile leg.

After the WAAA changed its rules in 1975, the first long-distance event in Scotland to admit women was probably the Annan 12-mile race in Dumfriesshire in July 1976.[42] In 1977, when Dale wanted to give women's road racing in Scotland a boost, she persuaded the organisers of the Round Cumbrae 10, on the Isle of Cumbrae off the Ayrshire coast, to put on a women's competition with a trophy. Four years before, in 1973, the magazine *Athletics in Scotland* had reported the presence of two ghost runners at the Round Cumbrae race: 16-year-old Moira O'Boyle and her mother Noreen, members of Victoria Park AAC in Glasgow, had run the race as unofficial competitors, crossing the finish line together in 1:17:19.[43]

After the Round Cumbrae organisers agreed to Dale's request for a women's race, she was aghast to find that she was the sole female entrant. It is a testament to Dale's powers of persuasion that just a few days before the race in September 1977 she managed to convince Palm Gunstone to enter, as Palm had given birth to her first child just four months before, had hardly run for a year and had never run a 10-mile race. Palm says that at the time women stopped running when they were pregnant and were 'not encouraged to rush back to training.' She had only run a couple of times since having her daughter. At the race start, Dale and Palm set off ten minutes before the men. As the male runners overtook Palm, they gave her lots of encouragement. Dale finished first with Palm a few minutes behind her. Dale was duly presented with the trophy and Palm was very surprised to find that she, too, was to receive a prize and went up to accept it holding her daughter. It was an unusual introduction to long-distance road races, but in the 1980s, after having her second child, Palm would make a return to road races and cross-country, winning many masters prizes. There were still only a few women competing in road races in Scotland and Palm was one of the pioneers. In August 1981, she was the first woman to run in the Alyth to Blairgowrie 12-mile race, winning a pair of running shoes. She carried on racing and, in April 1985, she won the Tom Scott 10-mile race in Wishaw and two weeks later finished twelfth in the Dundee Marathon in 3:17:39. When the first women's national 10-kilometre championship was held in Glasgow in June, Palm won the masters race and Liz McColgan, another Dundee Hawkhill Harriers athlete, was the overall winner. Today, Palm is still active and involved in her local parkrun in Dundee, where she has volunteered more than 100 times.

In 1978, Dale ran the Round Cumbrae 10 again with 50-year-old Aileen Lusk (née Drummond). Aileen, born in 1928, was nine years older than Dale and had been a leading Scottish athlete in the 1950s, winning the national cross-country championship three times from 1954 to 1956, and holding the Scottish mile record for nine years from 1953.[44] After marrying in 1956, Aileen retired from athletics at the age of 28 and had two children, before returning after a 10-year break.

The first Scottish marathon to admit women was the inaugural Aberdeen Marathon in September 1979, won by Leslie Watson. The first women's marathon championship was not held until 1983. By that time, Dale was no longer competing at the distance as she had seriously injured her feet in a swimming pool accident the year before.

In 1974, when she was 37, Dale closed down Tannahill Harriers, the club she had founded 15 years before. While she remained involved in cross-country running for women, both as an administrator and a competitor, she became more engaged in the emerging masters movement.

Dale's introduction to the world of masters running came through Walter Ross, who had founded the Scottish Veteran Harriers Club in 1970. The veterans movement, now usually known as 'masters', started in the 1960s in several countries. It was created for male athletes aged 40+. When women were eventually admitted, they were classified as veterans at 35. The first organisations, such as the Association of Veteran Long-Distance Runners (IGÄL), founded in Germany, Scottish Veteran Harriers Club and the Association of Veteran Athletes, founded in Britain, were exclusively for men.[45] This led to a situation where Dale was doing a considerable amount of administrative work to support a club, the Scottish Veteran Harriers, that she could not join.

Women in several countries were pushing for inclusion in masters events, and by 1974 IGÄL had decided to allow them to become members and enter events. Dale promptly joined and when the seventh World Veteran Distance Running Championships were held on 19 May, 1974, at Draveil near Paris, she was one of seven pioneering women among the 570 finishers in the marathon. Along with Dale were four women from Germany, one from Japan and one from Denmark. It was a hot day and the conditions underfoot were difficult as, unusually, the course included many miles on forest paths. Dale ran with Walter Ross and won the race, finishing in 3:45:21. She was presented with a cup engraved with her name and time which she kept all her life. The author of the race report in *Veteris*, the magazine of the Association of Veteran Athletes, devoted very little space to the female runners, referring to them as 'a sprinkling of women' and using the patronising headline 'The ladies – God bless 'em'. Clearly women were very much on the fringes of the masters movement.

An article from a local paper in Dale's scrapbook celebrated her victory calling it 'the most remarkable feat of the afternoon' and referring to Dale as 'Scotland's most amazing sportswoman.' The journalist listed all Dale's rulebreaking runs. Dale, as usual, downplayed her extraordinary running, framing it as a hobby: 'Now I just run for recreation, covering 80 miles a week. I don't see anything remarkable about that. It's a pleasant way to pass the time.' Unfortunately, Dale was unable to defend her title in 1975, as the championships were in Tokyo and she couldn't afford to travel there.

Women were not given full membership of the Scottish Veteran Harriers until 1982. Once again, Dale took the initiative, setting up the Scottish Women Veteran Runners Association in 1974. She organised a cross-country championship, held at the same venue and on the same day as the men's championship, but over a shorter course (5000 metres). The first, on 2 March, 1975, was won by Norma Campbell with Noreen O'Boyle (who ran the Round Cumbrae 10 in 1973) second, Dale third and Aileen Lusk fourth. It was held again in 1976 and 1977, but the association was short-lived.[46]

However, Dale continued to work in support of masters athletics. When the IGÄL World Veteran Distance Running Championships came to Glasgow in 1980 she was on the organising team. Organised by Scottish Veteran Harriers with the support of the Glasgow Sports Promotion Council, it took place over a weekend in August and was a hugely successful event, attracting over a thousand masters runners, men and women, from more than 20 countries to compete in the 10-kilometre race and the marathon.[47] Dale didn't have time to compete herself that weekend, but she did participate in more than a dozen other IGÄL road and cross-country championships in the 1970s and 1980s, including the World Veterans Marathon in Coventry in 1976 and in Berlin in 1978. Serving as IGÄL Assistant Secretary from 1982–87, she travelled to many countries both for races and meetings.

Aileen and Dale used to run together on Thursday evenings in Bellahouston Park in Glasgow, and it was Dale who encouraged Aileen to try masters road races, giving her a whole new running career in her late forties.[48] She competed in the IGÄL 10-kilometre races in Berlin in 1978 and Glasgow in 1980, finishing third in the v50 category both times. Aged 53, with Dale's encouragement, Aileen entered her first marathon, Inverclyde, in 1981, finishing first in her age category in 3:45:46.

Dale retained a lifelong connection with Ryde Harriers. In 2006, they invited her and Leslie Watson, who was the race record holder and had won seven times between 1980 and 1994, to attend the 50th running of the Isle of Wight Marathon. Dale and Leslie were driven round the course by car and attended a celebration dinner in the evening where, to Dale's bemusement, lots of people wanted a photo with her.

The club invited Dale again on the 50th anniversary of her run, in 2014, but she was not well enough to travel. Malcolm Ross travelled up to Paisley every year to have lunch with Dale and, at his suggestion, Dale, then in her late seventies, reluctantly agreed to say a few words on film to mark the anniversary. In the short clip, the warmth of her personality comes across as she thanks Ryde Harriers for what they did for women's running, saying that her world record run wouldn't have happened if Ryde Harriers hadn't been 'so forward-looking in letting women run' and never mentioning her own much greater contribution.

Who recognised and thanked Dale for all she had done for women's sport? In the years after her rulebreaking runs, with the exception of *Athletics Weekly* and Doug Gillon, a respected athletics journalist at the Glasgow paper, *The Herald* there was little media interest in her story or public recognition of her achievements. In interviews in the 1980s and later, Dale downplayed her role as a pioneer of women's running, saying she didn't run to prove anything and didn't look for plaudits: 'What nobody seems to realise was that I never considered myself as a pioneer, championing women's rights. I just ran for fun because I loved being outdoors.'[49]

In 1999, Dale was both delighted and astonished to receive an invitation from London Marathon co-directors Chris Brasher and John Disley to a special dinner celebrating the Notable 19 – British marathon runners who had held a world record or won a major title. Dale and Joyce Smith were the only women on the list. The invitation was for three nights at the Tower Hotel on the London Marathon weekend, with a champagne breakfast and passes to the finish line grandstand on the Mall on the day of the race. Among Dale's papers is her reply, which shows she was convinced that no-one would know who she was: 'I have enclosed one or two "press cuttings" by way of introducing myself since I'm sure no one will have a clue who I am! I feel like a "gate-crasher" beside all these great marathon runners you have lined up and whom I have admired over the years.'

Dale attended the dinner for several years, accompanied by Cynthia and her husband Alex until his death in 2002. Cynthia was by then not in good health and Dale cared for her devotedly for the last years of her life until her death in 2013. In her later years, Dale became close to Cynthia's sister-in-law Rosemary Kidd and Rosemary's daughter Niki Kidd. When Niki took up running, Dale encouraged her and was enthusiastic about her achievements. She was delighted when Niki and her sister climbed Ben Nevis and phoned her from the summit.[50]

Dale was inducted into the Scottish Athletics Hall of Fame in 2018, but didn't attend the ceremony. By then she had been ill with kidney cancer for a few years. Dale died on 12 May, 2019, aged 81, in a hospice in Paisley.

Dale's life was guided by the sense of duty and spirit of service she learned at school. Future generations of Scottish athletes benefitted from her work to expand opportunities for girls and women. Breaking barriers for women, she trained seriously. Long-distance runners today would recognise her as one of them – a committed long-distance runner, even though in the 1960s and early 70s society told her she couldn't be one. Her profile on the Scottish Distance Running History website sums her up as: 'a serious athlete who had a core of steel which enabled her to do remarkable things in the sport.'[51]

Dale led by example and inspired many other women both to challenge themselves and to free themselves from the pressure of social norms. Palm told me that Dale had a dry sense of humour, never gave up and never let anything defeat her, and she told Scottish Distance Running History website that Dale was the person who inspired her to compete in cross-country, road and hill running. Palm regards Dale as 'one of the most under-rated of athletes' and points out that, 'It's a shame that the majority of women competing in … mass events will never have heard of Dale', or know about the role she played in creating races for women.[52]

Doreen remembers Dale as, 'One of the most impressive people I've come across in my life … I'm 80 now, you look back on your life, on the people who have played a big part, and Dale is one of them. Dale … had a big influence on me … I learned to stand up for myself more. I was quite shy and I wasn't afraid to go out running, and [have] people shouting at me and things like that. Her way was to lead by example.'

Why is Dale so often just a footnote in the history of women's running or not even mentioned at all? While her modesty and reticence may have played a part, it feels like an act of collective forgetting of an extraordinary woman. But the next generation of female rulebreakers, women like Bridget Cushen, knew about her story and Dale inspired them to act.

4
OUT ON THEIR OWN

'Why on earth can't we run longer distances?'
– Bridget Cushen[1]

At 7 a.m. on Sunday 14 October, 1973, it was still dark. Bridget Cushen was getting ready to leave for her long Sunday run, the last long run before the Harlow Marathon on 27 October. She'd had some cereal and a cup of instant coffee. The weather forecast was cold and dry. Bridget was wearing her running t-shirt and shorts, with her tracksuit on top. Wearing tracksuit bottoms meant she got fewer wolf whistles, catcalls and comments from men and young lads. Bridget laced up her shoes and put on her gloves. A woolly hat covered her dark, curly hair. After stretching for a few minutes outside the front door, she set off on the familiar route from her home in South Wimbledon to Wimbledon Common. After crossing the common and reaching Richmond Park, she was intending to do two seven-mile laps of the park, to bring the distance to about 20 miles, a good long run before the marathon.[2]

Having been stuck at her desk in a civil service office in central London all week, Bridget was looking forward to getting away from the busy city streets to the open ground of the common, which gave her the feeling of being in the countryside. It was not, of course, anything like the countryside in County Carlow in Ireland, where she'd grown up, but running the mile or so across the heathland and through the woods revived her spirits.

It was light by the time Bridget reached the common. She crossed paths with Arthur Whitehead, the owner of a place called Lauriston Cottage, out for his morning run. They greeted each other, but Bridget knew full well that Whitehead disapproved of women like her, women who ran long distance. Male runners were welcome to use the outbuildings at his home to get changed, and he often invited them in for tea and biscuits. The cottage was the base for the Lauriston Runners Club, which Whitehead had formed, and runners congregated there before heading out. Women were not admitted to the club, to the group runs or to the cottage.[3] No cups of tea for them. Bridget sometimes wished that the men at her club, Hercules Wimbledon AC, were more supportive, but the men there kept away from the women – they probably thought a woman wouldn't be able to keep up with them. There were only a few senior women and none were interested in long runs. That meant she always went out on her own.

As she set off on the first lap of Richmond Park, Bridget said hello to two ladies walking their dogs. She saw them nearly every Sunday. Running along paths through the open grassland, her thoughts turned to the marathon. She'd never raced further than two and half miles on the road. She knew she was strong, she had the endurance, but would she run out of steam after 20 miles? Would the tarmac give her blisters? Would race officials prevent her from even starting?

After a few minutes, Bridget's cloud of worries dispersed as she turned her thoughts to the first match of the cross-country season for her junior girls' team. Managing the team and travelling to races took up a lot of her time in the winter. It was a shame that most of the girls dropped out of athletics in their late teens, though, because some of the junior team would make really good seniors if only they stayed on.

Bridget had entered the Harlow Marathon because she'd always wanted to have a go at the distance. Who knew how long she'd have to wait for the Women's Amateur Athletic Association (WAAA) to change the rules. She had pushed for the WAAA to add the 3000 metres on the track and that had taken long enough. On her entry form, Bridget wrote her name as 'B Cushen', but it wasn't a serious attempt at subterfuge as she had rung the race organiser beforehand.[4]

On the afternoon of Saturday 27 October, 271 male runners gathered on the track at the Harlow Sportcentre. The cream of British men's marathoning was there; Ron Hill, Colin Kirkham and Don Faircloth were the favourites. Not only was the race hosting the English and Welsh marathon championships, it was also the qualifier for the 1974 Commonwealth Games in New Zealand. BBC cameras were there to film footage for that afternoon's *Grandstand* programme and reporters from all the major newspapers were in attendance. At the back of the field stood 33-year-old Bridget, the lone female competitor, wearing her Hercules Athletic Club vest, yellow with a diagonal red stripe, and white shorts. The race started with two laps of the track, followed by one short lap and two long laps on undulating roads and cycle paths. It was a cool, bright, dry day – perfect conditions for marathon running.

Bridget was starting at the back of the field to avoid any criticism that she had interfered with the men's race. She was pleased when she realised that, 'The race organiser had spoken to his officials who had agreed that they would not see me. As I ran past them, I noticed they were all looking down at their stopwatches calling out the time to the runners as they came past.' While the officials knew a woman was competing, the male runners did not. An Irish paper, the *Sunday Independent*, reported that Bridget said she was surprised at the number of men who tried to chat her up when they discovered a woman was in the race, remarking that, 'So many of the runners had long hair that they hadn't noticed at first.'[5] The male runners alongside her were supportive and encouraging, though, and she ran with two for a large part of the race, until one of them dropped out and the other ran ahead.

A few miles in, Bridget realised she'd made a mistake with her shoes. She'd bought them at a local sports shop – there wasn't much choice – and had gone for the best pair they had in her size that fitted her narrow feet, but the shoes were too light, the soles were too thin and she could feel every bump in the road.

At the 20-mile point, Bridget was running at under 7:00 per mile pace; she was on track for a sub-three-hour time. Unfortunately, after taking an orange drink at one of the refreshment stations, Bridget, who was unaccustomed to drinking anything other than water during long runs, felt nauseous and had to slow down. She finished in 3:37:24. While she was not included in the official results, *Athletics Weekly* reported her time and said that she had finished in 199th place.

The big story of the 1973 Harlow Marathon was the breakthrough performance by Luton United AC's Ian Thompson, who astonished everyone by winning the race with the fastest debut in marathon history, 2:12:40, earning himself a place in the British team for the 1974 Commonwealth Games in Christchurch. But the presence of the media meant that Bridget's run did not go unnoticed. A single sentence in the *Guardian*'s long report on the men's race mentioned her participation, noting that 'A curtain was raised … on another era of marathon running', but it got her name wrong and referred to her as 'Margaret Cushion'.[6]

Unusually, things were reversed in the *Daily Express*, which devoted just three short paragraphs to Thompson and almost a third of a page to Bridget, announcing, 'Bridget runs 26 miles to keep up with men'.[7] Under the headline was a photo of Bridget during the race, running between two men. The reporter emphasised Bridget's feminine qualities, describing her, using a common stereotype, as 'a dark-haired Irish colleen' and 'the trimly attractive Miss Cushen'; and saying she finished the race with a smile and 'glided easily past blistered piles of weary, worn out male casualties.' This focus on femininity suggested that, while Bridget's participation in the race was unusual, disruptive even, it was not a challenge to traditional gender roles.

In Bridget's eyes, the ban on longer distances for women made no sense when there was nothing to stop her from 'going out and running 10 miles on a public road.' She told the journalist from the *Daily Express* that she'd always wanted to run a marathon and explained her motivation: 'I feel strongly that women, at present limited to 3000 metres track races, should be permitted to run 5000 metres and 10,000 metres. This was the best way to prove it.'

Based on her experience in the race, Bridget predicted that women would easily run under 2:45 soon. At the time, the world best was 2:49:40, set by American Cheryl Bridges at the Western Hemisphere Marathon in Culver City, California, two years earlier. Just over a year after Harlow, in December 1974, Bridget's prediction would come true when Jacqueline Hansen, a teammate of Cheryl's, would become the first woman to break the 2:45 barrier at the Culver City race.

When I interviewed Bridget, she told me that, although she did tell the reporter that she might run another marathon in the spring, she didn't feel at the time that she was part of a wider campaign. Hers was an individual act of defiance: 'You just did it. You didn't think about publicising it and drawing more attention. You just wanted to prove that you could do it and that was the end of it.'

An article in the *Evening Standard* two days after the race pictured Bridget, smiling brightly and looking up from her typewriter at her civil service job, smartly dressed in an Italian black and white checked, short-sleeved dress with a red bow. She was, the article says, 'wondering what all the fuss is about.'[8]

My first interview with Bridget was in 2022, when I was writing an article for *Women's Running* magazine featuring four women rulebreakers: Dale, Bridget, Caroline Rodgers and Leslie Watson (more on them in later chapters).[9] Bridget, then 82, told me about her early life, her introduction to athletics and how she had disrupted the status quo in athletics. She described the 1970s as the 'pivotal era' when a huge wave of change occurred.

Bridget Cushen was born in rural County Carlow in southern Ireland in 1940, one of 13 children, seven boys and six girls. Her mother, Mary Fitzgerald, was born in Manchester. Her father Michael's family were from County Wexford. When Mary and Michael married in 1928, they moved to a farm in County Carlow that Mary had inherited, and made a living from growing wheat and other crops.

At the local school, there were no physical education lessons for either boys or girls. At break times the playing field was dominated by the boys who played football and hurling, a Gaelic Irish stick-and-ball game, which was hugely popular in the area. Bridget recalls that the girls' activities were more sedentary and social: 'We played hide and seek and rounders … We went by quite happy just sitting and chatting with the other girls and didn't compete in sport at all. It just didn't come into the equation.'

Bridget was aware that women competed in athletics at the Olympic Games, but the athletes all seemed to be university women. She didn't think athletics was for girls and women like her. In fact, Ireland did not send any female athletes to the Olympics until the 1956 Melbourne Games when Maeve Kyle (née Sharkey) competed in the 100 metres and the 200 metres. In 2016, Maeve, describing herself as 'the Irish suffragette of athletics', told *Athletics Weekly* about the resistance she had encountered in very conservative Ireland: 'You need to understand that at that time all sport was male-dominated and women played social sports rather than competitive sports.' [10] She experienced a lot of opposition from older women who disapproved of women taking part in sport. 'I think I made them feel uncomfortable,' she remarks. Someone even wrote a letter to the *Irish Times*, saying what a 'disgraceful hussy' she was going off to the Olympics, leaving her husband and small child behind.

After leaving school, determined to avoid getting stuck in low-paid shop work, Bridget learned shorthand and typing. In 1959, aged 19, she followed a path trodden by many of her contemporaries and left Ireland for London in search of better job opportunities. British employers used to place job ads in Irish newspapers. One of her sisters, Kathleen, was already working as a nurse in a hospital in East London.

For her first few years in London, Bridget didn't do any sport and it was a long-distance walking craze from America that led her to athletics. In late 1962, President John F Kennedy, concerned at the poor fitness of the nation, set US Marine officers a challenge of marching 50 miles in 20 hours.[11] The idea was taken up by the population at large and men, women and children were soon taking part in 50-mile hikes across the USA. The craze quickly spread to Britain. At midnight on Saturday 23 February, 1963, hundreds of intrepid men and women set off from Big Ben on a well-organised London to Brighton hike sponsored by the *Daily Sketch* newspaper. The *Nottingham Guardian* reported that thousands of well-wishers lined up along Brighton's promenade to applaud the 299 walkers who finished in less than 18 hours. The first female finisher was Miss Margaret Peart, a 24-year-old scientist at a radio research station, who finished in just under 14 hours. Margaret said that she'd been tempted to give up, 'but somehow I stuck it out, just to show the lads at work what a woman can really do.'[12] I can't help but be impressed by Margaret. She was working in a male-dominated field; she was determined to prove what she could do; and she walked fast, averaging three and a half miles an hour. She was precisely the kind of example to inspire another young working woman, Bridget. At that time, Bridget, 22, was working as a secretary at a manufacturing company based at London Bridge. Inspired by the walks they'd heard about in the press, a few dozen of the office staff and factory workers organised their own London to Brighton walk. Bridget recalls that the weather was dry – ideal for walking – and thinks it may have been late May, probably in 1963. In good spirits, they set off from Big Ben at 8 p.m. one evening with their rucksacks of provisions, hot drinks and sandwiches. Colleagues and friends were going to meet them at agreed points along the route.

By midnight the walkers had tramped through the suburbs of South London and reached Croydon, a distance of about 10 miles. Their feet were aching and many had painful blisters. Unsurprisingly, their enthusiasm was waning. The prospect of carrying on in the dark for several more hours was too much for some of Bridget's colleagues. They gave up and got lifts back to London. As the walk continued the group dwindled. Bridget remembers two young women from the factory who courageously got as far as Coulsdon, about 14 miles, before stopping. They had hardly done any training. Only two of the walkers had the tenacity, fitness and determination to walk the whole 50 miles to Brighton: Bridget and one of the men from the factory.

After the walk, Bridget's landlady suggested that, as she was clearly very fit, she should join an athletics club. When Bridget went along to the local athletics track at Tooting Bec, South London, she quickly realised that most of the clubs that trained there were men only. Just one club was mixed, Hercules AC – later called Hercules Wimbledon AC – so Bridget joined them and, aged 23, began competing in track and cross-country races for the first time in her life.

While still in her twenties, Bridget became involved in the running of the club. When she went along to the AGM one year, she was the only woman there and the committee asked her to become the women's captain. Bridget says it was hard to get other people to volunteer, but she was conscientious and wanted to make a good job of it, which was 'how I got lumbered with looking after the youngsters and doing everything else.' From this point, athletics became a big part of Bridget's life. Most weekends, she took the girls' teams to either cross-country or track fixtures, often racing herself, too, and she spoke in favour of longer distances on the track for girls at several annual general meetings of the WAAA. In this way, Bridget contributed to creating more opportunities for future generations of girls. By 1972, both juniors – girls under 15 – and intermediates – girls aged 15 and 16 – were allowed to compete at 1500 metres.

Within months of joining Hercules AC in 1963, Bridget was competing in cross-country races and finished a very creditable 11th in the Surrey County Championships that December, an event she would win in 1970. In the 1960s and 1970s she travelled to cross-country races across the Southeast and competed in the WAAA national championship each year. Clearly, longer distances were Bridget's forte. She competed on the track, too, but in the 1960s, women's athletics meetings usually had 880 yards as their longest race or, sometimes, the mile. While she was a strong performer over the mile, ranking in the UK top 20 for the year in 1967, for ambitious Bridget that was not good enough. She knew she would never rank highly at these distances. 'I became frustrated when I was running … I had not got basic speed so no matter how hard I trained I used to always get eliminated in the heats.' This frustration was translated into action when Bridget competed unofficially in a men's 3000 metres race at Hercules AC's annual trophy meeting at the Tooting Bec track in September 1966. Her coach at the club, Jim Braben, shared her view that women should be permitted to run longer distances and arranged for her to run in the race. Meanwhile, he and others were making the case at county and national level for the 3000 metres to become an approved event for women. Bridget ran the distance again at the club's 1967 trophy meeting and her time was recorded in the results in *Athletics Weekly*. In February 1968, the WAAA AGM agreed to recognise the distance. Later that year the first 3000 metres championship race was held. After this the WAAA began to make the case for the distance to be added to international competition.

Bridget was also willing to speak out for herself. In March 1971, *Athletics Weekly* featured a very long letter entitled 'Bridget Cushen "victimised"', accompanied by a photo of Bridget running in the national cross-country championships in 1969. What is extraordinary about the letter is that it was written by Bridget herself and she was clearly very angry. Women hardly ever wrote into *Athletics Weekly* and when they did they rarely expressed their opinions.

The cause of Bridget's anger was her treatment by the Irish athletics governing body. In 1967, when the International Cross Country Union had organised the first women's international championship race, Bridget, like Dale Greig a strong cross-country runner, had seen this as her best and only chance to gain international selection. And she had wanted to represent the country of her birth, Ireland. As she said at the start of her letter, the international championships gave women more incentive and enabled them 'to enjoy some of the privileges which men had enjoyed for so long.'

Bridget's complaint centred around the insistence of Irish athletics officials that if she wanted to be selected to compete for Ireland she would have to compete in the Irish national championship. Bridget's argument was that as she was an Irish citizen, she should be selected on the basis of her superior performances, not on whether she managed to travel to Ireland. In both 1967 and 1968, Bridget had been unable to travel to the qualifying race in Ireland and hadn't been selected, despite having consistently beaten some of the women who were selected, in cross-country races in England.

By 1969, she had become fed up with the situation. She had contacted the Irish officials in advance with evidence of her performances, drawing their attention to the fact that the English and Irish championships were happening on the same weekend. It was her strongest ever year – she had finished in the top three in every cross country race she'd run. Surely this was enough to secure Irish selection for the international championship in Clydebank, Scotland, in March? On Saturday 22 February 1969, immediately after finishing third in the English national, her highest-ever placing, she was told on the telephone that if she wanted to get into the Irish international team she would have to go over and compete in the championships the next day. Bridget had already qualified to run for England, but was so determined to represent Ireland that she made the journey from Aldershot to Mallow in Cork, a round trip of over 600 miles. Bridget placed fifth. Describing what happened next, she said in *Athletics Weekly*: 'I was brought before a committee of old men who asked me if I thought I was capable of beating the Americans at Clydebank. I returned to London that evening still not knowing whether or not I was going to be selected!' Bridget was finally put out of her misery and offered a place on the team, but, unfortunately, the recurrence of a stress fracture she'd had in 1968 prevented her from running. She blamed this on the physical stress of competing in two races within 24 hours combined with the long journey, reflecting bitterly: 'Again I saw a whole winter's training go to waste and was advised that I had only a remote chance of ever being able to run competitively again. What a penalty to pay for being dedicated to sport.'

To get ahead of the situation, in both 1970 and 1971, Bridget had got in touch with the governing body in Ireland, but they had refused to clarify whether she needed to travel to Ireland for the championship. In her letter, she accused the officials – 'those few old men who administer women's sport in Ireland' – of deliberately discriminating against Irish athletes living in England, preventing them from competing internationally. Bridget never did compete at the international cross-country championships, but she had spoken out powerfully, challenging the male-dominated athletics establishment. In the years that followed she would use this fire, this conviction and this confidence to campaign for the right of women to have greater participation in athletics through the masters movement.

Bridget's was not the only voice raised in protest. A few weeks before her fulminating letter appeared in *Athletics Weekly*, on International Women's Day 1971, thousands of women, and some men, had marched through London in the first Women's Liberation demonstration. They were voicing the four demands drawn up by the first Women's Liberation Conference held in Oxford a year before: equal pay; equal educational and job opportunities; free contraception and abortion on demand; free 24-hour nurseries. The movement was not just about campaigning on issues; women were seeking to transform themselves, their lives and society.[13] New, progressive legislation such as the Abortion Act (1967), the Divorce Act (1969) and the Matrimonial Proceedings and Property Act (1970) gave women more control over their bodies, their property and their lives, contributing to changing social expectations. Women like Bridget felt empowered and began to dream of wider horizons, to expect more and to demand change. Yet as Rafaelle Nicholson notes in her history of women's cricket in Britain, 'There remained a vast gap between women's sport and the second-wave feminist movement.'[14] The Women's Liberation Movement largely ignored the unequal treatment of women in sport and the feminist journals, such as *Shrew* and *Spare Rib*, made almost no mention of sport.

While the movement didn't engage with women's participation in sport, female athletes, whether or not they identified with feminism, felt less inclined to accept the status quo, which had imposed frustrating limitations on their participation for decades. The press called them 'athletic suffragettes' and 'women's libbers', which is not surprising, because by running on the roads they were embodying the right of women both to run long-distance and to be in the outdoor space. It was a radical, political act. They were challenging the deep-seated belief that women's place was in the home. Through individual and, occasionally, collective action, and by using their voices, they were effecting change.[15] As Nicholson notes, 'These women may not have been self-defined feminists, or involved in overtly 'political' campaigns, but their ideas and actions fed into the feminist movement.'

Despite these progressive legislative changes, in the early 1970s women were still deprived of basic rights which we take for granted today. In 1971, women could be sacked for being pregnant. They were not entitled to maternity leave or maternity pay. Employers could still pay women less than men for doing the same job (the Equal Pay Act would not be implemented until 1975).

Service providers could discriminate freely against women. Some nightclubs, restaurants and bars had dress codes that banned women from wearing trousers. Some pubs refused to serve women at the bar, or even to admit them to the bar room, obliging them to use a 'ladies lounge' instead. Working women were routinely refused mortgages or were granted them only if they could secure the signature of a male guarantor. Women could be refused credit, such as hire purchase. Annoyingly, even when they were paying for the item, it had to be their husband's name on the paperwork.[16] Only when the Sex Discrimination Act came into force at the end of 1975 were women legally entitled to the same services as men.

After turning 35 in 1975, Bridget became part of the growing masters athletics movement, competing in track, cross-country and road races at British, European and World Masters Athletics Championships. Generally, unlike traditional athletics, athletes didn't have to be selected to compete in masters events, although road races might have cut-off times. In June 1978, Bridget finished fourth in her age category – 35 to 39 – at the World Veteran Road Championships marathon in Berlin in 3:14:57.8. Dale Greig finished 14th in the 40 to 44 age category. Three months later, running nine minutes faster, Bridget won her age category in the European Veterans Championships marathon in Via Reggio, Italy, in 3:05:49.

A natural organiser and experienced administrator, Bridget soon became involved in the governance of masters athletics, in the UK and internationally. When the first steps towards the formation of an international governing body for masters athletics, the World Association of Veteran Athletes (WAVA), were taken in 1975, Maeve Kyle, who had competed for Ireland in the 1956 Olympic Games, was chosen as the only female member of the steering committee.[17] In 1983, Bridget was elected as the women's representative – the only woman on the association's all-male committee.

Four years later in 1987, Bridget was nominated as a member of the newly formed veteran committee of the international governing body, the International Amateur Athletic Federation (IAAF). For 75 years, the IAAF had perpetuated male control of international athletics with all the key posts held by men. The only women elected to the organisation were those who served on the women's committee. Bridget was astonished to realise that her appointment to the veteran committee had broken the established order – she was the first woman to be elected to a role outside the women's committee.[18]

Disappointingly, this didn't lead to an opening of the floodgates for women. It took another eight years for a woman to be elected to the council: in 1995, former athletes Abby Hoffman of Canada and Nawal El Moutawakel of Morocco took up two of the 27 places on the council, the key decision-making body in the IAAF. In 2016, 21 years later, the IAAF added minimum gender targets to its constitution with a plan to move towards equal representation on its council. In 2019, it elected its first female vice-president. In 2023, the association, by then renamed World Athletics, achieved its target of 50% women on the council. Yet, in its 113-year history, World Athletics has never had a female president.

In the 1980s, while the javelin, shot and discus were an accepted part of women's competition, there was no triple jump, hammer, steeplechase or pole vault for women in the WAAA Championships, the World Championships or the Olympics. The notion that these were not suitable events for women still held sway.

The masters movement became a driving force behind the introduction of more events for women. Bridget and others ensured that new events were included in the World Masters Athletics Championships, starting at the 1985 Rome championships with an exhibition women's hammer throw. At subsequent championships, female athletes enthusiastically took up the chance to compete in the triple jump and the steeplechase. Bridget presented videos of these events to the IAAF women's committee as evidence in support of their introduction to international competition. But progress was grindingly slow. The reasons for this were two-fold. Firstly, the committee did not have the authority to add events to the international programme itself. Instead, it had to make proposals to the IAAF Council, but the male-dominated council retained power by finding reasons to throw out the women's proposals or just completely ignored them.[19] Secondly, before an event could be added to international championships, individual countries had to introduce it to their athletics programmes and women had to train and compete nationally.

After the triple jump was added to the WAAA Championships in 1989, it took seven years for it to appear on the Olympic Games programme at Atlanta in 1996. The hammer throw and the pole vault were added at Sydney in 2000. Steeplechase took even longer. The first women's Olympic 3000 metres steeplechase was not held until the 2008 Beijing Games.

In 1988 Bridget was nominated for the *Sunday Times* Sportswoman of the Year award for her service to international athletics at the IAAF. When I interviewed her in 2022, she was about to step down from the position of honorary secretary at the British Masters Athletics Federation, after over 50 years' service to the sport.

In the early 1970s, Bridget was not the only woman to break the rules and run in men's races. On Sunday 10 March, 1974, a few dozen runners huddled together near the start line of the Milford 21-mile cross-country race at Cannock Chase in Staffordshire. The open expanse of the common afforded them no shelter from the biting, cold wind. Among them stood one of the best cross-country runners in the West Midlands, a small figure with dark, wavy hair. She had no right to be there. It was a men's race. Christine Readdy was a 21-year-old trainee teacher from Stafford. She'd won a cross-country race the day before and, earlier that winter, she'd become the Staffordshire cross-country champion. Not only was Christine breaking the rules by running in a men's race, but she was also about to attempt to run 17 miles further than the longest women's cross-country race in the calendar.

As the pack of runners set off over the common, the unremitting wind lashed their faces with showers of sleet. A small group of men pulled away. Christine was running well in the main pack of men and feeling confident. This was her home turf, where she did her long runs of 10 to 15 miles on Sundays. At the 10-mile point, Christine was well up in the field. Here the course entered a switchback of sharp, 100-foot climbs on loose sandy paths. On this tough four-mile section, the runners were forced to slow their pace. Christine realised she was too cold to carry on.[20] While dropping out of the race was a disappointment, it wasn't a failure. Several men dropped out, too, and Christine had proved she was tough enough to take on the course. Confident she would be able to finish under better conditions, Christine told the local paper so. And, in 1976, she returned to the race and finished it.

I was keen to interview Christine because she ran in some of the first official women's races (more on this in Chapters 5 and 6). I wasn't sure how to find her, but when I discovered her married name was Kilkenny, I realised that we were both members of Midland Masters AC and I asked the chair if he would connect us. When I interviewed Christine in 2024, when she was 71, she told me she was still active in athletics but was taking an enforced break from running due to an injury. As we talked, she revealed that she had been a ghost runner in many men's races in the 1970s.

In the early 1970s, Christine sometimes used local men's races as training runs, joining in behind the main group of runners. Just two weeks after the too-chilly Milford 21, she took part in a seven-mile road race at Newcastle under Lyme, beating a dozen of the men.[21] She seems to have passed under the radar of the athletics authorities, perhaps because her participation was not noted in *Athletics Weekly*. Christine was a well-known local athlete and this probably meant the clubs that organised races didn't make a fuss about letting her run. She recalls that the male runners didn't mind as long as she didn't get in their way and she enjoyed chatting to them.[22]

Christine was born in Stafford in 1953. At 14, she joined Stafford AC. Initially she did the sprint distances, which she didn't enjoy, progressing after a year to 400 metres. In her late teens, she began to race the 1500 metres, which had just been introduced for girls her age, and did cross country to build her stamina for track.

From 1972 to 1976, Christine attended Madeley College of Education, near Stoke-on-Trent, to train to be a PE teacher, and joined City of Stoke AC. Christine knew that Bridget had run in the Harlow Marathon and that women were running marathons in the USA. She came across some athletics booklets in the college library with articles by American women making the case for women doing longer runs. 'I remember reading those articles before I did my first marathon,' she says.

Christine probably read about Bridget's 1973 marathon when it was reported in *Athletics Weekly*. The magazine also listed breakthrough road-running performances by women in other countries in its international news section. In February 1973, a few months before the Harlow Marathon, the magazine featured a three-page article by Cliff Temple headed, 'Women are no strangers to the marathon'.[23] Temple was involved in club athletics, was the athletics correspondent of the *Sunday Times* and was a regular contributor to *Athletics Weekly*. Both Temple and the *Athletics Weekly* editor, Mel Watman, supported women running long distance.

In the article, Temple charted the progression of the world record for the marathon, mentioning Dale Greig's time at the Isle of Wight in 1964 and her London to Brighton run in 1972 – 'a double marathon'. Although the numbers of women participating were still small, by 1973 dozens of American women had run a marathon. Temple noted that, as American women were now officially accepted in races, 'if ever there is a *women's* marathon in the Olympic Games then the USA has a flying start.' He was, however, doubtful that change would come soon in the UK: 'Will we ever see a similar situation in Britain? Not for a long time, is my guess. And if women are allowed at some stage to race marathons it would have to be under tighter age regulations than exist in the USA.' Like most people in athletics in the UK, he disapproved of children being able to run marathons. In the USA, girls and boys as young as six were sometimes allowed to compete in them.

The organisation of races in the USA differed from the UK, where the governing bodies had a tight grip on the athletics clubs that put on road races. By contrast, in the USA, it was quite a confusing picture. Three organisations claimed to have jurisdiction over road racing and there were lots of race organisers who operated outside the control of any of these three bodies.[24] This looser set-up explains how the New York City Marathon was able to admit women to its inaugural race in September 1970, when it wasn't an approved distance for women under Amateur Athletic Union rules.

In May 1971, following protests by women at road races, those rules were relaxed. Women were permitted to compete in road races up to 10 miles and, rather oddly, 'selected women' – in other words those with experience – were allowed to run a marathon. The pressure continued and within a year the union permitted all women to compete in marathons. Every year since 1966, when Bobbi Gibb had been a ghost runner at the Boston Marathon after being refused an official entry, women had been competing unofficially in the race. Finally, in 1972, women could enter officially for the first time, as long as they had run a marathon in under three and a half hours – the same qualifying time as for men. Eight women ran and all eight finished. The first official champion was Nina Kuscsik, one of the women who had led the campaign for women's long-distance running. Nina finished in 3:10:26, with Elaine Pedersen of California second and Kathrine Switzer, who had famously raced Boston in race numbers in 1967, third. In an interview in 2013, Joan Ullyot, one of the American marathon pioneers, remembered being able to race every weekend in California in the early 1970s. Women in the UK – limited to races of four miles – really were missing out.[25]

Christine, too, was hoping for change but like Temple she wasn't optimistic it would happen. Before going to college, she represented her club at Midlands WAAA committee meetings. She recalls that most of the officials were old and conservative, and just wanted to make sure things ticked over smoothly. She doesn't think they were opposed to women's long-distance running as such, but says, 'I think they felt that there wasn't really a demand for it.'

Margaret Tunstall's early athletics experiences were similar to Christine's. Born in 1954 in Workington in Cumbria, Margaret started athletics at school, aged 12. She competed at long jump and hurdles. Her talent for longer distances became apparent at the school sports day. She ran the 800 metres, standing in for a friend who was ill, won the race, broke the school record and never went back to sprint distances. In 1969, when Margaret was

15, the school allowed girls to run cross country for the first time. Margaret qualified to run for Cumberland in the English schoolgirls cross-country championships at Leicester, which had been introduced in 1968. She joined a newly formed club, Lakeland AC, and competed for them in track and cross country.[26]

My first contact with Margaret came in October 2020, when she replied to one of my Facebook posts about women's running history. We have exchanged emails ever since and she has answered my questions about her athletics career and her experience of rulebreaking. In 1972, 18-year-old Margaret moved to Southeast England to train as a teacher at Bedford College of PE. She joined the local athletics club, Luton United AC, and competed in track and cross country. Her proudest moment was winning a 1500 metres race in 4:36.6, a time which qualified her to become a member of the elite British Milers Club. While at college, she ran unofficially in a few local men's road races and says, 'As far as I remember no-one was bothered, I joined in at the start without a number and didn't run through the finish. I can only remember encouragement from other runners and I timed myself.'

Once Margaret ran in a seven-mile men's cross-country league race as part of the Luton United AC team. There were no problems, perhaps because the race officials didn't spot her. Margaret married Ian Thompson, winner of the 1973 Harlow Marathon, in 1975. Like Christine, when road racing opened up to women in 1975, she was ready to grasp the opportunity.

In 1970, Joyce Smith turned 33. After taking time out of athletics in 1968, the year she gave birth to her first daughter, Lisa, she had returned to competition in 1969. The early 1970s were years of peak performances on the track and at cross country for Joyce. She finished in the top five at the national cross country for five consecutive years, 1970 to 1974, taking the win in 1973, aged 35. In 1971, she broke the world record for the newly recognised 3000 metres and won bronze at the international cross-country championships in Spain. In 1972, she won the international cross-country championships in Cambridge and reached the semi-final of the 1500 metres at the Munich

Olympic Games, setting the British record in her heat and then again in the semi-final. When the 3000 metres was included in the European Athletics Championships in Rome for the first time in 1974, Joyce won a bronze medal.

Joyce competed for Barnet AC and, as one of the fastest runners in the club, she often trained with men, as there were no women who ran at a similar pace to her. Her talent for long-distance was evident. Yet even Joyce could run into trouble.[27] In an interview in Gabrielle Collison's *British Marathon Running Legends of the 1980s*, Joyce recounts how this happened. In the winter of 1971–72, she was training at the track with the men from her club and would regularly go out for 10-mile runs with them. Joyce could keep pace and they told her she'd be very good at long-distance road races. However, there just weren't any for women to do. She did an inter-club five-mile road race at Alperton at one point, but somebody saw her and she got told off for running in a men's race.

It was common for female athletes who had gone to a men's road race as spectators to join in. They might run a bit behind the men, run on the pavement, or take shortcuts down side roads to see the men at different points in the race. This was generally tolerated by race organisers who liked to attract spectators. However, there were limits to this tolerance. It had to be clear that the women weren't there to race. If they had turned up in shorts and vests or had run alongside the men, they would have been reprimanded. They were to maintain the pretence of being spectators rather than runners. As was so often the case, it was clothes that made the distinction between passivity and activity. Nevertheless, women were no longer spectators holding the coats; just there to support men's sport. Now they had agency. Now they were on the path to becoming long-distance road runners themselves.

Why didn't British women go abroad to race? Margaret points out that there was uncertainty over how the governing bodies would react. The British Amateur Athletic Board (BAAB) was in charge of all international competition entries and Margaret recalls that her husband Ian was once threatened with sanctions from the BAAB when he ran a race abroad without asking permission first. The cost would also have been a deterrent. Travel abroad was expensive, most women were either working full-time or part-time, and some were caring for children. As British women had no experience as long-distance runners, they would not receive invitations to races, which usually came with the offer of paid expenses.

One British woman did compete in a road race abroad, however. In May 1974, Dale Greig won the women's race at the World Veterans Marathon Championship in France. Ironically, she would not have been permitted to compete in a marathon in her own country.

However, 1974 saw several other significant steps forward in women's road running. In February, the Amateur Athletic Union of the USA held its first Women's National Marathon Championship and 44 women finished.[28] In September, an international women's marathon was held in Waldniel in West Germany with 46 participants from seven countries, including West Germany, USA, France, the Netherlands and Sweden. It attracted 20,000 spectators.[29] In October, 56-year-old German Eva-Maria Westphal, who had competed alongside Dale at the veterans marathon in France in May and at Waldniel in September, became the first woman to win the Athens Marathon.[30] Another first came in October, when the inaugural Berlin Marathon counted 10 women among its 244 finishers.

A few women were running even further than the marathon. In the early 1970s, women in some Western European countries were officially competing in ultras, 100-kilometre races in West Germany, Switzerland, Denmark, Italy and Finland. In Dortmund, West Germany, women had competed in the Unna

100-kilometre race since it began in 1969.[31] Eva-Maria had won the first four races from 1969 to 1972 and finished third in 1973. She was third again in 1974. Although the number of female competitors was small that year – 15 female finishers as opposed to 690 male finishers – they were there and that was what mattered.[32]

There were, of course, no official female competitors in British ultras – races over marathon distance. Dale had been an unofficial competitor at both the Isle of Man 40 in 1971 and the 53-mile London to Brighton in 1972. On 24 August, 1974, a Canadian woman, Susan Taylor, followed her example when she completed the 36-mile Two Bridges road race in Scotland. The Scottish Distance Running History website describes the race as 'one of the real classics of Scottish ultra-distance running' and it attracted runners from across Britain and further afield.[33]

The route followed the north bank of the River Forth, crossing it at the Kincardine bridge, then running back along the south bank to cross over the famous Forth Road Bridge. In 1972 the Washington Sports Club in the USA created their own version of the race along the Potomac River, and runners from the USA and Canada began to come to the Scottish race.[34] In 1974 there was a team of three men from the Washington Sports Club, a man from New York Pioneers Club and one R Taylor from Vancouver, Canada. Among the finishers there was a woman, Taylor's wife Susan. The report in the Road Runners Club newsletter did not record her time, but noted: 'Canadian Susan Taylor also ran the course, although just over three hours behind her husband, but she still had plenty of energy left for that evening's activities.'[35]

Susan took around seven hours. We know nothing more about her, but at least we have a first name whereas her husband – Richard? Robert? Roger? – is missing his in the race report. Given her pace of 11:40 per mile, Susan must have had some running experience. It was, of course, a men's race and while her husband had entered in advance, Susan's participation was as a guest rather than as an official competitor. Nine years would pass before another woman ran in the Two Bridges – in 1983 three American women became the first official female competitors. In the final months of 1974, though, momentum was building for change and in 1975 more women would resort to rulebreaking to assert their right to race long-distance.

5
MAKING IT OFFICIAL

'The event, acknowledged as the most gruelling of athletic races, held no fears for them.'[1]

In the early hours of 1 January 1975, after seeing in the new year, Avril Jones and her boyfriend Peter Lewis went out first-footing round Cramlington New Town in Northeast England, visiting people Peter knew from his time as an undergraduate at Durham University. They were staying with one of Peter's friends from the university athletics team, Mike Bateman and his wife Angie. They remained out until 2.30 a.m., even though both Peter and Mike were going to run in the 13.6-mile Morpeth to Newcastle road race later that day. Fortunately, the race didn't start until the early afternoon and they were able to get a few hours' sleep.

Avril and Peter were both members of athletics clubs. They had met at university in Birmingham and were living together in Bromsgrove, not far from the city. Avril was 20 and in the last year of a degree in PE and German language and literature, and Peter was a postgraduate student. The previous year, she had been a spectator at the race and had hated standing around watching as she had got very cold. Determined not to repeat that experience, this year Avril was going to run. Of course, she hadn't entered the race, as women weren't allowed to race this distance. The longest road races Avril had done were women's relays, usually just two miles. Nevertheless, she was confident she could cover the distance as she trained six days a week, and she and Peter were in the habit of doing a long run of about 10 miles together on a Sunday.

Avril and Peter discussed what she should do and decided that the best thing would be for her to start 10 minutes before the men. She duly set off and, after a while, the men started to overtake her. Peter caught up with her at about seven and a half miles. She was enjoying running. The weather was mild and there were lots of people out watching the race. Many of them cheered her on, shouting words of encouragement. As she approached the finish funnel, she slipped off to the side to avoid going over the finish line with the men.

What happened next surprised Avril. The journalist covering the race for the *Newcastle Journal*, a daily paper which was sponsoring the race that year, had spotted a good story and made a beeline for her. Avril was quite shy and felt embarrassed, but agreed to be interviewed and to pose for a photograph.

A picture of Avril in her tracksuit sitting behind a massive, ornate, silver trophy appeared on the front page of the paper the next day with a short article entitled, 'Girl runner leads the way'. The paper reported her as saying, 'Women aren't allowed to compete in men's races, although I would like to if I could. I do some cross-country and middle-distance running, but I am a better competitor when I'm running against men. In America women run in the marathon, so why not here?' The *Newcastle Journal* gave Avril's time as 1:36:30[2] and said that had she crossed the line she would have placed about 150th out of 202 finishers.

When I interviewed Avril in 2024, she recalled that participating in the race was an entirely positive experience. There was no comeback or criticism from the race officials or the local Amateur Athletic Association (AAA). This may well have been because she and Peter were friends with several members of one of the local clubs, Morpeth Harriers. Mike Bateman was also a long-standing member of the Harriers.

My first contact with Avril was in 2022, when she commented on one of my Facebook posts about women's running history. I was keen to interview her because I knew she'd run in the first official British women's marathon in 1975 (more of this later in this chapter). However, I had no inkling that she had been a ghost runner in the Morpeth to Newcastle race. Fortunately, Avril had kept a scrapbook and was able to send me the newspaper clippings that filled in details she no longer remembered.

When I interviewed her on the phone, Avril was at home in Ontario with her husband Peter. They married in 1975 and moved to Canada in the early 1980s. Avril, now 70, was surprised and fascinated that someone was interested in her running 'after all this time', telling me that it was Peter, not her, who was the athlete of note – he had represented Great Britain at 800 metres. Whereas Peter has kept all his detailed training diaries, Avril hadn't made records of her training or races as an adult. It didn't seem important at the time, but looking back 50 years later she sees her rulebreaking and her pioneering races as part of a bigger picture of women's activism:[3] 'I am shocked it is so long ago, but glad I am still around to remember it. I remember how exciting and inspiring it felt to be a trailblazer in running marathons at this time. It was very empowering and gave me a lot of strength to face challenging times in my life.'

Avril had always loved to run. Born in 1954, she grew up in Haywards Heath in Sussex. When she was at primary school, she would challenge herself to run the mile to school without stopping. When she started at Haywards Heath Grammar School she didn't do well at athletics as she wasn't a good sprinter and sprints were the only races for girls in school sports. Everything changed when Avril was 13 and a man called Phil Nash came to the school. He was involved in setting up a new athletics club for young people at the local youth centre and he asked the teachers to get all the girls to run round the perimeter of the large school playing field. Avril wasn't fast enough to be invited to training and might have given up at this point were it not for something Nash said which stuck in her mind: 'We believe that girls can run and do just as well as boys, and they can run the same distances.'

Avril rang the phone number Nash had given out and started going to the new club, Haywards Heath Harriers, two evenings a week. She was coached by Tim French, a former Army physical training instructor and, true to Nash's words, the training was mixed. Avril recalls that the girls and the boys did everything together, which was unusual at the time, 'When we were training for the winter, we'd all do a gym session, then we'd all go out running together up to five miles around the roads.' Not all Avril's training was with the club, though, because living in the countryside she felt safe and would regularly run five or six miles on her own.

In July 1968, Avril was one of a team of 14-year-old Harriers girls who, along with over 900 other walkers, set off from the

Leatherhead Football Club ground to do the Tanners Marathon, a 30-mile countryside walk organised by Alan Blatchford who was involved in putting on many running and walking events in Surrey (more of him later in this chapter). The weather conditions were challenging, with heavy rain making the footpaths slippery. Accompanied by Tim French, Avril's father and another adult, the girls completed the trek within 10 hours, earning the finishers' certificate and demonstrating exceptional endurance.[4]

Scrapbooks of newspaper clippings collected by her mum record that in her teens Avril competed at track and cross country, representing the school and the club. She was picked several times to represent Sussex, and the Haywards Heath Harriers team won both the county and the area championships. After going to university in autumn 1972, Avril continued to compete in cross country and on the track and represented the University of Birmingham in the British Universities Cross-country Championships in February 1974. But April's Morpeth to Newcastle run on New Year's Day 1975 marked the start of a new chapter of road running for her.

On 15 January 1975, two weeks after Avril's run, United Nations International Women's Year was launched in the UK. There were many civic celebrations and campaigns. The year's aims of full gender equality and the elimination of gender discrimination were much discussed in the British press, with many female journalists voicing their opinions. One effect was to highlight just how far women were from equality. As one female journalist pointed out at the beginning of the year, only 27 of 635 MPs were women. Sexism and the objectification of women were still pervasive and ingrained in social attitudes, but women's legal rights were progressively improving, creating a platform for further social change. The Sex Discrimination Bill was about to make its way through Parliament and the Equal Pay Act (1970) would come into force at the end of 1975.

Allowing British women to race longer distances must have seemed an obvious and uncontroversial step to many, but it was to take a few more months and more rulebreaking, rebellion and resistance by women before the decision was made. One of these women, 24-year-old nursing student Adele Brignall, had had enough of not being able to race long distance on the roads and decided to organise a women's run herself. On 22 February, 1975 a small notice appeared in *Athletics Weekly* with the title '10 mile run for women'. It read:

> Any woman athlete who would like to join in a 10-mile run, same day, same course as the Tonbridge 10, but starting one minute behind the male runners in this event, should phone Miss A. Brignall (Tonbridge 3774) for further details.

It was a radical act. Placing a notice in *Athletics Weekly*, the magazine read by everyone interested in athletics, meant that not only would it reach women who might be interested in running, but it would also be seen by the officials of the Women's Amateur Athletic Association (WAAA). This was a step up from individual women crashing races: it was an open act of defiance.

Adele and her future husband, Dave Cross, were on the committee of Tonbridge AC, the organisers of the Tonbridge 10. In 2022, after I posted on Twitter about this race, a member of the club kindly offered to put me in touch with Adele. Much of the detail that follows comes from a video interview with Adele and Dave, during which we talked about the race, Adele's early interest in athletics and her running career.

After placing the notice in *Athletics Weekly*, Adele was pleased to hear from a dozen women who wanted to run. She was less pleased to hear from Marea Hartman, honorary secretary of the WAAA. The purpose of Hartman's letter was to enforce the rules governing women's road racing. Women were not permitted to run further than four miles and were not allowed to race against men. She stated that as the proposed 'race' was not covered by a WAAA race permit it should not go ahead. Adele boldly wrote in reply that it was a run not a race and so no permit was required. Adele knew she had the support of the Tonbridge AC chair and most of the committee members. She had even run the course one year, starting at the same time, but running in the opposite direction to the men.

The day of the Tonbridge 10, Saturday 8 March, was very wet and windy. Adele, Alison Blake, Betty Norrish, Sheila Ansell and Andrea Russell were getting changed into their racing tops, shorts and road shoes in a cramped storeroom. The men had the changing rooms in the Swanmead Pavilion. There were no changing facilities for the women. The five women chatted excitedly about the prospect of racing the 10 miles. It might not have been official, but it still felt like a race to them. Alison, Betty, Sheila and Andrea had all travelled a long way to be there. Alison lived in Plymouth, over 200 miles away, but didn't want to miss the chance to get a recorded time for 10 miles.[5]

Adele wasn't well but, having organised the run, she was determined to start. Standing behind the men, soaked to the skin by the heavy downpour, Adele felt a surge of pride at what she had managed to do. The field of about a hundred men set off on the two-lap course and a minute later the five women started. A photographer from the local paper was there and took photos. Alison went into the lead straightaway and was soon passing the slower men. At the halfway point, Adele was feeling awful and had to stop and go home.

About 10 metres before the finish line, each of the women went off to the side. Bill Collins, chair of Tonbridge AC, timed them all. Alison Blake finished in 58:24, ahead of about half the men in the race. It was an unofficial British record; she had laid down a time for other women to beat. Betty, who was in her forties, finished eight minutes after Alison. Sheila and Andrea both finished in under 73 minutes.

Adele was born in 1951. As a young child, she went along to sports days held by the bank where her father worked. Boys and girls ran in races together, and Adele remembers winning: 'I would run like mad and always win the prize for the fastest runner … I had that competitive edge straightaway – I wanted to win.'[6]

She joined Tonbridge AC in her mid-teens and was coached by Brian Mitchell, a senior British athletics coach, for the 1500 metres and cross country. She was the only woman he coached at the time. There were no other women running long distance at the club and Adele and Brian had lots of conversations about longer distances for women. She says, 'I was very much saying to Brian I wanted to do longer distances. I actually loved being out there and just running … I guess now looking back it was quite difficult being a woman wanting to run anything more than 800 metres.'

Adele went out on training runs with the men sometimes, 'hanging on to their shirt sleeves', and often ran on her own, fitting in runs with her nursing shifts. She ran four or five miles comfortably. Mitchell was willing to coach Adele to run longer distances, despite knowing that there would be no opportunities for her to compete unless the rules changed. She reflects, 'He couldn't see any reason at all why women couldn't run those events. I look back and I value his time because he wouldn't have got the credit for being one of the first people to coach a girl seriously.'

While Mitchell's support must have contributed to Adele's confidence as a runner, she also had an innate self-belief: 'I think there was just a negativity about women, per se, running. It was almost, "You're a woman, you weren't born to run," whereas I thought I was born to run and I was going to run.' Being a long-distance runner was a core part of Adele's identity, even before society was ready to accept that women could be endurance athletes: 'Women tend to be more determined in some respects because you've got to prove yourself as a female. I can remember running distances and thinking, "Why are people telling me I can't do this?"'

The *Kent and Sussex Courier* featured a long, favourable article on the women's run with a photo taken at the start showing all five women together, with Alison Blake in the lead.[7] Linking the run to the aims of International Women's Year, the headline read, 'Women join race for equality'. The journalist reported that the five women were all opposed to the ban on longer distances and quoted Adele saying, 'I am sure there are many women and girls who want to run the longer distance and if this run has done anything to improve their chances of doing so, then it is a good thing.'

Admirably persistent, Adele kept up her campaign. Unusually, the race results didn't appear in *Athletics Weekly*. Perhaps the club wanted to avoid the publicity. But Adele and Dave made sure that people knew about the women's run by writing letters to the magazine. Adele's letter, published in the 29 March issue, highlighted Alison Blake's performance, saying that with her blisteringly fast time she had 'proved that women are more than capable of running 10 miles-plus … more capable, in fact, than some men.' The race, she said, was evidence that 'women want to, and are capable of, running these distances'. Despite her impatience for change, Adele didn't expect it to be imminent and thought it might take another year for the WAAA to take action.

In his letter, Dave described how Alison Blake had overtaken him in the race, running comfortably – evidence that the women were as strong as the men – remarking, 'Even in these conditions I didn't notice any of the female runners having any troubles; in fact some of the male runners looked near death as they finished!' He encouraged others to organise their own run or write to the press.

Mel Watman, the editor of *Athletics Weekly*, endorsed the campaign, commenting that Britain was 'lagging badly' behind the USA and West Germany where women were permitted to run in long-distance races and exhorting the WAAA 'to reconsider its attitude.' He encouraged more women to write in and concluded: 'There must be hundreds of women athletes in this country who would welcome a broadening of their racing horizons, and train thoroughly enough to tackle longer distances.'

Over the next few weeks, women and men responded. Sheila Anne Smith and race walkers Judy Farr and Christine Coleman sent letters in support of longer distances. Sheila and Judy pointed out that they both regularly ran over 10 miles in training. Judy's frustration was evident: 'At last people are wakening up to the fact that ladies, myself included, think nothing of a 10-mile training run, but rarely get a chance to race above two and a half miles. The demand must surely be there as there are several of us in Wiltshire alone who would support longer road races.' Brian Mitchell, Adele's coach, added his voice with an article headed, 'Let women run longer distances'.[8] Comparing the British situation with that in the USA, he argued for 'the removal of outmoded rules' that were preventing women from racing.

There were no repercussions from the WAAA for either Tonbridge AC or Adele, but there was also no evidence that the governing body was considering a change to the rules. When the *Kent and Sussex Courier* approached Vera Searle, chair of the WAAA for her comments, she was dismissive. Searle was a member of Tonbridge AC and had been at the race as she was the race referee. She said that she wasn't against women running 10 miles, but, 'There were only five on Saturday … and that does not seem to indicate any great need for longer races. Women who want to run 10 miles are rather unusual.'

Searle stated that the WAAA always sought medical advice before introducing new events for women. Prior to introducing the 3000 metres in 1968 they had held races on a trial basis and doctors had examined the athletes after they'd finished, she explained. Despite all the evidence to the contrary, it was clear that the WAAA still had concerns over the impact of long-distance racing on women's bodies and their health.

The organised, advertised, collective action at Tonbridge emboldened other women to break the rules. Momentum for change was building as more and more individual women were crashing men's races. The most popular races in the 1970s were 10-milers and they became a particular target for women, as Jeanne Coker remembered in an interview for her running club's Hall of Fame in 2022. In 1975 Jeanne was in her thirties and had just returned to London after three years in Barbados, where she had been teaching PE and training teachers. She remembers an organised campaign of action in the London area: 'I got involved with the road running scene in 1975. I ran a 10-miler out at Maidenhead. There were a number of us running 10-milers around the place. The top runners couldn't do it, because it was all illegal, they would be banned from racing. So, we did 10-milers in different places and if anybody got caught and banned, we were all going to stand up and be counted.'[9]

Athletics Weekly supported women's rulebreaking. Race reports, usually submitted by club officials, sometimes didn't mention women running unofficially. If they did, Mel Watman pointedly highlighted women's participation by including the details in bold. This happened when Carol Gould (née Firth), who had been the first national 3000 metres champion in 1968, took part unofficially in her local 10-mile race, the Ipswich 10, on 22 March, 1975. Her time, 59:41, was included in bold at the bottom of the results.

On Sunday 20 April 19-year-old Jean Haigh, the women's captain of Huddersfield club Longwood Harriers, was busy cheering on her two younger sisters, Susan and Anne, in the junior girls road race at Stannington near Sheffield.[10] Jean was there for the women's two-mile race, which had attracted a strong field of Northern athletes. As her sisters crossed the finish line, someone told Jean that the women's race had just begun. Annoyed at her mistake, she decided there and then to join in the main event instead, the men's Stannington 10. At least that way she would get a training run done. Jean started behind the men. The *Huddersfield Daily Examiner* recorded her participation, noting that officially women weren't allowed to race further than four miles. The journalist Granville Beckett added that, given that Jean had finished 'fresh as a daisy' in 65:27, beating more than a quarter of the men, the real reason for women's exclusion from longer distances might be 'to save the men from being embarrassed.'

Why was the WAAA – an organisation led by women, for women – standing in the way of women racing long distance? Were the women who led the governing body really sceptical of women's abilities? There was, after all, so much evidence from other countries and from other sports, such as cycling and swimming, that women could excel in endurance sports. And they knew, of course, that Bridget Cushen and Dale Greig had run marathons; and that more and more women were ghost-running in men's races. Why didn't they act more quickly?

The rulebreaking women generally thought that the people running the WAAA were old-fashioned, inflexible and out of touch. Avril, the rulebreaker at Morpeth to Newcastle, recalls: 'I just thought they were really back in time. I remember Marea Hartman fussing over the kind of shorts we wore. And there was all these suggestions that we might do damage to our reproductive systems, because we were being physically active. It was disappointing that it would be a woman in charge saying a lot of things that I thought were backward-looking.'

One factor was that the WAAA certainly took a conservative approach to introducing new events, as evidenced by Vera Searle's comments after the Tonbridge 10, but really it was too late in the day to take that approach to women's road running. Another factor was the age gap, we could even call it a chasm, between athletes and administrators. This arose because of the difficulties of finding women who could take on the administration of the sport. Most women left athletics when they married or once they had children. This led to a situation where it was not unusual for women to remain on committees for decades.[11] The somewhat matriarchal 'we know best' attitude of some WAAA officials didn't always go down well with the teenage girls and young women athletes. In 1975, two of the women at the top of the WAAA had served the organisation for decades, fighting the corner for women's athletics: Marea Hartman and Vera Searle.

In 1975, Marea Hartman (1920–1994) was in her mid-fifties and had been honorary secretary of the WAAA for 15 years, having joined the committee in 1950. Marea joined Spartan Ladies Athletic Club as a girl in the 1930s and sprinted both for the club and for Surrey. Her fiancé was killed in World War II and she never married. After the war, she joined Spartan's committee. By 1950, she was honorary treasurer of the WAAA, becoming honorary secretary in 1960. She was a personnel officer at the paper manufacturers Bowaters in Knightsbridge, but, according to Arthur Gold who wrote her obituary in the *Independent*, she 'spent most of her waking hours working for athletics.'[12] She was energetic, sociable and liked to have fun, but she was also an astute negotiator who held powerful and influential roles in athletics nationally and internationally.

Vera Searle (née Palmer, 1901–1998) was in her seventies in 1975 and had been a member of the WAAA Executive Committee for nearly 50 years. In 1924, Searle was a founder member of the Middlesex Ladies Athletics Club. Her athletics career was brief but illustrious. In 1923, she set a world record, 35.4 seconds for the rather odd distance of 250 metres, when competing for England against France in Paris. At the 1924 English track and field championships, she broke the 440 yards world record with a time of 63 seconds, breaking it again the following year. In 1926, she was one of a small contingent of British athletes who sailed to Sweden to compete in Alice Milliat's Women's World Games in Gothenburg, where she finished second in the 220 yards. She retired from athletics competition that year and married Wilfred Searle but remained very much involved in the administration of the sport.[13]

It would be wrong to portray the WAAA as a reactionary, backward-looking organisation as British women were some of the first to compete in new track and field events. In the 1950s and 60s, Britain, along with the Soviet Union, led the way when it came to competition in the 1500 metres and the mile. And in the 1960s, Britain introduced the 3000 metres several years before it was accepted as an international event. Marea Hartman was elected a member of the women's committee of International Amateur Athletic Federation (IAAF) in 1958 and as its chair from 1968 to 1981 she sought to get new events recognised by the IAAF congress. Once this happened, they would be added to international championships and, eventually, the Olympics. Ironically, precisely at the time that women were rulebreaking in British long-distance races, the women's committee under Hartman's leadership was trying to get the women's marathon on to the programme for the inaugural world championships in 1983.

This brings us back to the question: why was the WAAA standing in the way of women racing long distance? It's possible that it may not have seemed that important, for two reasons. Firstly, in the 1970s track and field and cross country were the primary focus in athletics. Today, distance running and road running are by far the most popular form of athletics, with millions of people in the UK running regularly and thousands taking part in races each weekend. Then, races often had fewer than a hundred participants – all men, of course. Secondly, there was no real incentive to develop women's marathon running as there was no opportunity to compete in international championships. In other words, there were no medals to be won.

However, it does feel as if the WAAA was out of touch with what was happening in road running and did not foresee the huge changes that were on the horizon as jogging hit Britain. Unfortunately, though, the minutes of the WAAA committee meetings aren't in the athletics archive at the University of Birmingham, so we don't have a record of the discussions that took place.

Meanwhile, the officials expected that if women wanted change, they would use the existing structures to make their wishes known. This meant women would have to persuade their clubs to press for change by raising the issue with either the area committee or the national committee. As the rulebreakers were typically the only women in their club interested in long distance, this wouldn't have been easy. And, even if a female athlete had persuaded her club to take up the issue, it would have taken a long time to work its way through the bureaucratic procedures of athletics governance. Matters were further complicated by the fact that the WAAA had delegated responsibility for road running – and cross country – to an affiliated body, the Women's Cross Country and Race Walking Association.

In the end, it was something of an inevitability that after all the ghost-running, rulebreaking, letters and articles, the decision would be made to allow women to run longer distances. The momentum was building and could not be ignored. At long last, after an Extraordinary General Meeting held on 27 April, 1975, the Women's Cross Country and Race Walking Association agreed a new set of rules which would allow women and girls aged 17 and over to race long distance on the roads.[14] The permitted distances were:

Girls aged 17 and 18 – up to seven miles
19-year-olds – up to 10 miles
20-year-olds – up to 15 miles
21 and older – up to the marathon distance

The rules were experimental and to be reviewed after a year. This reflected the WAAA's cautious approach to change, particularly where women's physical health could be perceived to be at risk. Women were still not allowed to race against men, though. This meant there had to be separate men's and women's races. If men and women were going to race over the same course, 'the race for women should start not less than 30 minutes after the start of the men's race.'

While the insistence on separate starts might seem odd to today's runners, the women's governing bodies were concerned with protecting women's competition. Separate races and separate start times meant women's performances would be properly recognised in their own right. The women's results had to be scored and published separately from the men's. Without these safeguards, they felt there was a risk that women would merely be seen as 'also rans' in men's races, rather than winners in women's races; positioning women's racing and performances as secondary to men's. When the experimental rules were reviewed in March 1976, the 30-minutes rule was revised. For races of 10 miles or longer, men and women could now start together. However, the rules made it clear that the men's and women's races must still be acknowledged as separate events in adverts and race programmes, with separate results lists for men and women.[15]

After separate start times for women and men were done away with, the idea of 'the women's race', which the Women's Cross Country and Race Walking Association had tried to preserve, was eroded and diminished. You can see the impact of this in the BBC coverage of the first London Marathon in 1981. Unsurprisingly, most of the commentary focuses on the lead runners in the men's race. We are told the names of the first 10 to finish. The cameras picked out the leading three women – the commentators referred to them as 'girls' – among the male runners, from time to time. After leading the men's race from mile 16, American Dick Beardsley and Norwegian Inge Simonsen decided to cross the line together, holding hands, as joint winners. As Alison Hamlett writes in a blog post celebrating the 45th anniversary of the first race on the London Marathon website, when they did so, 'they created the first truly great image of London Marathon spirit.'[16] As Joyce Smith, the women's race winner, approached the finish line 18 minutes later, we see her being directed to the left side where officials hold out a short length of tape for her to break. Our view of her is obscured by a file of male runners to her right who finished around the same time. The prestige afforded to the men's winners is missing. The visual impact of a woman winning a major race just isn't there. The women's race is secondary to the main event: the men's. This doesn't just affect how the race was seen at the time; it affects how it is seen now. If you search online for images for this race, multiple versions of the Beardsley and Simonsen finish line photo will come up. Will you find an image of Joyce Smith, who broke her own British record that day? Only if you scroll down through dozens of images.

This is why the WAAA wanted separate starts for women. Their concerns find echoes today in women-led campaigns that have drawn attention to the unequal coverage of men and women in races. In 2022, British ultrarunner Sophie Power launched the SheRaces campaign to encourage races to be more inclusive of female athletes by taking their needs into consideration.[17] SheRaces has created best practice guidelines for race organisers, for example, allowing free referrals for pregnancy, providing period products and adequate toilets and using inclusive imagery. The guidelines also advocate for equal recognition for the women's race: 'Our competitive race should be given equal respect to the men's (or open) race. We train as hard. We race as hard. We deserve the same recognition.' This means equal coverage in race commentary and film footage; listing women's race results separately; allowing women their own space at the start line; and prizes of equal value and quantity for men and women.

Problem solved? Not quite. Yes, the rules had changed in 1975 but, despite this huge step forward, women weren't able to compete in many road races that year. They weren't automatically entitled to enter road races of their choice and the additional bureaucracy associated with having separate governing bodies for men's and women's athletics did not make it easy for clubs to organise races for women. Road races for men were organised under AAA rules with an AAA permit. If a club wanted to organise a race for women, it had to notify the Women's Cross Country and Race Walking Association and, if it was not affiliated, apply for a permit. Most clubs didn't do this. The new rules weren't announced until May 1975, and by that time many clubs had already organised and advertised their events for the year. Some clubs decided to wait and see what happened that year rather than jumping in and organising a women's race. Others no doubt didn't want to admit women, thinking that women didn't belong in their men's races.

There were some exceptions, though. A handful of clubs were commendably enthusiastic about women's long-distance racing and keen to play their part in encouraging women's participation. Nevertheless, women weren't welcome at most road races. They could compete in the shorter distance women's events that clubs sometimes put on alongside men's long-distance races, but if they wanted to race further than the two or three miles on offer, there was very little for them. After the rule change, there were just five official women's long-distance road races in 1975: the Reebok 6, Barnsley 6, Wycombe 5, Chelmsford 7 and Barnsley Marathon, plus the unofficial Masters and Maidens Marathon.

Sunday 27 July was an unusually warm summer day. By the time 12 women lined up for the start of the Reebok 6 for Ladies, it was already 26°C.[18] Angela Briscoe was excited about competing in the first long-distance road race for women since the rule change, but she hated running on hot days. Alison Blake was the favourite. Alison had finished ahead of Angela at the national cross-country championships in February and she'd run a very quick time at the unofficial women's run at the Tonbridge 10. Despite facing such a formidable opponent, 23-year-old Angela thought she could take the win as she had a lot of experience of training on the roads.

The course was a tough three laps with a long hill. Alison, Angela and 18-year-old Shiree Hines took the lead, but by the end of the first lap Alison had pulled away from Angela and Shiree. Angela tried hard to catch her but was struggling with the heat. Angela's husband Frank shouted encouragement as she reached the end of each lap. Alison kept her lead and finished 59 seconds ahead of Angela in 34:28. Shiree finished in 36:51, more than three minutes ahead of the next woman. Two women dropped out. Both said that it was the heat rather than the distance that had caused them to stop.

Angela and Alison had very different routes into road running. Angela (née Lovell) was born in 1952 and had joined Solihull AC aged 14.[19] She began by competing in the 800 metres and cross country. When I interviewed her in 2025, she told me that her love of athletics had started at a much earlier age, at primary school, and it came from her father, Charles. He had competed for Doncaster Plant Works AC and carried on running into his forties.

He was often called to officiate at meetings and took Angela with him from the age of 18 months. They watched the 1960 Rome Olympics together on TV. 'He was always interested, and it must have rubbed off on me,' she says. When she was 10, Angela's father trained her for the junior school sprint race, which she won.[20]

One summer in 1966, when Angela was 14, she and her younger sisters went to stay with their grandparents in the Lincolnshire countryside for a few weeks. Feeling bored, Angela decided on a whim to start running: 'I think one of the things that triggered me was I couldn't get in the school team for athletics. It was all sprinting. They didn't even do 800 metres. And although I was relatively fast, I wasn't that fast.' Every day, Angela put on her plimsolls and went out for a short run on the rural roads. It was a turning point: 'I just discovered that I loved running. I could do it. It was something I could do.' When she returned to school in the autumn, with a new-found speed in her legs, Angela got into the team.

By the time she was 15, Angela was routinely running for an hour or more on a Sunday. In her late teens, she became one of Britain's best 1500 metre runners. In 1970, aged 18, she represented Great Britain at the European Junior Championships in Paris, finishing fourth in the 1500 metres. In the early 1970s, she also competed as a senior in international track matches and at the international cross-country championships and earned the honour of a profile in *Athletics Weekly*. Angela remembers going to some races that her husband Frank was running in in the mid-1970s and taking part unofficially. One year at the Wigan 6, when Frank gave her the car keys to look after, she decided to join in at the back of the race. She overtook many of the men but steered clear of the finish funnel.

Alison, born in 1948, was four years older than Angela. Her path into athletics deviated from the traditional route taken by most of her contemporaries. She had only taken up running at 23, joining her local club, City of Plymouth AC, in January 1972, and then Aldershot, Farnham and District AC in 1973. She quickly made an impression in track and cross-country races. On the track, she excelled at the 3000 metres and was seventh in the British rankings for the distance in 1974. That year, she was selected to compete for England in a cross-country home countries international.

What was even more unusual about Alison was the fact that she was the mother of four small children. When *Athletics Weekly* published a profile of her in May 1975, its title was: 'Four children – THEN Alison Blake took up athletics'. It was common for women of Alison's generation to have children in their early twenties but having four by the age of 23 as she had was unusual.[21] Alison had a part-time job at a swimming pool and her husband was a bus driver working shifts. Despite these circumstances, she was managing to train seriously, running six days a week and averaging 35 miles. She had to be flexible, running home from work and doing training once the children had gone to bed. Her coach, John Gilbert, enabled her to train and compete regularly by baby-sitting the children when needed. Alison broke with the traditional pattern for women in athletics that had prevailed in the 1960s: get married, have children, give up competition.

Alison commented that women should be able to race over any distances they wanted and she was in favour of mixed road races 'where the involvement with men would help to raise the women's standards.' She also thought they would be more enjoyable, because there would be more competitors and more spectators encouraging the runners. Alison carried on rule-breaking after the Tonbridge 10. In April 1976, the *Western Daily Press* reported the 'unofficial entry of a girl' in the Bampton to Tiverton 8 Mile Men's Road Race. Alison, it said, had finished in a good time, 45:30, ahead of some of the men.[22] I would have liked to have interviewed Alison, but, unfortunately, I was unable to find her. Some of the women I interviewed remembered her, but none of them had kept in touch with her. And my other searches didn't yield any more information about her life outside athletics. Her unconventional route into athletics, the big impact she had in 1975, and the way she combined her running with family circumstances that would have defeated others, make for a fascinating story.

In 1974 a new athletics club had been determined to put the town of Barnsley on the road running map. On Saturday 10 August, 1974, the Barnsley Road Runners Club held the Barnsley six-mile men's race, which attracted a 'colossal entry of almost 500 runners' and featured on the BBC and ITV. The race captured the imagination of Barnsley's residents who had turned out in their thousands to watch.[23]

In 1975, the club wanted to go one better and make its six-mile race one of the first long-distance road races in the country to admit women. On 17 May, just three weeks after the rule change had been agreed, the club placed a notice in *Athletics Weekly* entitled 'Important notice to ladies who wish to race long distance'. The club wanted to know there was sufficient interest in a six-mile race for women before it committed to organising one, so the notice asked women to write to the club secretary to express their interest in participating. There must have been a good response from female runners, because soon afterwards an enthusiastic advert appeared in the magazine.

> This history-making race will be over the Barnsley 6 course and will start 30 minutes before the men's event. It is open to ladies aged 17 or over on August 10th, 1975. COME ON GIRLS – YOU ASKED FOR THIS RACE – GET YOUR ENTRIES IN NOW!

Christine Readdy from Staffordshire, who had been a ghost runner at the Milford 21-mile race in 1974, was one of the entrants. At the weekends, Christine and her teammates from

City of Stoke AC often travelled to races together, especially when there were prizes to be won. These could be road relays or the shorter distance races that clubs sometimes put on for women alongside men's long-distance races. It was fun travelling as a group and they usually had enough runners to make a team. Christine often won individual prizes and sometimes there was a team prize as well. On 20 April, she had won the 2-mile women's race at Stannington, where Jean Haigh had missed the start, and the City of Stoke women had won the team prize.

Christine got a lift to the Barnsley 6 from Arthur Shaw, who coached the female distance runners at the club. He had suggested that three women from the club should go as a team.[24] When they got to Barnsley, it was a sunny Sunday afternoon. There was a festival atmosphere with announcements being made over a loudspeaker and crowds of people milling around. The finish area was packed with spectators waiting for the boys' two-and-a-half-mile race to finish.

There were at least 30 women lined up for the start of the women's race at 2.30 p.m.[25] Christine found herself in a close contest with Carol Gould, the top-class 3000-metres runner from Barnet and District AC who had run unofficially at the Ipswich 10 in March. Alison Blake would no doubt also have been at the front of the race but unluckily after travelling the 300 miles from Plymouth to Barnsley, she had fallen sick with a stomach upset from sausages she'd eaten the night before the race. Christine judged her race well and finished 29 seconds ahead of Carol in 40:06. Margaret Ashcroft (who we met at the start of this book, crashing the Chris Vose 10) finished third, over a minute behind Carol in 42:00. Among the 30 women finishers was Sheila Anne Smith of Ipswich AC, who had written in to *Athletics Weekly* in support of longer distances.

Christine won a coffee table and a trophy. Wearing a winner's sash, she joined Mike Tagg, the men's winner, for a ceremonial lap of honour in an open-top Rolls-Royce.[26] She remembers that the coffee table had a glass top and they struggled to get it in the boot of Arthur Shaw's car. When she got home to her parents' house they made space for it in their front room. While coverage in the local newspapers was positive, the *Guardian* was critical, declaring that, 'The event was not a good advertisement for women's long-distance running' and that several of 'the girls' had 'found the heat and distance too much, and finished exhausted.' For nearly all the women it was their first experience of competing in a road race longer than two miles. It was a hilly course and a hot afternoon. It's not surprising that some of them were exhausted at the end. No doubt some of the men were exhausted, too. But the focus was on the women and, just as in 1928, there were plenty of commentators seeking to validate their view that women were unsuited to long-distance running.

Alison Blake had better luck at the Ladies 5 Mile Race at Wycombe in Buckinghamshire on 21 September, the third of the official women's races in 1975. She finished second behind Joyce Smith, who was soon to become Britain's best long-distance runner (more about her in the next chapter). Race walker Judy Farr, who had written to *Athletics Weekly* in support of longer distances for women, was among the 20 women who finished. Participation in these early races was important, as it demonstrated that the demand for longer distances that Judy had described in her letter was real. Another finisher was Bridget Cushen, the ghost runner at the 1973 Harlow Marathon. The fourth official race was a 7-miler at Chelmsford on 18 October, where eight women competed.[27]

The Masters' and Maidens' Marathon took place in Guildford on 19 October. It was organised by Alan Blatchford, a long-distance walker, runner and athletics club member who we met earlier in this chapter organising the Tanners Marathon. His philosophy was long distance for all – runners and walkers, the young and the old, men and women. Blatchford did not apply to the AAA for a permit. The advert he placed in *Athletics Weekly* made it clear that it was not an official race: 'Open to women and men who have not beaten 3 hours, and veterans. No prizes, certs. only. Not a race but a timed run over 26M. 385yds.'

The name of the event indicated its non-elitist nature. It was aimed at older runners, the 'masters' (men aged 40 and over) and women (the 'maidens'). Blatchford presumably chose 'maiden', an old-fashioned word meaning girl or young woman, because of the alliteration. It wouldn't go down well today, but at the time calling adult women 'girls' was so common as to be unremarkable. The time limit was a generous five and a half hours. Men's marathons at the time usually had a three-and-a-half or four-hour limit.

Masters and Maidens had the spirit of a community event. The 136 participants included under-21s who were too young for official marathons. Seven teenagers, aged 14 to 17, an 18-year-old and a 19-year-old took part.[28] The inclusion of children might seem surprising today, but at the time some race organisers and athletes felt that children should be allowed to cover long distances, as they sometimes did in the USA.

Five years before the 'marathon boom' began in the UK, Blatchford's event was revolutionary, as he highlighted in the race programme, calling it 'the first marathon of its kind in Britain.' Masters and Maidens, he said, was aimed at slower and first-time entrants who might have 'lacked the courage to enter a top class event for fear of failure in the great pressure to achieve fast times.' He concluded triumphantly, 'Now we have given such runners the chance to test themselves in a non-competitive run over the traditional distance.'

Blatchford had been involved in the long-distance walking community for more than a decade. In 1972, Blatchford, his wife Barbara and friend Chris Steer had founded the Long Distance Walkers Association (LDWA). Its aims were to provide information about existing long-distance countryside challenge events and to organise new LDWA events, as well as social walks for members. The association grew rapidly and by 1975 it had more than 1500 members. Open to men and women from its inception, women participated in events on the same basis as men and a few women were involved in running the organisation.

Long-distance walking events were usually 20 miles or more. LDWA events were not races and there were no prizes. However, results were published with the finishing order and participants' finishing times and splits at the main checkpoints. Running was permitted and some participants would run the whole route. It was an opportunity to run off-road in a more relaxed event, outside athletics' strict rules. In the early 1970s, LDWA events gave a few women, such as Adele Brignall, their first opportunity to try long-distance running. Adele, the organiser of the women's unofficial run at the Tonbridge 10, did her first LDWA event in 1975 with her fiancé Dave Cross.

Miriam Bescoby, a 26-year-old biology teacher, was one of the 14 women and girls gathered at the start of the first Masters and Maidens Marathon. When she and her boyfriend David Rosen heard that Blatchford was organising the event, they were keen to take part in the first marathon-distance road race for women. But now, on the day, faced with the prospect of 26.2 miles, Miriam was apprehensive. She had covered longer distances, up to 30 miles, in LDWA events, but they were off-road challenges not road marathons. She wasn't in an athletics club and had no experience of racing. Miriam was worried she wouldn't finish within the five and a half hours cut-off, but David, who had run his first marathon the year before, reassured her, telling her that if she set off slowly she'd be able to keep going.

Adele Brignall and Dave Cross had travelled from Tonbridge for the event. Adele led the women from the start, going through the 10-mile checkpoint in just under 69 minutes, three minutes ahead of the eventual winner, Anne Clarke. But she dropped out after 10 miles. Another woman dropped out at around the same point. Adele would return in 1977 and complete the marathon in just under 4:20.

After Adele dropped out, Anne Clarke led the field. Her time of 3:11:54 was over 15 minutes faster than the mark set by Dale Greig in 1964. While *Athletics Weekly* acknowledged it as a women's best time, it was not in an official race. Caroline Falla of Bournemouth AC also finished within the previous British best and Scottish athlete Leslie Watson was third in just over three and a half hours (more about Leslie later in the chapter). Remarkably, all three of the girls who started, finished. Glenda Chell, 17, and Shirley Bennett, 16, ran most of the race together, finishing just under, and just over, four and half hours respectively, while 15-year-old Patricia Paige finished 35 seconds under the five-hour mark. Miriam was proud to finish in just over five hours and to receive her finishers' certificate.[29] The last woman, Sheila Ferriman, was 10 minutes behind her.

The women who were members of athletics clubs received letters from the WAAA after the marathon, reprimanding them for taking part and threatening them with suspension from competition. In the view of the governing body, Masters and Maidens was a race because it was timed. It contravened the rule that men and women could not compete against each other, and it didn't have a separate start for women.

When I interviewed Miriam and David in 2025, Miriam explained that as she wasn't a member of an athletics club, she was not a target of the WAAA's ire, but she heard about it through friends and was bemused by the governing body's reaction: 'I rather naively assumed that the WAAA would be delighted that women wanted to run marathons, so I was really quite surprised when they started threatening all these things.' In Miriam's eyes, 'It was extraordinary to see how behind the road-running scene was compared to orienteering.' She had taken up orienteering in 1969, while studying at the University of Bangor, and in orienteering men and women raced over the same course. Another of the women in this chapter, Avril Lewis (née Jones), the rulebreaker at Morpeth to Newcastle, also benefitted from orienteering's inclusivity, competing in long orienteering races, where you might end up running 15 miles or more to cover all the control points.

In 1976, Blatchford omitted the surnames of women who were members of athletics clubs as well as the names of their clubs from the results for the Masters and Maidens Marathon, explaining it was 'because by taking part in this event they are under threat of "suspension" by the WAAA.' The LDWA was the pathway into long-distance running for Miriam. It gave her the confidence to attempt the marathon distance, but it was Masters and Maidens which gave her the opportunity. Blatchford hoped that some participants would 'discover a liking for the distance and go on to greater things.' This was what happened to Miriam. She returned to the race in 1976 and ran it every year until 1984, winning it four times. From 1975 to 1997, Miriam ran 36 marathons, including the London Marathon eight times and the Barnsley Marathon six times. Today, Miriam and her husband David are very active in orienteering and travel frequently to events in the UK and abroad.

In October 1975, Margaret Thompson (née Tunstall), who had been a ghost runner in men's races in the early 1970s, travelled to Finland with her husband Ian, the British marathon record holder, who had received an invitation to the Korso Marathon in Helsinki. After winning both the Commonwealth Games and European Championships marathons in 1974, he had eased back on training and racing, turning down lots of invitations to marathons, but he accepted the Korso invitation because it would be a friendly, low-key event and because Margaret was able to go, too.[30]

Margaret told me that she had read about women being able to run marathons in Germany and the USA, and was aware of Dale Greig's and Bridget Cushen's unofficial runs.[31] She planned to use the Korso Marathon as a trial run for the Barnsley Marathon in November, which was to be the first official marathon for women in the UK. Having turned 21 four months earlier, she just met the minimum age for competition.[32]

In the weeks before Korso, Margaret did her normal training for track and cross country as well as a couple of two-hour runs off-road. When it came to race day, Saturday 25 October, she hoped to finish in under three hours. With no experience of racing such a long distance, Margaret made the mistake of going off much too fast, passing the halfway point in under 1 hour and 20 minutes. When I interviewed her in 2020, Margaret said, 'I have always regretted being too impetuous in that race, as I think I would easily have run under three hours if I had been more sensible.' The fact that she didn't feel too stiff afterwards and went ice-skating with friends the next day suggests that her assessment is correct.

Margaret's time, 3:07:47, was a new British women's marathon best performance. Both Margaret and Ian were now holders of the British marathon record. Reflecting on the race today, Margaret concludes that her training 'was nowhere near enough and was probably one of the reasons I faded so badly in the race.' Despite this disappointing first experience, Margaret was determined to run at Barnsley the following month.

Given that the Barnsley Marathon was held in the winter and that the route was tough and hilly, it's not surprising that there were only six women on the start line on Sunday 30 November. After all, only a few dozen women had taken part in official long-distance road races by that point and the pool of women who felt ready to run a marathon must have been quite small. Another reason for the absence of some of the women who had crashed men's races already that year was that most English counties had held their cross-country championships the day before. There was an established timetable for championships with all the county events usually held on the same day to allow time for athletes to be selected for the Northern, Southern and Midlands area championships. I can only imagine that most women wouldn't have wanted to do a marathon the day after racing in their county championship; and for those who lived at some distance it would have simply been too difficult to get to Barnsley in time.

This was the first marathon for women in the UK with official race permits. Could a new British record be set? All eyes were on Margaret whose target was to win in under three hours.[33] The other women in the race were newly married Avril Lewis; her Bromsgrove and Redditch AC teammate and training partner, Bronwen Smith; Hilary Matthews from Blackburn Harriers; 47-year-old Norma Campbell from Berwick-upon-Tweed; and Leslie Watson who had finished third in the Masters and Maidens Marathon. Twenty-two-year-old Hilary had won the Lancashire cross-country championship the day before. She'd travelled the 60-odd miles from Blackburn that morning with her mother, who had come to watch. In an interview with BBC Sheffield marking the 50th anniversary of the race, Hilary, now 72, said that, rather annoyingly, a journalist from a local paper had got hold of the race programme and rung her the week before the race, asking her 'stupid questions', such as 'Don't you think it's too far?' and 'What will people think?'[34] Hilary said that she didn't care and just wanted to have a go, although she was annoyed at the limitations placed on women.

When the large field of more than 160 runners gathered for the start at noon, it was chilly but there was brilliant sunshine. BBC and ITV film crews were there to cover the story of the first women's marathon. Unfortunately, the weather quickly changed and after 10 miles a thick fog descended, with visibility down to about five metres at some points. Margaret dropped out somewhere around the 11-mile point due to a pulled muscle and the effects of the cold, which she described in an email to me as: 'hypothermia due to freezing fog – I had icicles on my hair when I stopped!'

Bronwen Smith also dropped out. Despite inadequate preparation, Avril made it to the finish at Barnsley Town Hall in fourth place. When I interviewed her in 2024, she said that one of her clearest memories from the race, 49 years before, was needing to use the bathroom during the race: 'We were running past some terraced houses and so I asked if I could use the bathroom and was shown to the back of the house by a spectator.' How very different from marathons today, where runners can expect to find portable toilets at various points along the course.

The *Barnsley Chronicle*, one of the race sponsors, reported enthusiastically on the first three women finishers, mentioning International Women's Year and saying the race made the argument for 'marathon equality'.[35] However, the tone of the article reflected the pervasive sexism of the time: 'New statistics, some may say vital ones, were added to marathon racing on Sunday when four women … successfully completed the 26 miles 385 yards of the second Barnsley Marathon.' The 'vital statistics' were, of course, the women's bust, waist and hip measurements. Carrying on in the same vein, the unnamed reporter couldn't resist commenting on Leslie Watson's appearance: 'Anyone daring to argue that marathon running is damaging to physique should take a long look at the third-placed Lesley Watson from London Olympiades. Quite a girl is Lesley. And quite a runner too.' Hilary was pleased with the win but didn't fully appreciate its significance until her copy of *Athletics Weekly* arrived on 28 December. She was still in bed when her mother picked the magazine off the doormat and shouted up to her, 'You've made it.' Hilary's photo was on the front cover of the magazine.[36]

Hilary's time was 3:13:27, so Margaret's British record was safe for a while longer, but despite the general celebrations, the governing body was displeased. The headline in the *Huddersfield Daily Examiner* read, 'Marathon first may bring top-level rap.'[37] Athletics journalist Granville Beckett reported that Barnsley Road Runners might receive a reprimand from the Women's Cross Country and Race Walking Association as the club had not fully complied with the new rules by allowing the women to start with the men. Beckett speculated that Barnsley Road Runners had ignored the rule for publicity reasons, so that the television cameras could film the women and men setting off together.

In 1975 there were dozens of men's 10-milers across the UK – it was the most popular race distance at the time – but none of them admitted women. If women wanted to race 10 miles, they were forced to crash a men's race. Several women did just that, including Christine Readdy at the popular Michelin 10 in Stoke-on-Trent on 3 May. She knew the route, joined in near the start and avoided going through the finish funnel.[38] Whenever she ran in men's races, Christine tried to keep a low profile, running alongside the men, but keeping out of their way. She wanted to avoid 'any nastiness and upset'. In contrast, Jean Lochhead wanted to make her views known. On Monday 12 May, on a page in the *Huddersfield Daily Examiner* covering men's football, speedway, athletics, horse racing and pigeon racing, there was one article about a woman with the headline 'Protest likely after world best'.[39] It reported that on Saturday 10 May Jean had set an unofficial 'world best' for 10 miles at a race at Croxdale in County Durham. However, the article noted, 'Her efforts seem likely to bring recriminations instead of a bouquet.'

One of the male competitors had objected to a woman running in a men's race and was going to make 'an official protest to the athletics authorities'. Unafraid of the threat, Jean did not hold back when asked her opinion, saying defiantly, 'It needs some of us to stick our necks out to get things moving. If someone is going to be so narrow-minded as to get me disciplined for this, I'll go back to cycling where we can compete with the men.'

Despite setting off a few seconds after the men started, Jean worked her way up to finish ahead of at least 20 of the men. Her time of 58:22 was two seconds faster than the time Alison Blake had run at the Tonbridge 10 in March. When the race results appeared in *Athletics Weekly*, the report drew attention to her participation by recording her name and time in bold. It wasn't the first time that Jean had run in a men's race, and it wouldn't be the last. When I interviewed Jean in 2024, she told me that she didn't hear anything from the governing body, saying, 'I think the person who was in charge realised there was not much you could do with me.'

Twenty-eight-year-old Jean from Huddersfield had been representing Wales in the international cross-country championships since a women's race was introduced in 1967. She was eligible to represent the country because her mother was Welsh. Two months before the Croxdale 10 she had competed in the third IAAF World Cross Country Championships in Rabat, Morocco. In 1974, she had been part of the Welsh team at the Commonwealth Games in Christchurch, New Zealand, competing in the 800 metres and 1500 metres. Jean was used to running more than 10 miles in training. At the time, it was not unusual for female track and cross-country athletes to run a weekly mileage as high as some marathoners do today.

As 1975 drew to a close, the pages of *Athletics Weekly* were full of adverts for men's road races, occasionally put on with races for boys, but still only very rarely with a race for women. In December, an event highlighted that while opportunities were opening up for women – thanks to some favourably disposed race organisers – most races were still for men only. The Hog's Back 10 in Surrey was a long-established race which attracted a top-class field. On 20 December, the men were joined by two unofficial female competitors, Louise Day of Verlea AC and Ginette Williamson of Epsom and Ewell AC, both 16. They ran together, finishing in 70:32.[40] In 1976, would more races open up to women? And would more women take on the challenge of long distance?

6

WOMEN GO THE DISTANCE

'They said that on no account was I to run in any of their races again.'[1]
– Margaret Lockley

'Christine is a cracker!' declared the Daily Mirror on 17 April, 1976. The day before, Good Friday, 23-year-old Christine Readdy had won the first women's marathon to be held in the UK, the Feltham Ladies Marathon, and she had set a British record, too.[2]

Christine's mother had persuaded her to enter the race. She'd come across a newspaper article about the marathon that mentioned the British record held by Margaret Thompson and was convinced that her daughter could do the distance. In an interview in *Stride Out* magazine, Christine revealed that other people were more sceptical, asking her, 'How far will your marathon be? Not the same as the men's?' and telling her, 'Women don't do marathons!'[3]

Christine was well prepared. Just eight days before the Feltham marathon she had run the full distance in training, finishing in three hours. She trained on her own, as she didn't know anyone who wanted to do very long runs, and by race day she was confident she could beat Margaret's British record of 3:07:47. Four weeks before, she had returned to the 21-mile Milford cross-country race in Staffordshire, which she had dropped out of in 1974. Once again, she had been an unofficial competitor, joining in at the back. *Athletics Weekly* reported that the weather was atrocious 'with rain and sleet chilling competitors and turning what had been the day before, a bone-dry course, into a quagmire.'[4] This time, Christine ran the full 21 miles. On reaching the finish, she ran wide of the funnel in sight of the race officials and was surprised when they gave her an unofficial time.[5] Christine placed 84 out of 122 runners, averaging under 7:30 per mile over the hilly course and finishing in 2:37:05. When I interviewed her in 2024, she told me that she worried about repercussions when *Athletics Weekly* reported her unofficial participation: 'I thought, "Oh, dear, hope I don't get suspended because I've taken part in a men's race." They were very particular about sticking to the rules in those days.' But she didn't hear anything from either the men's or women's governing bodies.

On Good Friday, 16 April, 1976, 18 competitors arrived at the Feltham Arena in the London Borough of Hounslow for the Feltham Ladies Marathon, which had been organised by Lyn and Dave Billington of Feltham AC. Six of the runners had already raced a marathon: Bridget Cushen had run unofficially in the Harlow Marathon in 1973; Margaret Thompson was the British record holder; Anne Clarke was the winner of the 1975 Masters and Maidens Marathon; Hilary Matthews was the winner of the 1975 Barnsley Marathon; Norma Campbell had been runner-up at Barnsley; and Leslie Watson was the only woman to have run two marathons, both Masters and Maidens and Barnsley. Margaret Thompson's training had gone well and she'd been feeling confident that she would get under three hours until an Achilles tendon injury recurred. Despite this, she was there on the day: 'I should not have run, but wanted to be part of the first all-women's race,' she told me.

For seven of the other women, including Lyn Billington and Caroline Rodgers, it was their first official long-distance road race. I was very pleased when Jill Danskin, another of the runners I interviewed (more of her in Chapter 8), offered to connect me with Caroline. I had written about Caroline in my 'Rulebreakers' article for *Women's Running* magazine but had not managed to trace her at the time. Born in 1949, Caroline grew up in London and took up athletics in her late teens after her doctor recommended exercise as a way of improving her asthma.[6] She joined Highgate Harriers, but found sprint training hard. Her performances improved after her coach suggested moving up to 400 metres, although she was initially apprehensive, thinking, 'That's a long race. I can't race a whole lap of the track'. In the early 1970s, Caroline competed in cross country, short road races and road relays for the Harriers. As the decade went on, it was the opportunity to compete at longer distances which kept her in athletics, first in the 3000 metres on the track and then long distance on the roads.

Caroline and Lyn were friends, and it was Lyn who suggested that she take part in the all-women marathon. When Caroline told her coach at Highgate Harriers, Jack Bayliss, that she wanted to do the marathon he told her she needed to train properly. Caroline duly started doing long Sunday runs with the men from the club in preparation. She remembers the approach that Bayliss took to getting the best from his athletes. Anne Clarke was her teammate from Highgate Harriers, and she and Caroline were quite competitive with each other. Bayliss liked to set them up against each other, so before the marathon he told each of them that the other one was going to beat her. It worked, because when he told Caroline, she thought, 'Well, I've got to beat Anne. I can't let her beat me.'

The race started on the cinder track at Feltham Arena. A photograph from the *Middlesex Chronicle* shows a scattering of spectators in the stands and a leading pack of 11 women who are about to leave the stadium. Once on the roads, they ran two laps around the outside of Heathrow Airport before returning. There was not much traffic as it was a bank holiday.

After two miles Christine moved to the front, closely followed by Caroline and Lyn, who had 'done so many long, agonised runs together in preparation for this race.' They ran side by side until the 15-mile point. After that Caroline moved into second place. Christine stretched her lead over the other two women. At 20 miles she was more than three minutes ahead of Caroline and 'tired, but … spurred on by encouragement from spectators.' Despite sore knees and blisters on her toes, Christine was running six-and-a-half-minute miles, well within Margaret's British record pace.[7] Dave Billington's report for *Athletics Weekly* described Christine's finish: 'Entering the arena, Christine Readdy was still full of running and within minutes of finishing was giving interviews on how she had just sliced 16:52 from Margaret's Thompson's British best.'

Her time of 2:50:55 was fast enough to place Christine ninth on the world all-time list, the first British woman to make it into the top 10. More than six minutes later, Lyn finished, having caught and passed Caroline in the final mile. All three women achieved under three hours. Caroline's teammate Anne ran over nine minutes faster than at Masters and Maidens, finishing fourth, also within the previous record. Margaret had dropped out at nine miles due to her tendon injury and Bridget at 20 miles because of blisters. Jeanne Coker, one of the women who crashed 10-milers in 1975, was running her first marathon and was the only other runner not to finish.

In her hometown of Stafford, Christine's feat was met with disbelief. When she told some of the male runners at her club, Stafford AC, her time, they replied incredulously, 'No you haven't,' but others had seen her on TV and confirmed that she had indeed run that fast. The race was evidence that there was a cohort of British women with the fitness and ability to race fast times if they were given the opportunity. Christine told the *Daily Mirror*: 'I suppose some people might not think this is very feminine. But at least I have proved that women have the same endurance as men.'[8] Christine was 23. What might she have achieved in the marathon if she had been given more assistance after Feltham? We will never know. There was no support from the governing bodies and no pathway to international competition. Lacking in opportunity, Christine chose to focus on shorter distances and didn't run another marathon for five years. Her British record remained unbroken for over two years, until Rosemary Cox ran one second faster at the Rugby Marathon in September 1978.

Lyn Billington was born Carolyn Sheehan in Gloucester in January 1945. From her late teens, she competed in canoeing in endurance races of up to 35 miles and was included in the 'possibles' squad for the 1968 Olympic Games but wasn't subsequently selected.[9] It was through canoeing that Lyn met her first husband, Martin Bosher, also a British international canoeist. They married in 1967 and lived in Yateley, a small town in Hampshire. While training with the GB canoeing team, Lyn discovered her talent for running. On days when the weather was bad, the canoeists would go for long runs to build endurance.

Lyn found that she could beat the men. Eventually she shifted her focus to running. 'When I realised I was not going to be good enough for the elite level at canoeing, I thought I'd take up running instead,' she says.[10] After joining Aldershot Farnham and District AC in the winter of 1968, she began running in cross-country races for the club, competing in her first national championships in February 1969 at Aldershot.

By 1972 Lyn had moved to Hounslow in West London and joined Feltham AC, where she was coached by club stalwart Dave Billington. From 1972 to 1975, she competed for Feltham in cross-country races, track races, short road races and road relays. On the track she most often competed at the longer distances, 1500 metres and 3000 metres. For part of this time she served as the ladies' captain and was awarded the trophy for outstanding service to the club in 1973. She and Martin divorced, and in December 1975 Lyn and Dave were married. Lyn didn't take part in any of the official women's road races in 1975, but, frustrated at the lack of distance events for women, she and Dave decided to organise the 1976 Feltham Ladies Marathon, a breakthrough event, as a showcase for British running talent. Lyn and Dave worked hard to attract club runners to the race. Two months before the race they put a notice in *Athletics Weekly*[11] with the headline 'Attention, women marathoners'. It stated that there was going to be a pre-race training run around the course on 7 March. The run was to be one lap of the course, which was 13 miles. The notice also listed the entries already received: Margaret Thompson, Norma Campbell and Leslie Watson. Knowing who had entered would encourage more women to sign up. Free overnight accommodation was also offered.

After Feltham, Lyn continued to race, mainly at distances of 10 miles or longer, finishing first in several events, and in 1977 she gave up her full-time secretarial job, preferring to work freelance from home as this allowed her to concentrate on her training. She was being coached by her husband and running between 70 and a 100 miles a week. When Lyn and Dave travelled to New York in November 1977 for the marathon, she had her sights set on Christine's British record. She finished seventh in a field of 179 women, with another sub-three-hour time, but fell short of the record – her time, 2:58:51, was over a minute slower than at Feltham.

In the years after the 1975 rule change, women were forced to carry on rulebreaking and ghost running as they were still excluded from most races. Lyn was one of them. In spring 1977, she asked Portsmouth AC for permission to run in their 25-kilometre Chichester to Portsmouth race, explaining that she wanted to get the experience of racing the distance, something she couldn't replicate in training. She wrote later in *Jogging* magazine about the club's response: 'I received a polite reply to the effect that although my reasons were appreciated they could not allow me to run with the men. They condescended to admit that they couldn't stop me running in the road section of the race, but they could, and would, stop me finishing on the track.' Lyn ran very nearly all of the race, apart from the last 1000 metres which were run on the track. 'How petty it all seems!', she commented.[12]

On Sunday 12 June, 1977, a 'tough new cross-country race … said to be one of the hardest in Britain' took place. The Offa's Dyke 15 was along the Offa's Dyke long-distance footpath from Hay-on-Wye in Powys to Kington in Herefordshire and was 'over mountain ridges of up to 1300 feet'. A local paper reported that two women had run in the race unofficially, finishing towards the back of the field. They were Avril Lewis and Pauline Brearley.[13] When I interviewed her, Avril did not remember much about the race, except that it was muddy. She chose to do it because it would be a personal challenge. However, this didn't mean it was just a training run. She and Pauline, one of her training partners from Bromsgrove and Redditch AC, took it seriously: 'I never would just have been going to stroll. If I was going to do it, I would have done the very best I could.' In contrast to many other runners' experiences, Avril's rulebreaking never led to any difficulties with race officials. She thinks that by 1977 it was becoming easier for women to participate: 'Dale Greig probably had to put up with a lot of stuff, but by the time I was doing it [it] was on the edge of it becoming more acceptable … people like Bridget Cushen pioneered the way. They did the difficult stuff. And when I was able to do it, it was more, "Okay, we're going to give you a chance." And, of course, we got to the end and we didn't die … the worst didn't happen.'

Avril's friend, Pauline, broke the rules again when she returned to the Offa's Dyke 15 in June 1978, accompanied by another Bromsgrove and Redditch AC member, Bronwen Smith. Bronwen finished in 2:07. *R.A.C.E.* magazine reported: 'Both were delighted to finish and found "the scenery beautiful – but not the hills". Next year it may well be that the race will be open to ladies.'[14]

On the 15 April 1978, Margaret Lockley (née Ashcroft) found herself in hot water. She was due to compete in the first women's national marathon championship, which was taking place on the Isle of Wight on 20 May, and she wanted to see what it was like to run hard over a long race. But there were no long races for women so, she told me, 'All the lads in Luton AC were going down to the Finchley 20, and I thought I'd just run round alongside the men, as a training run, while they were running the race.' On the way down to the race, one of the men said he didn't feel like running and Margaret said she would take his number. Her thinking was that this would make it easier for the race officials when she ran through the finish funnel.

Everything might have been fine if Margaret hadn't run so fast that she finished as the sixth Luton AC runner. It was the Southern Counties Championship and the fastest six runners from each club counted as a team. Had she been slower, Margaret's participation might not have been spotted. When her identity was revealed, it caused 'quite a kerfuffle' as Margaret puts it. The race organiser, Hillingdon AC, received a reprimand, probably from the Southern Counties AAA. Hillingdon AC sent a letter to Margaret's club, Luton AC. 'They said … that on no account was I to run in any of their races again, or in any men's race again', Margaret recalls.

Born in Wallasey in 1947, Margaret joined the local athletics club, Wallasey AC, as a teenager. During her teens and early twenties, she competed for them in track, cross country and road relays, as well as in some of the short road races which were put on for women. She favoured cross country because it was the longest distance women could do.

In 1965, aged 18, Margaret went to teacher training college to become a PE teacher. She met her future husband, David, through Wallasey AC. After college, she worked as a teacher in Liverpool and carried on competing for the club, until she and David moved down to Luton in 1976.

At the time of the Finchley 20 in April 1978, Margaret was 30 and recently married. She was the Cheshire cross-country champion and competed on the track in 3000 metres races and in occasional road races. She and David were both members of Luton AC and she was working at the Luton Regional Sports Centre. Twenty miles was a good distance to race in preparation for a marathon. Men had their pick of 20-milers with dozens of races put on each year. Yet when Margaret was preparing to run her first marathon, she couldn't find a single 20-mile race that officially admitted women. In a 1979 article on women's marathon running in *Athletics Weekly*, Cliff Temple noted that there were probably more marathons open to women runners than half marathons, 15- or 20-mile races.[15]

The most popular race distance at the time was 10 miles. There were dozens of 10-milers in 1978, the year of Margaret's rule-breaking run at the Finchley 20. However, women still couldn't run in most of them as they were men-only races. On the track, the furthest race distance for women was 3000 metres. Men raced 5000 metres and 10,000 metres, which provided a good progression route for longer distances, as it does for athletes today. Don Shelley, the newly appointed British national marathon organiser, commented in 1979 on the lack of events for women:

'Women have no official intermediate races, but jump from 3000 metres on the track to the marathon.' He said it would help if there were 10,000-metre track races for women and if more of the 10- and 20-mile road races admitted women.[16] Margaret's view was that if women's road running was to be taken seriously there needed to be more support for women's races. She wanted to see more women racing distances of 10 miles and more, and international races for the best women. Of course, for this to happen the way athletics was organised had to change. She highlighted that attitudes had to change too: 'A lot of people do take women marathon runners seriously, but many others regard us as a bit of a joke.'[17]

Unsurprisingly, the Women's Cross Country and Race Walking Association was far less relaxed about rules being broken. In July 1978, three months after Margaret's race at Finchley, it issued a directive to its affiliated clubs forbidding women's unofficial participation in races: 'Reports have been received of an increase in 'ghost running', so-called time trials, and of athletes not eligible to compete running the course and running out at the funnel … such activities will be in direct contravention of the rules and action against offenders may be taken.'[18]

Ghost running could cause havoc for race organisers, particularly if runners without numbers went through the finish funnel. This was many years before chip timing was invented. Runners' numbers had to be noted in finish order as they crossed the line and matched up with the times that had been recorded. It could take hours to sort out the results if there were ghost runners messing up the finish positions.

Of course, women were only ghost running in small numbers and most ducked out before the funnel. It is more likely that male ghost runners, using races as 'time trials', were the ones giving race organisers headaches. In 1977, the chair of Vale of Aylesbury AC wrote a letter to *Athletics Weekly* about the club's Rex Foulkes 20-kilometre race. Ghost runners, presumably mostly men, had caused problems for the past two years, he said. Their misdemeanours included: running with duplicate race numbers; going through the finish funnel; and even worse, taking the finishers' reward – a dozen eggs. 'Please do not do it,' he implored.[19]

While the Women's Cross Country and Race Walking Association threatened action against female ghost runners, it may have been impractical to see it through. After all, the runners had to be identified by race officials and reported to the association. Also, the governing body may have been overwhelmed by the scale of the rebellion. It lacked the resources to reprimand every ghost runner individually. And while many women received reprimands, I have not found any evidence that any were suspended from competition.

However, it would be wrong to think that the athletics governing bodies issued empty threats – other rulebreaking was taken very seriously, particularly when it came to the thorny issue of amateurism. At the time, strict amateur rules meant that athletes were unable to accept cash prizes or indeed to make any money relating to their athletics careers, for example from promoting products, giving talks or writing books. Deviation from the rules was rarely left unpunished and no-one was immune. Dorothy Hyman was Britain's most successful female sprinter ever when she decided to retire from athletics in 1964, aged only 23. She had won medals at the Olympic Games, European Championships and Commonwealth Games. In *The Official History of the WAAA*, Mel Watman recounts how what might seem like a minor transgression led to Dorothy losing amateur status.[20] After retiring, she published her autobiography, *Sprint to Fame.* Because she was making money from the book, the Women's Amateur Athletic Association (WAAA) barred her from competition. After coaching athletes for four years, a voluntary role, Dorothy reconsidered her decision to retire and applied to the WAAA to be reinstated. The governing body agreed, as it had decided that her book 'did not contravene the amateur rules as far as home meetings are concerned.' Dorothy was allowed to return to domestic competition and in 1969 regained her position as Britain's top sprinter. However, the WAAA never selected her to represent Britain again. Discouraged, Dorothy retired from sprinting for good as there did not seem to be much point in continuing when she couldn't compete internationally.[21] This waste of talent might seem harsh and ridiculous to us now, but amateurism was one of the cornerstones of athletics nationally and internationally, and that wouldn't start changing until the 1980s.

On a hot, sunny afternoon on Saturday 20 May, 1978, a crowd of holiday sightseers and locals gathered on Ryde Esplanade to watch the start of the Isle of Wight Marathon, the race where Dale Greig had set a world record time in 1964. The 1978 race had a big field of over 200 runners. And among the men were 11 women, attracted to the race by the fact that it was the inaugural WAAA National Marathon Championship. Margaret Lockley had trained hard for her first marathon. Following the plan set out by her coach, she'd increased her weekly long run to 20 miles a week for the previous eight weeks, running 90 miles a week on average. And she had done some 20-mile training runs, including her notorious appearance at the Finchley 20. Sub-three hours was her goal. Could she break the 2:50:55 record set by Christine Readdy at the Feltham Ladies Marathon in 1976? It would be a big challenge on this hilly course with over 1300 feet of ascent.[22]

Gillian Adams would be her main rival today. She'd run two sub-three-hour marathons in the USA in 1977, one of only four British women to have achieved a sub-three time. Margaret Thompson, the former British record holder, was also there. She'd run a fast 10-miler the month before, but since Korso in 1975 hadn't finished another marathon. She'd given birth to her first child in 1977. She'd only heard about the Isle of Wight race in February, when she'd met Leslie Watson at the men's national cross-country championships. Talking to Leslie 'ignited a spark' and Margaret decided to enter. Leslie knew the course well, having competed in the marathon in 1976. She'd run more marathons than any other British woman, but none of them had been under three hours.

Before the race started, the press got the women to line up in front of the men for photographs. At 2 p.m. prompt they were off to the cheers of the crowd. As they ran west through the streets of Ryde, which were lined with spectators, Gillian took an early lead. For the first five miles the two Margarets, who were good friends, ran together, with Leslie Watson close behind. At the five-mile point, Gillian was still in their sights, about 300 metres ahead. By the time Margaret Lockley reached the refreshment station in the village of Shide, close to the 10-mile point, she had left Margaret Thompson, who was about a minute behind her; Leslie Watson was out of sight further back. As Gillian approached the refreshment table, she glanced over her shoulder and saw that Margaret Lockley was closing on her and, by the time she'd found her drinks bottle, she'd been caught.

Race rules in the 1970s prohibited refreshments – water, other drinks or food – in races of under 10 miles. In longer races you couldn't carry your own refreshments or take any refreshments from anyone, except those provided by the race organiser. In marathons, refreshments were provided from seven miles and every three miles thereafter. There were 'sponging points' with water in between the refreshment stations. You could have your own drinks at the refreshment stations as long as these were approved by the race organiser and handed in before the race start. Angela Briscoe recalled that the races she competed in didn't have many drinks stations and this put her off running marathons as she struggled with thermoregulation. Most runners just drank water or sometimes very diluted orange squash – electrolyte powders were available but not widely used. Lydia Gould (née Kirk) recalls that, 'It didn't occur to anyone that you ate food.' However, some runners used dextrose tablets for energy.

After running with a few men for a while, Margaret and Gillian ran side by side, south along the Newport Road, chatting occasionally. There was little shade and with each steep hill they found themselves overtaking men who had stopped to walk. The picturesque village of Godshill marked the halfway point.

Negotiating their way along the narrow roads choked with cars and coaches, they were applauded by the day trippers.

The route turned east to the coast, arriving at the seaside resort of Shanklin. After taking the coast road for two miles, just after passing through another resort, Sandown, Margaret and Gillian reached the 20-mile checkpoint. They had been running for two hours and 12 minutes, averaging 6:38 per mile. They were both running well and it seemed as if they might have to take it to a sprint finish back at Ryde Esplanade.

It was not to be, though. Somewhere after the 20-mile point they encountered what seemed like an endless hill. Margaret noticed that Gillian was starting to slow. 'Come on, Gill, we'll make it to the top,' she said, but Gillian was broken, 'No, I can't, I can't do another step'. She stopped dead in the middle of the road. When Margaret reached the top of the hill on her own, she spotted Gillian's coach, Cliff Temple, and told him that Gillian needed his help. She now faced running the last miles back to Ryde on her own. Margaret felt dehydrated and a throbbing pain was coming from a large blister on the ball of her foot. Her pace slowed a little, but was still under 7:00 per mile. As she approached the finish in front of the Esplanade Pavilion, she could hear the applause of hundreds of spectators. Margaret was the first national marathon champion and had achieved her goal of finishing in under three hours. It was over and it was a huge relief.

Margaret Lockley's time was 2:55:08, just over four minutes slower than Christine Readdy's record, which had been set on a flat course at the Feltham Ladies Marathon in 1976. More than 20 minutes later, Margaret Thompson finished, having been struck by cramp at the halfway mark. She had walked for a bit and some of her male club mates had encouraged her to carry on. Leslie Watson was two and a half minutes behind her. Five more women finished: Judy Farr, 46-year-old Kathleen Wartnaby, Miriam Rosen, Bridget Cushen and Sheila Smith. Margaret Lockley was now second in the British marathon rankings.

'I always wanted to do a marathon, but I thought it would be my "swan song" before I retired completely,' Margaret told *Athletics Weekly* later.[23] She was encouraged by male club members at Luton AC and her coach, Harry Wilson, who was Britain's national middle-distance coach. He was coaching Tony Simmons, who'd finished fourth in the 10,000 metres at the 1976 Montreal Olympics, and Steve Ovett who'd set the British 1500 metres record in 1977. Despite women's marathon running being in its infancy in the UK, Wilson took it seriously. When Margaret mentioned she was thinking of running at the Isle of Wight, Wilson said he'd put a training programme together for her. When I interviewed her, she told me, 'He wasn't dismissive. Considering he was coaching Olympic athletes, I thought it was good of him really, because I was just somebody who wanted to have a go.' Wilson even travelled to the Isle of Wight for the race, which Margaret hadn't expected him to do.

Margaret felt that women's distance running was always an afterthought and that the people with power in athletics, and a lot of the press, didn't consider it to be important. She found it strange that road running was lumped together with cross country and road walking under the auspices of the Women's Cross Country and Race Walking Association. 'We were a bit of an oddity,' she reflects. Margaret's impression was that: 'There were such negative vibes about the whole thing of women doing marathons that I thought it would never happen. I thought they wouldn't bother. They'd have a token one on the Isle of Wight and then, because we were so bad at it, they just wouldn't bother having another one.' It is probably true that the women's governing bodies were not that interested in women's road running. There were, after all, no international women's championships. Why develop athletes' talents when there was no international pathway for them? However, it seems less likely that the Women's Cross Country and Race Walking Association deliberately chose a marathon in a difficult-to-get-to location and with a hilly course in order to put women off entering.

Margaret was not the only woman dissatisfied with the organisation of the championship. A row broke out in the letters pages of *Athletics Weekly* after a hectoring letter from John Symonds, chair of Ryde Harriers, the race organisers, appeared in the magazine a week before the race, criticising women, 'athletes of the "fair sex"', who had campaigned for change and were now being 'strangely reticent' about entering the race. He stated that the club had received only seven entries and described the national championships as a 'fiasco'. He rounded off with the patronising exhortation: 'So come on girls … the future of British women's distance running is in your own hands: don't let the rest of the world beat us before we've started.'

Four weeks later, replies from three women were printed: Jill Standerwick, Lyn Billington and Hilary Matthews, winner of the 1975 Barnsley Marathon. They were all fuming. Hilary's letter summarised the main issues. There had only been six weeks' notice that the race was to host the WAAA championship, she wrote, which was insufficient time to train for a marathon. Additionally, some women would have needed to save up for their train and ferry tickets. In response to Symonds' condescending closing words, Hilary retorted: 'So it's not come on girls, it's come on organisers. Give the women advance warning as necessary for such an event and they will give you support.' Three years after the rule change, it seemed that some race organisers would be only too happy to see women's road races fizzle out and to blame it on women themselves, rather than to consider making changes to their events. Despite all the bad feeling around the race, her win did lead to Margaret Lockley getting her first international vest. The Road Runners Club (RRC) hosted an annual international men's marathon. It was agreed that the 1978 race, held in Milton Keynes, would also serve as an international women's team race.

Vera Duerdin, the honorary secretary of the Women's Cross Country and Race Walking Association, contacted Margaret to let her know that she had been selected to compete for England in the race on 8 July, just seven weeks after the Isle of Wight Marathon, although it wasn't all plain sailing. Female cross-country and race walking athletes picked to represent England received national vests and tracksuits. When Margaret asked about getting her England vest for the race, she was told the governing body didn't have any women's racing vests (the men, of course, had vests) and would send her a cross-country vest instead. When the vest arrived, it was made of Bri-nylon and had a high neck. When Margaret complained that the vest was totally unsuitable for racing a marathon in July, she was told to 'go and buy a men's vest from Marks and Spencer's, and we'll send you a badge.' When the red rose badge arrived, Margaret sewed it on to the plain white V-neck vest she'd bought for the race.

The attempt to inaugurate an international team race at short notice was, rather inevitably, unsuccessful as England was the only country to muster the four athletes required to make a team. But there was a good turnout generally, with 13 women, representing England, Wales, Scotland, West Germany and the USA. Five of them had competed at the Isle of Wight: Margaret Lockley, Margaret Thompson, Gillian Adams and Judy Farr, representing England; and Leslie Watson representing Scotland. During the race, Margaret Lockley gradually increased her lead over the West German runner Gisela Schneider, finishing over three minutes ahead of her in 2:51:09 – just 14 seconds outside Christine's British record. The report in *Athletics Weekly* described Margaret and Gillian, who was third in 2:59:26, as 'running attractively as ever'. It's impossible to imagine a male runner being described in that way. Margaret Thompson had picked up a serious knee injury during training and had been receiving treatment at a rehabilitation centre in the run-up to the race. After receiving a cortisone injection, a week before the race, she had run her best ever 20-mile time in training, but by the day of the race the injury was painful again and she was forced to drop out.

In late September, Margaret Lockley received a last-minute invitation to race the New York City Marathon on 22 October, the world's largest marathon, but it did not come from the Women's Cross Country and Race Walking Association. Instead, Empire International Restaurants, a British restaurant chain with a restaurant called Richoux of London in New York, offered to pay all her expenses, as long as she was willing to wear a branded Richoux vest for the race.[24] Unaware that runners were supposed to ask permission to compete abroad, Margaret didn't advise the athletics authorities in advance. There was no come-back afterwards, perhaps because it was a fait accompli.

Grete Waitz of Norway won in a world record time of 2:32:29. Margaret was sixth and her time of 2:50:58 earned her third place in the British all-time rankings. She was joined in New York by Glynis Penny, who finished ninth in her debut marathon despite having hit 'the wall' at 20 miles, Gillian Adams, who was 15th, and Leslie Watson, who was 39th. The race had 8549 finishers and must have been an overawing experience for the British women. There was nothing like this in the UK, where 200 finishers was considered a big number. What's more, the women's field was huge with 769 finishers and the standard was high – the first 23 women ran under three hours. While the British women showed they could hold their own against a mainly American field, the top American women were far more experienced at this distance and weren't excluded from road races in the way British women still were. For example, 34-year-old Sue Petersen who finished third had already run 10 marathons that year, eight of them in California.

When I interviewed her, Margaret said that New York was the most prestigious race she had been part of and reflected on the sense of validation it gave her: 'When I did New York, that was the first time I really felt as though I was running and it was important.'

While British men could set their sights on the 5000 metres, 10,000 metres and the marathon at the European Championships, Commonwealth Games and Olympic Games, there was no development path for elite female athletes as they had no opportunity to compete at those distances on the international stage.

Women were not on the start line when these events were televised or covered in the press, effectively consigning women's long-distance racing to a secondary importance. As Bryan Smith, Joyce Smith's husband and coach, commented, there was no real incentive to train for a marathon, but 'If there was an Olympic or European marathon for women, you'd see the times coming down quickly, just as they did when the 1500 and 3000m distances became international.'[25]

Going to race abroad was also not straightforward. Firstly, you had to have permission from the British Amateur Athletic Board, which was responsible for British participation in international events. Secondly, you had to have the money to do it or find a sponsor. Finally, you had to have the time to train, travel and compete. Most athletes were working full time; a few, like Margaret Thompson and Joyce Smith, had young children.

Not long after Margaret's participation in New York, there was a hopeful sign that more support for women's marathoning was on the horizon. In late 1978, the British Amateur Athletic Board appointed Don Shelley as its first national marathon organiser.[26] His role was to ensure that the top male and female runners got proper coaching support and opportunities to compete internationally. Shelley announced the new men's and women's national squads. The men's comprised 24 runners, split into an A squad and a B squad. The women's consisted of six runners who had all run sub-three races: Gill Adams, Lyn Billington, Rosemary Cox, Margaret Lockley, Caroline Rodgers and Leslie Watson. In March 1979, Shelley organised a get-together at Sandbach in Cheshire and all but Caroline, who was unavailable, attended. They had a guided run around part of the course for the Sandbach Marathon, which was going to be the national women's championship that year, with a group discussion afterwards about their individual training and racing plans.

Both Margaret and Caroline told me they felt the squad did not live up to its promise, but this may partly have been down to a lack of funds. They had hoped for training weekends and team trips to races abroad, but both commented that it was not until 1982, when Evian became involved as a sponsor, that more support was provided.[27]

Of all the long-distance pioneers, Lyn Billington was one of the most consistently outspoken. In February 1979, when an argument broke out over a group of women being prevented from starting a five-mile race, 34-year-old Lyn was right at the centre of it, vehemently defending women's right to race. On Saturday 17 February, she and four other women turned up at the Hillingdon Express 5. The organisers, Hillingdon AC, hadn't put on a separate women's race, but the women expected to join the men's race, running unofficially as they had done at other races. The race director was willing to let them run, but unexpectedly, on the start line, the race referee pulled them back, telling them they would have to start one minute behind the men. As the *Sunday Mirror* reported, Lyn was furious and said: 'I was extremely angry and upset. I know I could have beaten half the men there. I have run in about 30 men's races. Women are running longer distances and men have to accept it.'[28]

For Lyn, the intervention was an unnecessary, petty application of the rules by an overweening male referee concerned to keep women out of men's racing: 'It is the odd bumptious official who takes it upon himself to exercise His Powers, even though you may be on the actual start line all geared up for a fast time. What devil takes hold of them? Do they feel threatened by the sight of the women taking on the men? Do they think that by waving the rule book they'll make themselves more secure?'[29]

Lyn wasn't going to race under these conditions. Nor was she going to take it lying down. She contacted Léon Stork, a journalist at her local paper, the *Staines and District Chronicle*. His article, 'Angry Lyn hits out at out-of-date officials', appeared within a week, opening with: 'Men and women may be considered equal in most aspects of daily life these days but in long distance running discrimination is as bad as ever and Hounslow's marathon runner Lyn Billington is furious at the latest slight on her ability.'

The *Sunday Mirror* interviewed Lyn and reported that she had complained to the Equal Opportunities Commission, the independent public body established under the 1975 Sex Discrimination Act. A spokeswoman for the Commission was quoted as saying, 'Women are very much discriminated against in sport. We'll investigate her complaint and take appropriate action.'

The paper noted that Lyn had received an apology from Hillingdon AC, but a WAAA spokesman was unsympathetic, saying, 'Women are banned from competing with men. It is a world-wide ruling, but some clubs are breaking it.' Unfortunately, the *Sunday Mirror* didn't report the outcome of the Equal Opportunities Commission investigation, if there was one.

In view of the lack of races for women, should race officials have turned a blind eye and allowed women to run in men's races? This was what Lyn and many others thought. They viewed the rules as obsolete and race officials as inflexible, out of touch and anti-women. But race officials were trained to follow the competition rulebook. If you didn't respect the rules, how could you ensure the integrity of the sport? It was a clash of intransigence and impatience.

Lyn could see that speaking to the press was not going to be enough to change things. Another way to have influence was to be on the inside of the athletics establishment, on the committee of one of the governing bodies. Lyn probably felt that her dissenting voice would not have been welcomed by the Women's Cross Country and Race Walking Association, an organisation that was only peripherally interested in road running anyway. In the 1970s, the lead organisation for the governance of road running was the RRC, so this was where Lyn directed her attention. The club set performance standards for its members and promoted its own races. Its focus was distances of 10 miles and more, the marathon and ultra-distance events, which at the time were run on the track and roads.

In 1976, the RRC members voted in favour of allowing women to join as full members, but for many years women made up a tiny minority of the membership. In 1977, the club's council co-opted Leslie Watson when they decided that 'a lady's voice … would be advantageous', as their newsletter puts it.[30] But for unknown reasons Leslie only remained on the council for a few months. It was Lyn who, in 1979, became the first woman to be elected to the council. The club had over 2600 members and described itself as the largest athletics club in the world. When Lyn was elected just 42 of the members were women – less than 1.5%.[31] She no doubt used her voice to encourage more events to be opened up to women, and by writing race reports for the club's newsletter, she ensured that readers knew that women were running long distance. She was a lone female voice on the all-male council until 1984, when she stood down. There was no woman on the council for a year until Lyn Fitzgerald was elected for 1985–86.

At around the time Lyn Billington joined the RRC Council in 1979, the International Runners Committee was formed in the USA. Sponsored by shoe brand Nike, the committee's first objective was 'a full program of women's distance races in the 1984 Olympics, and in all other international championships leading up to the Los Angeles Games'. The committee was led by Jacqueline Hansen who had set the marathon world record twice: in 1974 and then again in 1975, when she ran 2:38:19 at the Nike Oregon Track Club Marathon in Eugene. In her memoir, *A Long Time Coming*, Jacqueline writes about her dawning realisation that she and other women long-distance runners couldn't compete in international championships: 'I was keenly aware by now that my new distance events did not afford me the opportunity to try out for the Olympic team … I came to realize the injustice of having no place to advance to the highest level of the sport. Naively I imagined that a few letter-writing campaigns, circulating petitions and speaking out in the media would "get the job done". Little did I know that it would be a 10-year ordeal before seeing the marathon in the Olympics.'[32]

It was this personal experience that led Jacqueline to become an activist, campaigning for future generations of women runners to have the same opportunities as men.

The International Runners Committee recruited members from the USA, Brazil, West Germany, Hungary, UK, New Zealand and Japan. Lyn was the British representative. Their role was to lobby their respective governing federations to push for women's distance races to be added to the programme of the Olympic Games. This wasn't just about the marathon. They were fighting for the 5000 metres and 10,000 metres too.

In August 1979, *Jogging*, a new magazine, published a one-page opinion piece by Lyn: 'Let women run on equal terms with men'. Describing some of the progress achieved in the USA, she contrasted it with the cautious, sluggish approach to change in the UK: 'Sadly, we don't seem to have learned anything from the Americans … Only now are our officials beginning to accept that women can not only run at longer distances, but on equal terms with men.' Lyn accused the WAAA of being out of touch: 'Why did it take so long for this decision to be made? Didn't the committee concerned look at the training then being undertaken, or did they just remember 'their' day when women only raced over short distances?' As there weren't enough women competing yet to make women-only races viable, Lyn's view was that they should be allowed to run in men's races. She offered women some advice on how to make this work and avoid criticism. A woman who wanted to run in a men's race should write to the organiser in advance requesting permission to run. She should also offer to turn up in her running gear so that there would be no requirement to provide changing facilities for her. Lyn concluded with a rousing call to action:

> Make a stand. Don't be belittled by any male. Remember you have trained hard and the only way to acquire fast times is in a 'racing environment' … Turn up and run. The more the better. Only when we have sufficient numbers will we be taken seriously.

So where did things stand at the end of the 1970s? In her article in *Jogging*, Lyn estimated that only about 40 British women had run a marathon. It definitely took time to build a cohort of women who wanted to run long-distance road races (of any length); for women to create their own long-distance running stories, having missed out on decades of road races; and for role models to emerge to inspire younger generations.

In the mid-1970s, the pool of women was quite small. And standards were high. You had to be fast to race. Most of the pioneers came from athletics clubs. But many girls left athletics in their late teens and young women often left when they got married or when had their first child.

So women training for long-distance often found they had no other women to run with. To run with groups of men, women had to be fast and confident of their ability to keep up. At Wallasey AC, Margaret Lockley and her training partner, Barbara Banks, did a long run of 8–10 miles together on a Sunday. During the week, they went out on the roads with the men, finding a pace group that suited them. Margaret told me: 'We used to run when the men were going out on a run … If it was a cold, dark night, we'd all stick together and run five miles, quite hard. There wasn't a lot of easy running. You went flat out all the time, because that's what you thought you had to do. Every night was like a race.' For many runners, women and men, training miles were all hard miles. When I interviewed Angela Briscoe, who finished second behind Alison Blake in the Reebok 6 in 1975, she told me that when she went to Leeds University in 1970, she found there wasn't a women's cross-country team so she trained with the men's team. She reflected that the long road miles she did may not have been good for her: 'I didn't do many easy runs … It makes sense now, but nobody knew. They hadn't done the science so that was the way it went. I know I ran too hard.'

In mixed clubs, the women's section had to compete with the larger men's section for funding for transport to fixtures, track time and coaching. In a 1978 interview published in *Athletic Review*, a magazine focused on athletics in Northern England, Angela described the situation at her club, Stretford AC: 'The men are pretty much anti-woman! We don't see them that much there's so many separate fixtures. It's like two separate clubs really … The men seem to think they're more important and some of the women's officials have a similar attitude on their side.'[33] The men on the committee had recently decided that there would no longer be coaches put on to take girls to races. This had resulted in a big drop in the number of girls participating.

Gillian Burley did athletics at school but focused on competitive swimming during her undergraduate degree at Sheffield University as the athletics club wasn't interested in women athletes. A move to Newcastle University for postgraduate study in engineering reignited her interest in running and she joined Gateshead Harriers, one of the top clubs. In April 1979, 22-year-old Gillian qualified for the 1980 Boston Marathon when she ran 2:58:09 at the Duchy of Cornwall Marathon, the 14th-fastest time by a British woman that year. The club was subsidising a team of three men to travel to the race. Gillian was funding her own trip. When she approached the club committee and asked if they'd consider giving her a token contribution to her expenses, they turned her down.[34]

In 1976, Joyce Smith, Carol Gould and several other women split from their mixed club, Barnet and District AC, setting up a separate club for women, Barnet Ladies AC. In an interview on the *Marathon Talk* podcast in 2014, Joyce explained why: 'As a ladies' section we found we weren't doing very well and not getting a lot of encouragement, so we broke away.'[35] They were coached by Joyce's husband, Bryan Smith. Yet, mixed clubs worked well for some women, like Adele Brignall and Margaret Lockley, who benefitted from the access that being in a mixed club gave them to male coaches (as women's long-distance was in its infancy there were not yet any female coaches).

When the plans for a specialist British Marathon Runners Club were published in December 1977, it was immediately clear that no thought had been given to women. For one thing, the proposed qualifying standard for membership was a marathon time of under 2:20 or you had to have finished in the first 10 in the AAA marathon championship, even though 2:20 was 15 minutes faster than the women's world record and the AAA marathon championship was a men's event.[36] However, the inaugural meeting on 29 January 1978 rectified this by adding a qualifying standard of 3:10 for women. They weren't to be left out after all.

Public attitudes were still quite negative towards women running long distances. Margaret Lockley says that people generally thought she was 'bonkers' for wanting to run a marathon. Gill Adams, who had lived and raced in the USA, compared the attitude there with that in the UK: 'If you live in California, you're accepted as a female marathon runner … Over here people still think you're strange.' She attributed this difference to the popularity of jogging in the USA. She said she was disappointed that more British women hadn't taken part in races, commenting, 'There still seems to be a stigma about women running in long road races.'[37]

As the decade neared its end, one runner was to redefine British excellence in long-distance running and narrow the performance gap to the international best: Joyce Smith.

As soon as women were allowed to compete in long-distance road races Joyce quickly made her mark, winning the Wycombe 5 on 21 September, 1975, aged 37, with 'a huge margin of supremacy', over one and a half minutes ahead of Alison Blake. After having her second daughter, Lia, in 1976, she broke the UK 10-mile record twice in 1977, lowering it to 56:27. Joyce continued to compete on the track, but after her last international event in June 1978 realised that she wasn't enjoying it any more and decided to train for running a marathon in 1979.[38] At the beginning of that year, she told *Jogging*, 'I hope to run a marathon this year, because it is something I always wanted to do before I retire.'[39]

In 1979, now in her early forties, Joyce ran not one but three marathons, winning all of them and breaking the British record twice. The second WAAA national marathon championship, sponsored by Avon Cosmetics, was held at Sandbach in Cheshire on 17 June in conjunction with a men's race. The field of nearly 30 women included some new challengers – notably Carol Gould and Kath Binns who were both running their first marathon – and most of the country's top marathoners, all of whom had run sub-three times: Margaret Lockley; Gillian Adams; Alison Blake, who had run her first marathon two months earlier in 2:55:02; Lyn Billington; Gillian Burley; Leslie Watson; and Caroline Rodgers. Rosemary Cox, the British record holder, was absent because of illness. Caroline had a big lead in the race for the first 12 miles, but by the halfway point Joyce had caught her. Joyce's emphatic win exceeded expectations. Sandbach was a breakthrough race for British women's marathoning. Mel Watman wrote in *Athletics Weekly* that Joyce had 'helped revolutionise women's marathon running in this country.' Not only had she knocked nine minutes off the British record, but three other women, Gillian Adams, Carol Gould and Kath Binns, had finished inside the old record too.[40] Caroline finished fifth in 2:54:37, knocking four minutes off the personal best she had set at Feltham in 1976. Margaret Lockley finished sixth in 2:54:50 and Jean Lochhead, running her first marathon, was seventh in 2:55:16. Lyn was the ninth woman to finish in under three hours with 2:58:03.

Joyce's win earned her an invitation to Avon International Women's Marathon in Waldniel, West Germany, held on 22 September. It was the second in a series of international women's marathons sponsored by Avon as part of its campaign, spearheaded by Kathrine Switzer, to get the women's marathon into the Olympic programme. The first race in the series had been held in Atlanta in the USA in 1978. No British women had competed there. These races were seen as the unofficial world championships for women.

The Waldniel race attracted over 200 runners from 24 countries. Joyce won in 2:36:27, regaining the British record which Gillian Adams had briefly held, and placing sixth in the world all-time list. The UK won the team competition, too, with Carol Gould third and 23-year-old Suzan Hassan 15th in her first marathon. Lyn finished 35th in under three hours. Suzan had won her paid-for trip to the race by finishing first at an Avon-sponsored cross-country race on New Year's Day.

Around this time, the international governing body, the International Amateur Athletic Federation (IAAF), took two major steps forward on the path to a women's Olympic marathon. In August 1979, the IAAF congress agreed to the women's committee's request to include the women's marathon in the inaugural athletics world championships in 1983, and in November the addition of the women's marathon to the European athletics championships was approved. It was now up to countries worldwide to encourage women's marathoning and to put on international women's races.[41]

Joyce's third marathon win of 1979 was the Tokyo International Women's Marathon on 18 November. Aged 42, she finished in 2:37:48, with 24-year-old Gillian Adams second in 2:39:28. That year, Joyce also set British records at 10 and 20 miles. Forty-six years later, her 20-mile time, 1:57:00, is still the British record for the 40–44 age category and the eighth best British performance of all time.[42]

Joyce made the most of the opportunities that became available to her as women's distance running developed. They motivated her to keep competing and extended her career as an elite athlete. She said, 'Because the events slowly came in, I just moved up a step each time and it was a new event, a new achievement. There was always something new to do … New horizons kept opening up.'[43]

Did women have equal access to road races as the decade ended? Still no. It took several years after the rule change in 1975 for more races to admit women. Although in 1979 things were opening up, most road races were still men only. It was really the growth in popularity of jogging in the late 1970s, and the advent of the marathon boom in the early 1980s, that transformed both public attitudes to running and the way races were organised. The huge new contingent of 'leisure runners' regarded the exclusion of women as archaic. New race organisers were also keen to attract as many runners as possible, so excluding half the population no longer made any sense whatsoever.

7
JOGGING HITS BRITAIN

'I find it wonderful for keeping life in perspective – all your problems can be thought out in peace.'[1]

On Sunday 1 October 1978, there was a mass gathering in Hyde Park in central London. It wasn't for a parade, a pop concert or a carnival. Instead, 11,822 men, women and children were there to take part in the *Sunday Times* National Fun Run and 30,000 people had come to watch.[2] Twenty-nine-year-old Miriam Rosen was among the crowd of fun runners queuing to pick up their numbers. It was all a bit disorganised. People were getting anxious that they would miss their slot and the organisers had to delay the start time of the first run by 15 minutes. Miriam was in the fun run for women aged 19 to 29. There were 12 other runs catering for all ages. The youngest participant was four and the oldest was 80.

Miriam, whose first long-distance running event had been the Masters and Maidens Marathon three years before, was now a member of Barnet Ladies AC. She'd never done an event with quite so many participants and when I interviewed her in 2025 she told me how astonished she was to find that many of the women were complete beginners: 'A lot of the women were walking round, because I don't think they'd really run before and they'd been cajoled by friends or workmates to enter this.'[3] The route was a twisty four kilometres in Hyde Park finishing near the Serpentine. The day ended with a celebratory mass jog for everyone over the same course.

The *Sunday Times* National Fun Run was not the first mass fun run, but it was the biggest by far. It marked the point where jogging had got a grip on the nation and it was only going to get bigger. It had been advertised many months ahead and teams from newly formed jogging clubs had been training for it, as well as many other groups. A reporter from the *Liverpool Echo*, Charles Lambert, who ran in the men's 20 to 29 fun run, described a diverse assortment of groups: 'Taking part was the thing, for where else could you run side by side with such varied teams as the London Society of Magicians, the crew of the nuclear submarine Churchill, the Guild of Professional Toastmasters and the Bethnal Green Town Hall PR Staff?'

Lambert noted that he had finished ahead of 'two men dressed in monkey suits, a magician, staff from a London hotel running in chefs' hats and Buzby, the GPO mascot.'[4] Clearly the British penchant for running in fancy dress was already well established. How, in the space of a few years, had jogging changed from an activity for sportspeople who wanted to keep fit to a national craze involving all the family?

Jogging had taken off in the USA in the 1960s amid concern that Americans' increasingly sedentary lifestyles were causing ill health with the middle-aged, particularly middle-aged men, perceived to be most at risk of coronary heart disease. Bill Bowerman, a track coach at the University of Oregon, is generally credited with popularising jogging. During a visit to New Zealand with the university's track team in 1963, he was inspired by the training approach of the highly successful track coach Arthur Lydiard, who invited him to join his newly formed Auckland Joggers Group one January Sunday morning. The group's aim was to improve the physical fitness of men over 40 through non-competitive group running at a relatively slow pace. Bowerman, 51, was shocked to realise that he wasn't as fit as he thought he was. Despite running with the slowest pace group, he struggled to keep up with men 10 and 20 years older than him who had had heart attacks. Something had to be done, so on his return to Oregon Bowerman devised a jogging-based fitness programme for himself and started a men's and women's jogging group, which proved hugely popular.[5]

Exercise physiology in middle-aged adults was poorly understood and Bowerman realised that research was needed to establish the impact of jogging on health and understand what type of training worked. In 1965 he established a research project at the university looking at the effects of regular jogging on previously sedentary men aged over 30. The outcomes were an article on the benefits of jogging published in a medical journal and the creation of a jogging programme suitable for sedentary people. Bowerman subsequently described this in a book written with a cardiologist, Dr Waldo Harris. *Jogging: A Physical Fitness Program for All Ages* was published in 1967 and its front cover proclaimed its benefits: 'Reduce the waistline – Improve your appearance – Help prolong your life'. It became a best-seller.

Jogging was said to be suitable for all ages, even children and the elderly. It provided a path to good health and fitness if it became a daily or regular habit. It was easy to do. You did not need more than a pair of comfortable shoes. And you didn't need a coach as you could follow a gradual programme laid out in one of the many books available. You could go jogging on your own or with others. There was no need to join a club.

Increasingly, rather than the state being responsible for the health of the nation, individuals were being encouraged to take responsibility for their own health. Jogging quickly became about more than just fitness; as sociologist Neil Baxter notes, it could be part of 'a holistic self-improvement strategy – a technique for becoming a better, happier, more authentic human being ...'.[6]

In *The American Marathon*, Pamela Cooper describes how jogging quickly spread across the USA, with fun runs organised by the Road Runners Club of America; newspaper and magazine articles promoting the benefits of jogging; and upper-status individuals and celebrities becoming fitness runners and entering marathons.

The UK was also concerned about the impact on health of sedentary lifestyles, but it took a bit longer for jogging and fitness to grip the public imagination. Part of the impetus came from the government, which from the late 1960s started to take an interest in sport, both at national and local level. There was a new focus on fitness rather than elite competition as being of most benefit to the nation. The government was putting money into sport and local authorities took a growing role in sports provision. Following its formation in 1972, the Sports Council launched its Sport for All programme and invested in community leisure facilities. As a consequence, from 1972 to 1981, the number of British leisure and sports centres increased from 27 to nearly 800.[7]

While there was an awareness of jogging in the UK from the late 1960s, it was not widely known about and journalists felt the need to explain what it was. In July 1971 the *Staffordshire Evening Sentinel* reported on the formation of Stone Jogging Club, which it described as 'possibly the first jogging club in the country'.[8] It explained jogging as 'simply running easily with a group' and said it was 'suitable for anyone in normal health from 18 to 80 years of age.'

From a slow start, jogging started to gain momentum in 1975. 'Jogging along … on the crest of a craze' was the title of an article in the *Daily Mirror* on 10 January in which journalist Christopher Ward proclaimed that he had taken up jogging in the park on New Year's Day and had been putting on his tracksuit and running around Regents Park in London every morning since: 'Besides the pleasures of socialising at 7 a.m., a gentle run round the park is considered by many doctors to be the best form of exercise for the desk-bound modern man.'[9]

In February 1975, athlete Brendan Foster started holding twice-weekly lunchtime 'Jogalong' sessions at the Gateshead athletics track. Foster was still at the height of his athletics career, having won gold in the 5000 metres at the European Championships in Rome the previous year, and as the sports and recreation manager at Gateshead Town Council he was involved in the organisation of numerous sporting events.

The *Newcastle Evening Chronicle* reported that the first jogging session attracted 'more than three dozen assorted bodies trying their hand at the latest in keep-fit ideas' including 'two attractive office girls'.[10] Eventually up to 150 people were attending – men and women. The idea of the mass fun run probably originated in Gateshead and on 27 July a mass Jogalong for charity at the Gateshead Stadium attracted 385 participants. Foster's initiatives in Gateshead featured in a Tyne Tees TV documentary, *Everyone's a Winner in Gateshead*, broadcast a month after the Jogalong.

A further fun run at Gateshead Stadium on 29 October 1977 attracted around 600 participants 'of all ages and sizes'.[11] It was billed as one of the first in the country. Participants were promised the chance to 'jog along with Big Bren.'[12] Those who completed the two miles in under 18 minutes would receive a certificate signed by Foster.

The idea caught on and in 1978 a fun-run craze swept the country. The town of Boston in Lincolnshire kicked it off with a New Year's Day fun run organised by Boston and District Sports Council. January saw the first fun run in Northern Ireland held in Mallusk, in conjunction with an international men's cross-country race. Scotland joined in with a fun run in Inverleith Park, Edinburgh, in February. The craze spread as towns and cities across England and Wales held their first fun runs. By April, fun running had even reached as far north as the Shetland Islands.

The media really started to take notice. Newspaper references to jogging increased more than threefold, and radio and TV programmes began to talk about jogging.[13] By this point the term had become ubiquitous and journalists no longer felt the need to explain what it was.

Jogging offered women who did not see themselves as 'sporty' an opportunity to get fit. You started from where you were with a mixture of walking and jogging. You could jog on your own or join one of the new, informal, mixed jogging groups that were springing up everywhere. Women who would never have joined an athletics club found their way into running and road racing through jogging.

The fifth finisher in the women's 19 to 29 fun run at the *Sunday Times* National Fun Run in 1978 was 22-year-old Lydia Kirk. Unlike Miriam, Lydia had no experience of long-distance races. Her only running event had been the Metro Radio Fun Run in Gateshead four months earlier, where she had been the first woman to finish, wearing her first pair of running shoes – 'plastic' Whiz-Kids children's trainers. Lydia, who was 5 foot 2, had chosen them because they were cheap – only £5 – and came in small sizes.[14]

Until her mid-teens Lydia was at a girls' boarding school in Cambridgeshire. She enjoyed sport, played in the hockey team and took part in swimming competitions. She was also keen on horse riding. But there wasn't much in the way of athletics at school. Although the girls did cross country, they didn't compete against other schools. When I interviewed Lydia in 2025, she said, 'I'd always enjoyed running at school ... but no one ever took athletics seriously.' Habitually late, she often had to run the two miles to and from school and knew that sprints were not her forte.[15] 'Like most people who are not super talented, I looked for something that I might be good at,' she told me. Having won several short cross-country races at school, Lydia knew she favoured longer distances.[16]

When Lydia did the Metro Radio fun run in June 1978, she was a fine art student at the University of Newcastle. She hadn't found any opportunities to run there, but knew she wanted to test herself over a distance that she thought would suit her and she timed herself. A few days after the fun run, she managed to run five miles and the idea of running a marathon crept into her thoughts, but it would not be realised for another year.

On a sunny Saturday morning, 19 May 1979, the ferry from Portsmouth to Ryde was bustling with people, many of them runners destined for the Isle of Wight Marathon that afternoon, the notoriously hilly race where Margaret Lockley had won the inaugural national marathon championship the previous year. As the vessel left the dock, Lydia gazed out of the window at the boats moored in the harbour. A middle-aged man dressed in a tracksuit and trainers was standing next to her. Lydia asked him if he was going to the race. The man introduced himself as John Disley and said that he was going to the island for the marathon, but that he was not running it. Lydia explained that she was planning to watch the race and hoped to chat to some of the female runners as she wanted to run a marathon herself one day. Disley told her that on-the-day entries were available for the marathon. Lydia was doubtful about entering as she didn't have her running gear with her and only had gym shoes. She couldn't imagine running 26.2 miles in jeans. Disley encouraged her to ask if any of the women on board could lend her a pair of shorts. Lydia duly went round the ferry looking for the female runners. Eventually she came across a friendly woman who looked as if she might be a good runner. The woman was very helpful, saying, 'If you really want to do it, I've got a spare pair of shorts in my kit bag'. She also lent Lydia a sleeveless top. Lydia decided she could manage to run in her gym shoes.

After paying her entry fee and getting her race number, Lydia began to feel quite nervous. While she hadn't done many races, she had started training seriously, running up to 70 miles a week. Some of her long runs had been over 20 miles. At the start line on Ryde Promenade, she chatted to one of the other women and told her that as it was her first marathon, she'd decided to start at the back and go at a slow pace. The two women ran together for a long time. Lydia enjoyed every minute of the race and recalls, 'We just chatted and laughed and joked all the way around and looked at the scenery … It was relatively easy … It was much slower than I was training at. I was jogging compared to my training pace.' For most of the race, she was running more than a minute and a half slower per mile than her usual training pace of 7:00 per mile. At the 10-mile checkpoint she was the last of the 232 competitors, but at 20 miles Lydia had overtaken one of the women and 11 of the men. She then picked up her pace in the final 6.2 miles, averaging 7:35 per mile and passing two more of the women and 29 more men. Lydia finished sixth out of nine women in 3:43:52. Australian Linda Thompson from Leamington Spa Cycling and Athletics Club, an experienced marathoner, finished first in 3:10:50 and Bridget Cushen was second.

The Isle of Wight Marathon marked the start of a remarkable five months of racing for Lydia. In June, she competed in the Women's Amateur Athletic Association (WAAA) Marathon Championship at the Sandbach Marathon, finishing 17th in 3:18:20, a 25-minute improvement. She now had some proper running shoes from the American brand PONY. At the beginning of September, Lydia won the Rugby Marathon and three weeks later brought her marathon time tantalisingly close to sub-three hours, finishing second in 3:00:40 at the International Milton Keynes Marathon. Another second place followed at the Harlow Marathon in October. After competing in just two fun runs in 1978, it was a remarkable transformation, especially as Lydia wasn't in a club and was training without the benefit of coaching.

In March 1979, a magazine launched which sought to tap into the jogging craze. *Jogging* was very different from the athletics magazines available at the time. It was more like a specialist lifestyle magazine with recipes, cartoons, humorous features and profiles of celebrity joggers alongside the more traditional running advice and information. As public health historian Alex Mold has noted, jogging was promoted to women in a highly gendered manner – as a way to get fit, lose weight, become more attractive and even improve your sex life. She quotes James Hewitt, author of one of the many popular jogging books published in the late 1970s: 'Women should not consider it "unfeminine" to jog: such a view is old-fashioned and unwarranted. Jogging leads to a more shapely figure and a more youthful and attractive appearance.'[17]

In June 1979, *Jogging* published an extract from a forthcoming book called *Jogging*, by the journalist John Bryant. Although no doubt his aim was to encourage women to take up jogging, Bryant's view was that women had fewer preconceived ideas about 'running style' than men, which he saw as an advantage: 'Perhaps because they've been less sports-orientated at school, women tend to see jogging less as a sport and more as a health and beauty treatment – which is good, especially in the initial stages when the great aim is to enjoy it, to ease into it, to establish the habit of exercise.'

Bryant proceeded to list some of the benefits of jogging, his basic premise being that losing weight would make women more attractive to men. They didn't need to worry about their appearance becoming 'masculinised' either, because, he reassured them:

> The women who've taken up jogging have been delighted to find that: it doesn't produce bulging muscles – it *does* take off weight; it doesn't make their breasts sag – it *does* firm up the figure; it doesn't lead to the whole world laughing at them – it *does* lead to envious glances and enquiries as to what they've been up to.

Clearly some of the benefits both Hewitt and Bryant identified were as much for men as for the women themselves and, of course, they didn't stop to ask women what they themselves wanted.

Unlike rival publications such as *R.A.C.E.* (later *Athlete's World*), *Jogging* had women on its editorial team. Rosemary Cox, who had set the new national marathon record in 1978, was editorial assistant for the first eight issues and contributed occasional articles, as did the production editor Eve Martin. Although the magazine to a certain extent reflected the prevailing sexist attitudes of its time, it was groundbreaking and innovative in the topics it covered. The May 1979 issue included a feature entitled, 'Running A Family', with interviews with four female runners about how they combined running and motherhood. This was probably the first article in an athletics magazine to ever look in depth at the practical issues women had to deal with if they wanted to make time for running. Even though women were in the minority of joggers, from the very first issue *Jogging* published content that was aimed at them.

What did women themselves say? The magazine was bought mainly by men, but there is plenty of evidence on the letters pages from 1979 that women were reading the magazine, too, and many correspondents shared their new-found love of jogging, no doubt inspiring other women to try it themselves. For example, Mrs Moir, a teacher from Southampton, explained how buying the magazine had given her the confidence to try jogging again. She had attempted it the previous year but given up after two weeks 'because of jeers from husband and family'. Her motivation to keeping going this time included: 'the realisation that though fair, fat and 40 *I am not alone* in my desire to feel better and get slimmer. I have lost 11½lbs in a month through jogging and diet.' She was beginning to feel the benefits of persisting with jogging: 'I know I look better, and feel better, than I did a month ago … I don't think I'll give this up. The dog and I enjoy it too much already, and people laughing haven't put us off yet!'

Margaret Park from Malvern wrote that she had started jogging after her 'superfit cycling-cum-running addict of a husband' had brought the first issue of the magazine home. She'd borrowed his tracksuit and training shoes and gone out for a jog. Six weeks later she was still jogging, pushing herself harder, and had given up her 30-cigarettes-a-day habit (around 40% of women smoked at the time). She proclaimed, 'Gone is the fatigue. I now feel alive, and it's all down to you, *Jogging*.'

Mrs E Blake from Guisborough in Yorkshire described the pleasures of her early morning jogs: 'I jog alone at 6.15 a.m. through the quiet streets, my only companions being the birds and the squirrels …'; and the solitude that gave her time to think: 'I find it wonderful for keeping life in perspective – all your problems can be thought out in peace.' After having a shower, she prepared breakfast for her husband and son as her husband would get back from his jog in time to eat.

Sylvia Jenkins from Clywd in Wales wrote that she had started competing in races in January 1978 at the age of 30, when her daughter was eight months old. She noted, 'Before that I was a keen jogger, and jogged all through my pregnancy, running round country lanes until I was seven months pregnant. Then embarrassment at my shape drove me to run round the garden for 10 minutes, twice daily!' Sylvia clearly felt the magazine was for her, saying 'It's great to be able to indulge my running fanaticism with other jogging and running converts.'

While women were part of the jogging craze, it was, like most sports, a predominantly male activity. Stone Joggers was founded in the market town of Stone in Staffordshire in 1971 and was a men's club until 1975, when Lyn Hawkins, the wife of one of the club's founders, set up a ladies' section. In a profile of Stone Joggers in the May 1979 issue of *Jogging* she recounted, 'When we started in 1975, we were just half a dozen wives of the joggers … Our husbands were going out so often, we thought it must be something good!' They persisted, despite the men not taking them seriously, and eventually more women joined.[18] However, for the women in the club being keen did not mean being competitive. Lyn contrasted the women's approach with the men's: 'They're very competitive, always seeing how far they can go, and who they can beat. For us, it's more social.'

Clubs and groups offered women moral support and safety, helping them overcome some of their concerns about exercising outdoors. Lyn explained that a lot of women were very embarrassed about jogging, saying that it took some six months to pluck up the courage to come along to the club: 'I think some women imagine they'll look silly, or something, especially if they're a bit plump. But, you know, size has nothing to do with jogging.' It's clear that contrary to the assumptions of many male 'experts', women joggers themselves believed that well-being was more important than weight loss or appearance. The feeling of being part of a community of joggers also mattered, whether it was by joining a group or through the pages of the magazine.

As Lyn, ladies captain at Stone Joggers, explained, one problem facing women who wanted to start jogging was what to wear. Tracksuits were for sport. They hadn't yet become street fashion, so most women didn't have one hanging up in their wardrobe. Some beginners borrowed their husbands' tracksuits, but that didn't work for everyone. Lyn advised women they could start in jeans and a sweatshirt. It must have been incredibly uncomfortable, but it meant they didn't initially have to spend money on specialist clothing.

In response to the growing popularity of jogging, manufacturers developed clothing, shoes and other products to meet the needs of this new consumer market. The second issue of *Jogging* (April 1979), featured adverts for several brands of jogging shoes; joggers' pedometers; the Mr President jog suit from the USA, made in heavyweight cotton/acrylic; a very expensive indoor Campri Sport 'jogging machine' that looks like a set of sprung scales; a keep fit cycle; and many other products related to health, fitness and slimming.

New joggers often ran in plimsolls or canvas tennis shoes. Traditionally, shoe companies' products had focused on training and racing shoes for male road runners. By the end of the 1970s, several shoe companies were targeting joggers, for example Tiger (now ASICS), Mitre and Gola all produced shoes called 'Jogger'.[19] However, it wasn't always easy for women to find running or jogging shoes. As most runners were men, some brands didn't make sizes smaller than a six. And some sports shops didn't stock smaller sizes. As Christine Kilkenny (née Readdy), winner of the 1976 Feltham Marathon, told me, many women just had to make do with what was available, buying a small men's size: 'For a long, long time, there weren't women's shoes … I take a size six in a shoe and that was at the low end of the men sizes. I could get a shoe, but they didn't have a lot in stock at that size and you just tied the laces tight.' Other women told me that they stuffed paper in the toes of shoes that were too big.

Finding a bra suitable for jogging and running was another problem. Christine said, 'They didn't do women's running bras. You just ran in your everyday one. And if the straps came down, you could safety pin them to your vest.' In 1977, two American women, Lisa Lindahl and Polly Smith, devised the first sports bra, the pull-on 'jogbra' with straps that crossed at the back and a supportive, elasticated band beneath the breasts, made using a new polycotton/Lycra fabric.[20]

In 1978, the department store Debenhams sold the first sports bra in the UK. It cost £1.99 (about £16 today). Advertised with an image of tennis player, it was 'for the girl who takes sport seriously.'[21] In 1979, Australian lingerie brand Berlei launched its British-made sports bra, their version of the jogbra. The new bra attracted a lot of publicity as Berlei had sponsored the British athletics team to test it out and, according to the *Daily Mirror*, was offering cash prizes to sportswomen.[22] *Jogging* announced the imminent launch of the new bra in its May issue. It was even featured in an article about getting fit, 'Are you in the running?', in the UK's biggest-selling teen magazine, *Jackie*.[23] At £4.50, equivalent to £35 today, it was pricier than the Debenhams one, but a lot cheaper than most running bras available today. However, none of these innovative bras catered for women with a chest size over 38 inches or a cup size bigger than C. It seems that manufacturers assumed that women with larger busts wouldn't want to play sport or jog, and it would be more than a decade before sports bras in larger sizes became available.

Male authors' advice to women was based on their assumptions about what women's daily lives were like. In his book *Jogging for Fitness and Pleasure*, published in 1977, the athletics journalist Cliff Temple describes an archetypal 'Tonbridge man', a sedentary middle-aged office-worker at high risk of heart disease. He describes his daily life and that of his wife, 'Tonbridge woman'. She is running the house, looking after two school-aged children and driving her husband to and from the station, but she has plenty of time during the day to sit down and read magazines, drink cups of tea and eat biscuits. Temple really had a thing about biscuits. He describes Tonbridge woman doing housework, but even that is interrupted by biscuit-eating: 'There is a ring at the doorbell, and her next-door neighbour, Janet pops in. Janet's husband also goes to London every day, so the pair of them sit down for a chat, and pretty soon they are both clutching cups of coffee and munching chocolate biscuits.'[24]

Women's work in the home and for the family was both unrecognised and undervalued. Clearly clueless when it came to childcare, Bryant, in his book, nevertheless didn't hold back from giving women some advice. He acknowledged that getting out of the door can be difficult for 'the house-bound housewife', yet he wonders whether women are just making excuses. His evidence is a conversation with one mother who told him that a lot of women 'use the children as an excuse not to jog', and that their real reasons for not jogging were 'embarrassment, laziness or both.'

For women who do not have 'understanding husbands' or anyone else to mind the children, Bryant has a helpful suggestion. Women could take their babies and toddlers with them in their prams or pushchairs, 'park them on a playing field or in the corner of a park, and jog around without ever losing sight of them.' He suggests that once they are bigger they'll want to join in anyway, which in his view will be an excellent childcare solution. In Bryant's world view, women have to accept that they may never be truly free of their family responsibilities and should not expect any time to themselves. If they can't get fit, he believes they are to blame and, 'Like other obstacles to jogging the problem of fitting it in to your all too busy day can be overcome if you're determined enough.'

What if women just wanted time for themselves? Time to think? Time to be themselves unconstrained by their social roles as mothers, wives and daughters? Women's lives were changing dramatically in the 1970s and the middle-class, married, stay-at-home housewife described by Bryant and Temple was not representative of the real experiences of the majority of women. Since the war, the proportion of married women in paid employment had steadily and significantly increased, from

26% in 1951 to 49% in 1971, and this figure would rise further to 62% by 1981. Improved access to contraception and abortion was a significant factor as it made it easier for women to plan motherhood and to limit the number of children they had.[25] Additionally, new domestic appliances reduced the hard physical labour of housework, freeing up time. When Joyce Smith was interviewed by *Jogging* for its 'Running a Family' article, she mentioned several things which reduced the time she spent on housework: fitted carpets, an automatic washing machine and duvets. Joyce was fitting in many hours of training, part-time accountancy work, and caring for her daughters Lisa and Lia. She commented that 'You must have a husband who understands your needs and co-operates.'

Women's lives may have been changing dramatically, but social attitudes didn't keep pace. As a result, even when most women were working, both men and women continued to see housework and childcare as primarily female responsibilities. This led to women bearing the dual burden of wage-earning and unpaid work in the home, and this is borne out in women's letters to the magazine. Margaret Park, the woman from Malvern with the 'cycling-cum-running addict of a husband', felt compelled to distance herself from the stay-at-home housewife stereotype, saying that she wasn't a 'bored housewife who's jogging to pass the time'. In fact, she was working five 10-hour night shifts a week, and looking after her seven-year-old son and a large house and garden. It sounds exhausting.

Sylvia Jenkins from Clywd was fitting in running 40 to 50 miles a week and racing once a month alongside working part-time as a nurse, and looking after her toddler and the family home. She, too, describes her husband's support as essential: 'If I sit down and think about my life I wonder how I fit it all in … I know that if I didn't have an exceptional husband I'd never manage.'

Susan Fletcher, one of the 'running wives' featured in the *Jogging* article, had taken up running at 27 in 1976, despite the disapproval of her husband, Roy. 'He thought I was crazy,' she notes. She was working full-time as a clerk for British Rail, commuting into London, leaving at 7.30 a.m. and getting home at 5.30 p.m. She didn't always feel like going out running in the evening and her husband wasn't encouraging. Susan explained that she was training two nights a week with her club, Enfield Harriers, but had to 'give Roy his tea first.' At weekends, she had to manage her time carefully as she had to fit in shopping, laundry and housework. She would try to go out running when her husband was out with friends or at football matches. It's a miracle she managed to fit it all in. Perish the thought that Roy might make a meal or do any housework. His time at home was for leisure, whereas Susan's was largely for unpaid work.

Men who saw women's jogging as being just about fitness, socialising and losing weight, underestimated just how transformational exercising outdoors could be. Every time they went out, female joggers were confronting social norms of what women should do, what women should wear, what women should look like. They were claiming their space on the streets. And they were claiming time for themselves, away from the home and the family.

Was jogging equally accessible to all women? Writing in 1984, feminist historian Jennifer Hargreaves asserted that working-class women were much less likely to engage in active leisure outside the home and that, 'The fitness boom is in large part illusory: it has not touched vast numbers of women in our society at all …'[26] While jogging may have been a predominantly middle-class activity, it's possible that initiatives like the Gateshead fun runs and the first People's Marathon in 1980 did attract a wider cross-section of the population.

Racism was pervasive in British society and culture in the 1970s. *The Black and White Minstrel Show* drew on a long tradition of 'blacked-up' white men singing and dancing. Despite complaints, this grotesque caricature was peak-time TV for the BBC until 1978. Sitcoms like *Till Death Us Do Part* on the BBC and *Love Thy Neighbour* on ITV were awash with racial slurs and crude racial stereotypes.[27] For Black and Asian women in the 1970s, the prospect of being subjected not only to sexual harassment but also to racist abuse may have deterred them from jogging.

It's rare to come across examples of women of colour jogging in the press coverage from the time. One exception was Louise Springer, a 20-year-old audio typist at Berkshire County Council, who was born in the West Indies. In April 1978, in the *Reading Evening Post's* Monday fashion section, Louise is described at the time as a jogging enthusiast. The paper was starting a weekly lunchtime 'jog-in'. Louise is pictured in sporty poses modelling jogging clothes, tracksuits and shoes, all available from a local sports shop. Keen to appeal to a non-sporty readership, the female journalist notes that 'a lot of these clothes would look equally good for ordinary casual wear.'[28] Louise had another reason for featuring in the article. She was one of the 12 finalists in the newspaper's Model of the Year contest and was hoping to become a professional model. Louise appeared in the paper several times over the next two years as she also entered the contest in 1979, although there was no further mention of jogging as one of her hobbies.

On a more positive note, the emergence of jogging may have contributed to changing attitudes towards wheelchair athletes. By the end of the 1970s, there was an organised structure for disability sport in the UK. Regional competitions for athletes with disabilities enabled them to qualify for the national games held at Stoke Mandeville, the spinal injury centre which, in 1952, had founded the International Stoke Mandeville Games, the precursor to the Paralympics, but the races in these competitions were limited to sprints.

Initially, wheelchair athletes competed in the same chairs as they used every day, but these did not offer the manoeuvrability or speed that they were looking for. Wheelchair athletes in the USA were becoming expert at modifying their wheelchairs to make them better for racing and in 1975 former wheelchair athlete and wheelchair designer Bob Hall was the first official wheelchair competitor at the Boston Marathon.[29] Racing in an adapted chair, he finished in under three hours.

In October 1978, 20-year-old Mark Agar, a wheelchair basketball player from Aston in the West Midlands, started the Harlow Marathon, but had to withdraw with exhaustion after 14 miles. He was accompanied by another wheelchair athlete, Tim Marshall. In his book, *Wheelchairs, Perjury and the London Marathon,* Marshall explains he had been due to compete but had been unable to start due to an injury. At Easter that year, Marshall had completed a circuit of Derwentwater in the Lake District, almost exactly 10 miles, in his wheelchair.[30] A year later, in the spring of 1979, a Round Derwentwater event was organised for people with disabilities. This was probably the first long-distance event open to wheelchair users in the UK. Perhaps half of the 63 entrants completed the full circuit, including Marshall. In May 1980, the British Sports Association for the Disabled organised the Birmingham Open Wheelchair Races for juniors and seniors at Sutton Park. The *Birmingham Evening Mail* reported that these were the first races of their kind in Britain. There were more than 50 competitors; the senior race was seven miles. I haven't been able to confirm whether women participated in these groundbreaking events, although it seems likely that they did, but both events laid the foundations for wheelchair athletes to compete in road races in the 1980s.

In the 1970s, road running was transformed from a performance-driven male activity for the 'serious runner' into a 'sport for all' as hundreds of thousands of people took up jogging for fun, fitness and health. Women, older athletes and wheelchair athletes all contributed to these changes as road racing began to open up to a more diverse group of runners but access was not equal. Women did not benefit to the same extent as men and were less likely to race. Only 26% of the entries for the 1978 *Sunday Times* National Fun Run were women and women's participation in the road races that were finally open to them was low in the late 1970s – typically less than 5%.

As the decade ended, many of the new road runners were to turn their attention to the marathon. Its popularity started to grow in 1979 and in the early 1980s races proliferated, drawing thousands to test themselves against the distance. One woman more than any other was associated with the British marathon boom. Her name was Leslie Watson.

8

LESLIE WATSON QUEEN OF THE ROADS

'She was the catalyst for everybody else to do things.'[1]
– Jill Danskin

It was Sunday 19 October, 1975, and sitting in her friend Lawrence Brampton's car on the way down to the Masters and

Maidens Marathon in Surrey, wearing her London Olympiades vest and running shorts under her tracksuit, Leslie was regretting going out with friends the night before, particularly the bad red wine. She had drunk too many glasses of that. An hour ago, Lawrence had picked her up at her flat. There hadn't been much time for breakfast. Knowing that she needed to eat something to keep going for 26 miles, Leslie was snacking on chocolate and popcorn. She searched in her bag for her mirror, fixed her makeup and brushed her long, wavy, dark brown hair. She was annoyed to notice that the dark red nail varnish on one of her nails was chipped. Staring out of the window, Leslie remembered the 20-mile run she had done in preparation for the marathon. She'd felt OK at the end of the run, but it really didn't seem like enough.

Runners and a few supporters were milling about at the start. Leslie was surprised to find that there were more than a hundred participants. They were quite an odd assortment to find at a race. She'd never seen anything like it. While there were a few young men in club vests and shorts, many of the participants did not look like runners and, most surprisingly of all, some were teenagers, which went completely against the Amateur Athletic Association (AAA) rules. But this wasn't a conventional race, so perhaps that didn't matter. It was more like a challenge event for runners, joggers and walkers. Leslie realised that she was not the only one doing her first marathon. In fact, it seemed as if almost everyone was running the distance for the first time. She chatted to one or two of the other women. As the start time got closer, she took off her tracksuit and handed it to Lawrence. She began to feel sick with nerves. But there was no going back now …

Strangely, the start wasn't at the Bannister track in Guildford where the race would finish, but at the army training ground at Hankley Common, about 12 miles to the southwest. At noon, Alan Blatchford, the race director, set them off. They left Hankley Common, turning north along the road to the village of Elstead. By the time she left Elstead, Leslie's legs were aching and she felt exhausted. They were only three miles in! She had made the mistake of setting off too fast, covering the first five miles in 29 minutes.[2] By nine miles her feet were covered in blisters, thanks to the light, unpadded shoes she was wearing. Thank goodness that she'd thought to bring a spare pair. Lawrence was accompanying the race in his car and was able to stop so that she could change her shoes.

At the halfway point, Leslie began asking herself why on earth she had chosen such a hilly course, but there was no way she was going to give up. She stopped thinking about racing, instead trying to motivate herself by focusing on the weight she would be losing. Part of her reason for entering was that she thought running a marathon might be slimming.[3] The male runners around her gave her lots of encouragement and after 19 miles things felt a little easier. At mile 22, they started the steep drag up the Hog's Back. They ran along the narrow, undulating ridge before at last reaching the long downhill stretch into Guildford. Leslie's legs were stiff and although the downhill exacerbated her painful quads, she was exhilarated to be nearing the finish.

The first woman, Anne Clarke of Highgate Harriers, had finished nearly 20 minutes ahead of her, but Leslie was happy with her time, 3:31:41, and third place. These were the first steps of what was to become an extraordinary road running career, but this race gave her no inkling of what was to come. Whether intentionally or not, it was also a first act of rebellion.

A few days after the marathon, a letter arrived from the Women's Amateur Athletic Association (WAAA).[4] It informed Leslie that she should not have taken part in the event as it broke the governing body's rules. The letter threatened Leslie with suspension from competition for a year if she took part in the event again. This would have meant she could not compete in track, cross-country or road races for a year. Leslie thought this was ridiculous. Why shouldn't she take part? It wasn't an official race after all. And it had been the first opportunity for women to try the marathon distance. Defiantly she returned to the Masters and Maidens in 1976 and finished first. In 1977 she finished second behind Caroline Rodgers. The WAAA sent further reprimanding letters, but the threats were not carried out. Leslie was never suspended.

Leslie Mary Broadfoot Watson was born in Glasgow in the last months of World War II on 4 February, 1945. She was the only child of David Broadfoot Watson, a doctor, and Emily (née Kemp), known to her family as Millie, a dancer, who was 37 when Leslie was born. David was four years younger and serving as a captain in the Royal Army Medical Corps. The spelling of her first name was more common as the masculine form and, as a result, newspapers sometimes misspelled it as the feminine 'Lesley'. In an interview in 1982, Leslie explained that her father had made a mistake when registering the birth.[5]

Her parents had met when David was a medical student at Glasgow University. The circumstances of their marriage were unusual. On 18 September, 1937, the *Edinburgh Evening News* reported that the day before the couple had flitted to Gretna Green, arriving by car at 5 a.m., where they had been married by the blacksmith in a traditional 'handfasting' ceremony.[6] There was more than a whiff of scandal about marrying at Gretna. Due to differences in the laws in England and Scotland, English couples who wanted to get round the much stricter English marriage laws ran away to Gretna, the first village in Scotland. Why did David and Millie choose to run away to marry? It is most likely that one or both of their families disapproved of the marriage, but there is also an impulsiveness about the way that they drove overnight, more than 80 miles from Glasgow, to Gretna. When contacted by the paper, David tersely replied that he had nothing to say about it. Millie's mother was more forthcoming, saying that she'd never met the doctor, but knew he had visited the family home several times.

At the time of the marriage, David was working at the Stirling District Asylum in Larbert, 20 miles northeast of Glasgow, and Millie was a supervisor at the Royal Restaurant on West Nile Street in the heart of Glasgow city centre. The Royal was a famous, long-established Glasgow restaurant with dining rooms and bars. It was just round the corner from the Empire Theatre, the second-largest variety theatre in Britain, where Millie, a professional dancer, had previously worked.[7]

The marriage, however, didn't work out, and her father left Leslie and her mother when Leslie was still quite small. He travelled abroad and practised as a doctor in South Africa before coming back to the UK. Leslie did not see him for many years. Millie must have been quite self-reliant to bring her daughter up on her own at a time when single parenthood was both less socially acceptable and less financially secure than marriage. When Leslie was in her teens, Millie worked three jobs at once, in an office, a café and a pub, to make ends meet.[8]

Leslie's drive and determination was evident from an early age. She explained her love of racing started at five: 'I used to arrange races with my friends after school or after dancing classes. They always beat me so I went on and on, race after race, until eventually I outlasted someone.'[9] When she was ten, Watson joined Maryhill Harriers Ladies with a friend, Moira. She described herself as a 'scrubber', an athlete with little innate talent. She stuck at athletics despite this and in her teenage years started training with one of the club coaches, John Anderson, a PE teacher who later became a national athletics coach for England and Wales. Leslie attributed much of her success to his coaching and the fantastic club spirit he generated.[10] When *Athletics Weekly* profiled her in 1981, she said: 'Had it not been for exceptionally good coaching and motivation early on I'm sure I would have given up athletics years ago. Until being coached by John Anderson in 1961 I hadn't beaten anyone at any event.'[11]

Anderson was renowned for his tough approach to training, which included sprint intervals and weight training. His methods even provoked complaints to the Scottish WAAA that he was making girls work too hard. Leslie's friend Jill Danskin commented: 'He was criticised by other coaches for giving these lassies too much weight to lift. But they all seemed to do quite well out of it.'[12] Leslie recalled that on one occasion when they were training at the Meadowbank track in Edinburgh, the Scottish men's national football squad turned up. 'They were invited to join us, but took one look at what we were doing and refused. It is tough alright.'[13]

Although Leslie was training for sprints at first, Anderson's methods stood her in good stead for her future career as an endurance athlete. In her teenage years she began to compete in cross country. Six days after her 17th birthday, in 1962, Leslie finished fifth in the Scottish national cross-country championships, in a race won by Dale Greig, and aged 19 she was ninth in the English national. She became the Scottish cross-country champion for the first time in 1966 and retained the title in 1967, narrowly beating Dale in both races. In 1966 she became the Scottish mile champion on the track, with a time of 5:14.4. She finished ahead of fellow Maryhill athlete Cathie Kelly and Dale.

On leaving school, Leslie studied physiotherapy, probably at the School of Physiotherapy at Glasgow Royal Infirmary. After completing her training, she moved to London and at some time around 1970 she began working at St George's Hospital at Hyde Park Corner. It's not hard to imagine why Leslie was attracted to London. The city offered fashion, glamour, shops, restaurants and a freer social life, away from conservative Scottish society and the oversight of her mother Millie, who even decades later was given to vetting Leslie's boyfriends.

However, Leslie never felt happy in the NHS. Chafing against the constraints of working for a large institution, she wanted a more direct relationship with her patients and more control over her work. After just six months, she took the bold step of leaving to set up a private practice. Given her relative lack of experience, this must have been quite risky, but Leslie was good at making things happen for herself. She made connections with Harley Street doctors, who referred patients to her, and worked hard, seeing patients from 10 a.m. to 10 p.m. Soon her practice was thriving.

On moving to London, Leslie found it hard to train and race at first. She missed John Anderson's strict training regime and joined Ilford AC for a short while, because they trained harder than other clubs. But she had no car and little money, and the club was several miles from where she lived. She was also enjoying her new social life, which was a distraction.[14] She had, however, not lost interest in athletics. By 1972 she had joined one of the top women's clubs, London Olympiades AC, and enjoyed the traditional athletics programme of track, cross country and road relays, competing in everything.

Not long after this, Lawrence Brampton met Leslie when he came to a party at the flat she shared with a friend in Notting Hill. He told me that his first impressions of her were: 'Very attractive … very intelligent as well and knowing what she wanted in life … You could sense that she was a determined type of person.' After being in a relationship for a while, Leslie and Lawrence became lifelong friends. He supported her running and she supported him when he set up a new business. In 2022, after writing about Leslie for *Women's Running* magazine, I wrote about her on my blog, because I wanted more people to be aware of her remarkable story.[15] In the days following her death on 1 January, 2024, more than a thousand people read the article. There was no Wikipedia biography for Leslie at the time and the main two sources of information about her online were her profile on the Scottish Distance Running History website and my blog. A few months after Leslie's death in 2024, Lawrence commented on the article, then we connected and I interviewed him in June that year. Lawrence also introduced me to another good friend of Leslie's, Jill Danskin (more about her later in the chapter).

Leslie moved into a large, self-contained flat over two floors at 6 Upper Montagu Street, a prestigious address in the West End. She became friends with the building's owner and after a while he offered her the flat at a very reasonable price. She used the top floor for her physiotherapy treatment rooms and the ground floor served as her living quarters. Engaging, lively and persuasive, Leslie was good at making connections with people who could help her.

Perhaps some of her mother's self-reliance shows through in Leslie's choice of career and her independence. Being self-employed in a professional occupation, and owning her own premises and flat, gave her a degree of financial independence which most women could only dream of. As a qualified physiotherapist she was able to set her own prices, whereas employed women were more likely to suffer from the gender pay gap. Until 1975, when the Equal Pay Act became law, employers could pay women less than men if they chose to and many of them did. It was assumed that women were second earners in the family and the man was the main breadwinner. Even after the introduction of the Act, women earned just 76% of men's pay.[16] Leslie's situation gave her security, independence and freedom. She stayed at Upper Montagu Street for the rest of her life. This was the firm foundation on which her many adventures were built.

Leslie didn't let her difficult start at the Masters and Maidens Marathon put her off. Just two months later she was one of the first women to run another hilly marathon, Barnsley, finishing third in 3:18:46. Her marathon career was underway. In 1978 she ran under three hours for the first time and this was to be the first of many sub-three performances.

Leslie trained once a day, six days a week, and most of her runs were slow and steady. She was averaging 60 to 70 miles a week. Training was usually a social activity with men and women meeting for group runs starting from Leslie's flat. It was around this time that Caroline Rodgers, who had finished third at the Feltham Ladies Marathon in 1976, got to know Leslie: 'I used to run down from where I lived in Highgate to her house near

Baker Street, do a training session with her round Hyde Park or Regents Park and run home.'[17]

Leslie raced most weekends and always said that she preferred racing to training. During the winter it was mostly cross-country races. Every February she travelled up to Scotland for the championships, always finishing in the top 10. At first there weren't many road races open to women, but as the decade went on more opportunities arose.

Not content with racing only on one day at the weekend, Leslie would often race on both Saturday and Sunday, even when a considerable amount of travel was involved. For example, on Saturday 26 November, 1976, she competed in the Middlesex women's cross-country championships at Ruislip, finishing seventh. She then travelled the 170 miles north to Barnsley to compete in the marathon, which started at noon the next day. Still fresh enough to run the hilly course in 3:02:24, Leslie won the race, finishing just before a violent thunderstorm broke. The race report in *Athletics Weekly* noted that she finished in front of over 70 male athletes, demonstrating 'the quality and guts of her running'. Afterwards Leslie said she had run the marathon very comfortably and it was this that made her realise she could run a lot faster. Until then she had thought that she would never run much under three hours.[18]

Barnsley was Leslie's second marathon win, her first having come at the Masters and Maidens Marathon a month before. It was around this time that Leslie started to keep count of the marathons she ran, something she would do for the rest of her running career. Starting with two marathons in 1975, the numbers she ran went up nearly every year and in 1979 she ran 12 marathons, winning eight of them. By the end of the decade, she had run 31 marathons, including trips to the New York City Marathon in 1978 and 1979.

In the 1970s women in Britain could not take part in ultramarathons – races longer than the marathon distance. The few ultramarathons that existed were exclusively male races. Dale Greig had run the Isle of Man 40 in 1971 and the London to

Brighton race in 1972. And in 1974 Canadian Susan Taylor had run the 36-mile Two Bridges race in Scotland. However, these unofficial runs had not led to women being accepted in the races. In 1979 Leslie was one of four women who challenged the status quo by taking part unofficially in the prestigious 54-mile London to Brighton race, changing ultrarunning in the UK forever.

Lydia Kirk glanced at her watch for the umpteenth time. Thank goodness the taxi driver knew the way to Westminster Bridge where the London to Brighton race started, but it was now 6.50 a.m. and time was running out. Lydia knew they were close, but she couldn't see any signs for the race or any runners. The driver let out a frustrated grunt as they approached a road closure sign. 'I'm sorry, they've shut the road. You'll have to get out here. Will you be able to find your way?' Lydia thanked him and got out of the car. This last-minute panic was the culmination of everything going wrong. Why had she trusted the friend who had promised to meet her at King's Cross station the evening before? With the naïve optimism of a 23-year-old she'd expected everything to work out, but it hadn't. After hanging around at the station for an hour, she'd realised the friend wasn't going to come. She'd decided to start walking in the direction of Westminster Bridge and look for somewhere to stay. Instead of a decent meal at a restaurant, she'd had to make do with a kebab, and instead of sleeping in a comfortable hotel room, she'd spent the night in the kebab shop owner's spare bedroom with the door locked, worrying if she was safe.

Meanwhile, a crowd of runners had gathered on Westminster Bridge. Big Ben loomed behind them in the grey early morning clouds. A few men in tracksuits jogged up and down, others were gazing at the Thames, focusing their minds on the 54 miles that lay ahead. Cars driven by their supporters were parking along the bridge. It was Sunday 30 September, 1979. The 29th annual London to Brighton Road Race was about to start.[19]

London to Brighton was one of the Road Runners Club's flagship events. It attracted some of the best men from abroad and the 1979 race programme listed 46 Americans, one of whom, Allan Kirik, would be the surprise winner of the men's race.

In the 26th year of its existence, 1976, the club had finally agreed that women would be allowed to join as full members, but in 1979 women were still only a tiny minority of the membership – there were 42 female and 2632 male members.[20]

Three women stood on the bridge that morning with 137 men; three women breaking into this bastion of maleness – Leslie Watson, Ruth Anderson and Lyn Billington. Lots of the men greeted the women, particularly Leslie, whom many of them knew. 'Good to have you ladies in the race,' they said. 'See you at the finish.' A few muttered disapprovingly: 'Women in our race. They'll never make it to the finish.' Leslie, Ruth and Lyn were concerned to know what had happened to Lydia. Where was she? There was no time to find out, because the race was about to start.

They were going the distance, but this was, as so many times before, not an official women's race. The fact that they had got agreement to run was mainly down to the persistence of Ruth Anderson, an American nuclear chemist who had taken up running in 1972 aged 43. Ruth had pushed at the gates barring women from masters competition in the USA. Though there was no masters marathon championship for women, in July 1974 Ruth turned up at the men's championship race in Portland, Oregon, and ran it anyway. Having proved both that women over 35 could run marathons and that there were women interested in doing it, Ruth campaigned successfully to get the Amateur Athletic Union to create a masters category for women. And in 1976 she became one of the first women in the USA to race in an ultramarathon.[21]

By 1979, Ruth was an experienced marathon and ultra runner, and a seasoned campaigner in the cause of women's distance running. She had raced in masters competitions in the UK several times. In July she had won the v45–49 category in the 25-kilometre race at the Twelfth World Veterans Road Championship in Bolton.[22]

In April, Ruth had contacted the Road Runners Club (RRC) to ask for a London to Brighton entry form and the race information. She regarded herself as more than qualified to compete. To be eligible to enter, men had to have run a marathon in under three and a half hours. They did not need to have run an ultra-distance race. Ruth was able to demonstrate that she had already run almost as far as London to Brighton well within the cut-off time for the race. In February she had finished the Pacific Amateur Athletic Union (AAU) 50-miler in 7:25:05. 'But even my more than ample qualifying credentials couldn't overcome my being female,' she acknowledged, wryly. Her request to enter the race was politely declined.[23]

Not one to give up, Ruth engaged friends and contacts in the UK to make the case to the RRC on her behalf. She received further support from the president and international representative of the Road Runners Club of America who both sent letters to the RRC. The RRC Council held a special meeting and Leslie Watson, who had recently joined the council as its first female member, must have supported Ruth's campaign. According to Lawrence, Leslie 'was determined she was going to run London to Brighton, even though she wasn't really allowed to do it'.

The council agreed to allow women to enter London to Brighton unofficially. The women's race had not been advertised and was not in the official programme. No prizes would be awarded. But, despite being unofficial, the women would be able to use all the race facilities. Most importantly, they would be given numbers and their time splits would be recorded at the checkpoints en route, as would their finish times.

For Ruth, London to Brighton was her 'dream race' and her 'ultimate challenge'. Lyn was there to support women's participation in the event and planned to accompany Ruth for the first

30 miles. She had two recent marathons in her legs, having run the Nike Oregon Track Club Marathon in Eugene in the USA on 9 September and the Avon International Women's Marathon in Waldniel in West Germany on 22 September. When I interviewed her in 2025, Lydia told me that she had heard about the race from a member of the RRC and applied to take part as a personal challenge. 'Can I go that far? Or will I just crack up halfway? I wasn't really interested in … where I finished, just about achieving it and saying I've been able to run this distance.'

Leslie certainly didn't want to miss out on the opportunity to be one of the first women to participate in the race and she also thought she had a good chance of finishing first. According to Lawrence, 'She was determined she was going to run London to Brighton, even though she wasn't really allowed to do it … just to show that she could do it.' It is doubtful that any of the men had raced as much as Leslie had that month. Incredibly, by the time of the race she had already run five marathons in September – the British-American Marathon in Witney, Oxfordshire, Rugby Marathon, Aberdeen Marathon, International Milton Keynes Marathon and Rotherham Marathon – winning three of them. Lydia had also competed in two of them, winning at Rugby and finishing second behind Leslie at Milton Keynes. It will come as no surprise that Leslie hadn't rested the day before London to Brighton, instead preferring to compete in a cross-country fixture for London Olympiades.

As Big Ben sounded its first chime at 7 a.m. the runners set off. Lydia was still nowhere to be seen, but shortly after the runners had left she appeared, running towards the start. Race officials accepted her small bag of belongings, which would be taken to the finish. Lydia crossed the start line at 7.04 a.m., knowing she was going to have to catch up with the other runners. Habitually she started races slowly, but she couldn't today, because she had to get to the 10-mile checkpoint at Croydon before the cut-off time of 8:32 a.m. Although she had studied the route map published in the RRC newsletter, it was not going to be easy to find her way south of the Thames through London's streets to the A23 road to Brighton. Fortunately, spectators and officials gave her directions. Unsurprisingly, when Lydia reached the 3.5-mile point at Brixton Hill, she was dead last, but she reached the 10-mile checkpoint at Croydon well within the cut-off, having already passed a few of the slower men.

Ruth and Lyn led the race at the 10-mile mark at Croydon with Leslie about a minute behind them. By the 20-mile point at Redhill, Leslie had established a lead of more than four minutes over Ruth and Lyn and Lydia was moving up the field. However, around the halfway point Lydia began to feel very cold. She put it down to having had no breakfast. Her luck was about to change. The American man she was running alongside said that his wife was out on the course supporting him and when they got to her Lydia could have some of the electrolyte drink he was using. The woman gave her a bottle of the drink and a few snacks. Lydia couldn't eat much when running, but the drink revived her and carried her through the rest of the race.

Ruth was on her own from the 30-mile mark as Lyn had retired, and somewhere after 30 miles Lydia passed Ruth and moved into second place. Lawrence was following the race in his blue Jaguar.[24] At several points he overtook Leslie and then stopped to hand her a drink and chocolate, her preferred fuel on long races as it was easy to eat. Lawrence ran a few steps with Leslie each time, offering encouragement.

There was drama somewhere after the 40-mile point. Leslie was running downhill along a stretch of dual carriageway with an American runner, Peter Powers. The traffic had slowed because of the runners and their support cars. A white Mini sped down the outside lane, the driver slamming on the brakes at the last minute. The car spun round through the runners and traffic before crashing with a loud bang into a lamppost on the hard shoulder. Leslie and Peter, just 10 yards ahead, jumped on to the grass verge and turned to see what had happened. 'It was terrifying. For a moment I thought we were going to get hit,' she said afterwards to Tony Barnes in *Jogging*.

With around eight miles to go the route took the runners up into the hills of the South Downs. James Langton, writing in the *Shepherds Bush Gazette*, described Leslie's weariness during this last leg of the race: 'With six miles to go it was clear Leslie had problems. For the first time she was beginning to look tired. She was beginning to slow and her stride shortened. Her periods of walking became longer, and running shorter.' After the last descent, though, she was able to run the final two miles to the finish, where Lawrence and other friends were waiting for her among the cheering crowds. Tony Barnes, writing in *Jogging*, remarked that in the final miles of the race many of the men were in a state of 'shuffling exhaustion'. In contrast, Leslie was 'one of the freshest-looking'. Her relaxed pace as she approached the finish suggested that she was not suffering unduly. Her finish time of 6:55:11 would have placed her 43rd in the men's race. Ruth later admiringly described Leslie as 'this incredibly durable woman' and a picture of Leslie running with Peter Powers during the race appeared on the front cover of *Athletics Weekly* with the caption 'The astonishing Leslie Watson'.[25]

Nearly 35 minutes later it was Lydia's turn to run under the finish line gantry to applause from Leslie and a crowd of spectators. Her time was 7:29:43. Ruth followed in 7:46:16, delighted to finish well within the 8:23:00 time limit. Thirty-four of the 137 men who started the race didn't manage that. Three finished outside the time limit and 31 dropped out.

The men's prizes were presented by the Mayor of Brighton at a traditional tea at the Old Ship Hotel. All the finishers, including Leslie, Lydia and Ruth, received a commemorative certificate inscribed with their finishing time and signed by the race officials. Lydia was, of course, very hungry by then and when plates of cream cakes were placed at the end of the table where the civic dignitaries were sitting, she eyed them enviously. When it seemed that they might 'scoff the lot' without her getting one, Lydia nudged the male runner next to her who yelled out, 'There are some runners down here. Could we please have the cakes?' And Lydia duly got to eat one of the eclairs she had been coveting.

Top athletes raced far more often than they would do today. Lydia was surprised when I reminded her that she had done the International Milton Keynes Marathon the weekend before running London to Brighton. 'Nowadays they'd never let you run a mega race like that the week after [a marathon],' she said, adding, 'We never got injured, because we were tough in those days.'

Reflecting on her ultrarunning career later in her life, Ruth said that she regarded London to Brighton as her most memorable race:[26] 'My being allowed to participate in this previously men's-only race represented real progress towards the recognition of women runners as ultramarathoners.' Admitting women to the highest profile ultra in the UK was a milestone and once the gates had been opened they could not be closed again.

In 1980, the RRC put on the first official women's London to Brighton race with a trophy for the female winner. Leslie returned to the race and was joined by Caroline Rodgers. After winning the race, apparently none too fatigued, Leslie bounded up the steps to the stage to be presented with the new women's trophy to loud cheers from everyone there.[27] Caroline finished third behind American Donna Hudson. Caroline wasn't interested in ultrarunning, but this was one race she felt compelled to do. She ran it in memory of a friend who had always dreamed of doing the race, but had died of a heart attack before he got the chance. London to Brighton was her only ultramarathon.

Leslie ran other ultramarathons, too. In June 1980, she was the only woman to compete in the Grantham 100-kilometre race in Lincolnshire, finishing in 8:15:50. In December 1980, she wrote to Nick Marshall who published an annual US Ultradistance Summary which listed race results and forthcoming races, to ask him for help to find 'a 50-mile race in the USA which would be a suitable course to set a world best time.' She explained that the multivitamins company Pharmaton was sponsoring her to attempt an ultra-distance record and she didn't want to go for the 100-kilometre record.[28] Leslie didn't introduce herself in the letter, but Nick knew who she was, having seen her in running magazines. At Nick's recommendation, she travelled to Connecticut to compete in the Lake Waramaug 50-mile and 100-kilometre road race in May 1981. She had close competition in the race from the 100-mile world record holder, tough-as-nails American Marcy Schwam. Going out hard, Marcy led for almost 39 miles, only to be passed by Leslie who knocked nearly 10 minutes off the 50-mile road world record, finishing in 6:02:37.

In March 1983, Leslie set a 50-mile track world record in a RRC race at the Copthall Stadium in Barnet. Her time of 6:20:42 took 14 minutes off the previous best. Fellow Scot Don Ritchie set the men's world record in the same race.[29] Between 1979 and 1989, Leslie did 10 ultramarathons, finishing first in eight of them. The Grantham 100-kilometre was her longest distance.

On the evening of Friday 18 December, 1981, Lawrence Brampton glanced out of the window of his new running shop at 71 George Street in the heart of London's West End. The London Runner had only been open for five days. He was astonished to see a queue of people snaking down the street. There were dozens and dozens of them. He knew instantly who had attracted them there. The shop was hosting its first ever advice session for runners. The ad he'd placed in *Athletics Weekly* stated that Leslie would be there from 6.30 p.m. giving advice on running injuries. It was Leslie that these runners had come to see. The evening was a huge success. They sold lots of shoes and running kit, and Leslie was kept busy as everyone wanted to talk to her. She patiently listened to each runner's problem and gave them advice. One man had come all the way from Cardiff to see her.

In the six years since the Masters and Maidens Marathon, Leslie had gone from marathon novice to one of the best-known faces on the burgeoning running scene. In 1981, the year of the first London Marathon, Joyce Smith was leading the way in terms of women's performance on the roads, but it was Leslie, sixth on the UK all-time list, who was proclaimed the 'queen of the roads' in the race programme. It featured a full-page picture of Leslie posing in front of Buckingham Palace in racing briefs and vest, and wearing the race number 1. A brief profile stated that she had run 47 marathons and three ultramarathons with a best marathon time of 2:45:40 in New York in 1980.

The day before the race the BBC's Saturday afternoon sports programme, *Grandstand*, featured a race preview. Leslie joined the show's host, David Coleman, 'to explain the rigours that some of the less experienced entrants will face.' The *Radio Times* described her as 'a physiotherapist and leading contender for the ladies' prize,' but, unsurprisingly, it was Joyce who won the London Marathon in 2:29:57, improving on her own British record by 30 seconds. Leslie finished in 11th place and was the eighth British woman across the line in 2:48:06.

The *Radio Times*' description of Leslie neatly summarised the dual value that she offered programme-makers. She was both an experienced elite athlete and an expert who could give advice on training and injuries. In the 1980s and early 1990s, Leslie was invited on to many TV programmes. Another element of her appeal was her compliance with the conventional image of femininity. Leslie was always well presented with immaculate makeup and blow-dried hair.

At races Leslie attracted the attention of photographers and film camera operators alike. And she was always willing to give them her time, even at the race start where she might have preferred to warm up, as demonstrated in this account from another runner at the 1982 Loch Rannoch Marathon, published in the *Scottish Marathon Club Magazine*:

> As at the start of many marathons these days the main attraction for both male athletes and photographers was Miss Leslie Watson, who according to one newspaper was pre-race favourite to win outright! She had to pose in a crouched starting position for five or six photographers while we lesser mortals were jogging about nervously waiting for the start.[30]

The BBC Scotland coverage of the 1984 Glasgow Marathon picked out Leslie on the start line with the men, drinking from a large water bottle and passing it on to another woman. Brendan Foster, one of the commentators, described her as 'probably the most experienced marathon runner in Britain, including the men'. He pointed out that lots of men would use her as a pace guide. As races had few female competitors Leslie was easy to spot. Her times were consistent. If you were aiming for a sub-three-hour marathon, running with Leslie was a safe bet. You could have a nice chat with her and being close to Leslie gave you a good chance of appearing on race photos or TV coverage.

Leslie's willingness to work with the media made her a go-to source for stories, opinions and photographs. She featured in dozens of newspaper and magazine articles, and on the front cover of *Athletics Weekly*, *Jogging* and *Runner's World* magazines. She made money from appearing in adverts for the London Runner shops and for health and fitness products, and received sponsorship from Nike and several companies that supplied vitamins.

While Leslie didn't comply with conventional ideas of what women should do, the way she was presented in the press reflected the prevailing social norms of what women should look like. Male journalists invariably referred to her appearance, calling her the 'glamour girl of marathons' and 'Britain's pin-up of the sport'. A profile in the *Daily Express* in 1977 with the strapline, 'There's glamour in the marathon' referenced fears that sport would masculinise women.[31] In contrast, Leslie was presented as an example of how women could excel in a sport and yet still be feminine: 'In an age of sex changes, chromosome tests and fearsome female wrestlers, meeting Lesley Watson can come as a bit of a shock. She is, believe it or not, one Britain's leading women marathon runners.'

The large accompanying photograph shows Leslie sitting with her left leg drawn up, her elbow resting on her knee. She is wearing makeup, nail varnish and jewellery. Her fashionable, casual shirt is buttoned and hides presumably either racing briefs or very short shorts as her legs are bare. The photograph is cropped, but a racing shoe is just visible on her left foot – a mere passing reference to Leslie's athletic ability.

Worse still, journalists often explicitly sexually objectified Leslie. An egregious example was Chris Brasher's profile of Leslie in the *Observer* in December 1980, which opened with these words: 'Leslie Watson is a beautiful woman with a magnificent shape which is famous throughout the world of long-distance running: famous because its beauty brings a smile to all men who run with her.' This focus on Leslie's body and attractiveness casts her as decorative and there for men's pleasure. While Brasher clearly admired Leslie's powers of endurance, he also trivialised her by focusing on her appearance. It is hard to imagine him talking about runners regarding a male athlete 'with awe and with love'. Leslie was beating lots of men in marathons and competing in far more races than most men. This could be seen as disruptive, as powerful. By portraying Leslie as a conventionally feminine figure, Brasher removed any potential threat to the natural order of things in the male-dominated world of long-distance running.

But what did Leslie herself make of this relentless focus on her appearance? Was it tiresome? Did it make her anxious? Leslie always wanted to feel and look her best, and that applied to running just as much as to the rest of her life. For her, feeling and looking her best meant never leaving the house without her face made up and her hair looking good. She always had a hairbrush at the finish of a race and several times photographers captured her brushing her hair. Friends like Lawrence felt that she wasn't bothered about the attention the press gave her looks. He said, 'She never went out to seek attention … But she would never turn up at a race without her makeup on, putting on tan the night before and putting perfume on. She liked to look her best when she was running, but for her own personal satisfaction.'[32]

Her friend Jill Danskin, who joined London Olympiades in 1984 and travelled to races with her, was horrified to find that, when they went by train, Leslie spent most of her time painting her nails, including her toenails with her feet up on the table, the pungent smell of nail polish filling the carriage. When Jill remonstrated with her, Leslie was blithely unconcerned and would just continue with the task. In interviews, Leslie seemed to be preoccupied with her weight. For example, in 1979 she told *Scottish Marathon Club Magazine* that halfway through her first marathon, the 1975 Masters and Maidens, she 'stopped thinking about racing and thought about losing weight to inspire me to try harder,'[33] and a year later she informed the *Observer* that she had only entered the race because she liked wearing hotpants, but was 'a little too fat' for them and thought running a marathon might be slimming.[34]

In 1982, Leslie had another run-in with the WAAA in a controversy over racing vests. Along with other athletes, she had started to wear vests with a mesh panel at the front. The vests had thin material on the back and a three-inch panel over the bust. The rest of the front was mesh. The WAAA deemed them 'too revealing' and unsuitable for track and field events. When interviewed, Leslie was defiant, 'These vests are ideal and I am going to continue wearing them. So are all the other girls in my club and in other clubs.' She pointed out that the restriction was 'silly' as women were allowed to wear them for cross-country and road races.[35]

On New Year's Eve 1983, Jill Danskin, back home from London for the holidays, was busy ironing clothes at her parents' home in Dundee and watching the TV. She'd recently started running and had got the idea in her head that she might run the second Dundee Marathon in April after her Dad had told her how exciting it was to watch the first one. When she saw there was a programme called 'Marathon 83' on BBC Scotland she tuned in to watch it. And there was Leslie in the lead in the women's race at the Glasgow Marathon.

A month or so later, as Jill approached the finish line at a fun run in Regents Park, she heard a Scottish voice enthusiastically shouting, 'The first woman. Go on! Go on!'. As soon as she had finished Leslie appeared, first congratulating her and then asking, 'Do you belong to a club?' Leslie was always on the look-out for strong runners she could recruit to London Olympiades. Jill said she wasn't ready to join a club yet, giving the excuse, 'I'm not really a proper runner'. Never one to be put off, Leslie attempted to persuade her saying that she would improve if she joined the club. Jill explained that she was about to run a half marathon and if she did alright in that race, she would get in touch with Leslie.

Jill was one of several women Leslie persuaded to join London Olympiades. In the late 1970s and early 1980s Leslie built a strong team for cross-country and road racing, which included Margaret Lockley, Gillian Burley (who joined in 1981 after finishing her postgraduate studies at Newcastle University and moving south), Katie Fitzgibbon and Debbie Heath, all of whom won many road races. After doing the half marathon, Jill kept her promise and joined the club. She was living in central London and often joined Leslie on one of her evening group runs. Leslie's promise that Jill would improve if she joined the club proved to be true. Says Jill, 'I improved very quickly, because whenever I went out training, I was always the one at the back. I was always struggling just to keep up.' Jill hadn't been part of an athletics club as a teenager or at university. She had always wanted to run but found that, 'Nobody would go running with me. Girls, they just didn't want to run, so I was always on the lookout for somebody.'

Given Jill's aversion to mud, it is a testament to Leslie's powers of persuasion that she managed to persuade her to compete in cross-country races for London Olympiades, arguing it was good for building strength. Jill remembers, 'I bought lovely new spikes, and they looked like they were 20 years old when I finished. And you could never wear the socks again. The socks were brown forever in the mud. It wasn't my thing, but I went along and did it anyway.' Jill remained a road runner through and through, and, despite persistent efforts, Leslie never managed to make her into a cross-country enthusiast or to get her to run track races for the club.

It was a lot of fun to be part of Leslie's group of London Olympiades runners. Modest about her own achievements, Leslie encouraged others, praising their performances, and she was always at the finish line at races, supporting runners who finished after her. The team travelled to races together, both at home and abroad. When they raced in the UK, if there was a team prize London Olympiades usually won it. Jill travelled with Leslie, Caroline and others to run marathons in Northern Ireland, Ireland, Switzerland, the Netherlands, France and Barbados. Race organisers often invited Leslie to races, sometimes at the last minute. For races abroad, if she won the race or finished in the top three, she would be invited to run the following year, with expenses paid. Leslie was generous about creating opportunities for other women. If she received an invitation that she couldn't make, she would usually put one of the London Olympiades athletes forward as an alternative. Leslie was also generous with her time. As well as appearing on radio and TV, she was part of many advice panels for novice road runners. Wherever she went, at races, at the gym, on the street, runners approached her to ask for physiotherapy advice. A five-minute walk to the bank could easily turn into half an hour. Lawrence recalls how patient and kind Leslie was in these situations: 'At the gym that we used to go to, people knew she was a physio. And if they had a slight injury problem, they would come up and ask her advice. … She would never try and get away from them, or make an excuse … She always had time for people, even though it took up her own time.'

Gregarious, lively and full of energy, Leslie liked to be busy and throughout the 1980s and early 1990s she carried on racing every week, and racing was never just about fun – Leslie focused on competing. Caroline remembers: 'She was always quite relaxed and easy about stuff, but I think there was a steeliness about her.'

For almost all of Leslie's adult life, the media and the athletics authorities thought that she was three years younger than she actually was. As early as 1966, Leslie was giving the press a younger age. In June 1966, the *Daily Record* reported the extraordinary story of Leslie and a friend having been hit by lightning when training on the athletics track at Westthorn Park in Glasgow. Leslie's age was given as 19, but she was in fact 21.[36] Leslie always avoiding giving her age in interviews if she could. Journalists often remarked on her reluctance to reveal it. One wrote, 'The Marlene Dietrich of British sport, Watson is famously shy about her age.'[37]

It seems that by 1975, when she finished third in the Barnsley Marathon, she had settled on a birth date of 4 February 1948, three years after her actual birth date. The *Huddersfield Daily Examiner* reported her age to be 27.[38] When Leslie was profiled in *Athletics Weekly* in 1981[39], her date of birth was stated to be 4 February 1948. This date also appeared in all the marathon rankings lists. Given that when journalists did occasionally manage to get her to give her age, it was consistent with this date, clearly it was Leslie herself who was doing the rejuvenating. Mandy Mullan, the daughter of her partner, explains how this came about: 'Back in the days when passports were handwritten, her passport said 1945 and she changed the five to an eight.' All Leslie's subsequent passports showed her year of birth as 1948.

When Sylvester Stein interviewed her for *Running* magazine in 1985, when she was 40, he called her 'the Peter Pan of British and international marathon running'. Like Peter Pan, Leslie did not want to 'grow up' or grow old. He wrote, 'What next for the woman whose legs are still full of running, and who refuses to acknowledge the passing years? Though over 35 ... she doesn't want to be considered in the veteran category. She says she doesn't feel her age, even when running two marathons back-to-back on the same weekend. "I would *hate* to be old," she says.'[40]

Clearly a firm believer in the social convention that you should never ask a woman her age, Leslie kept hers a secret for most of her adult life.

One of her scrapbooks contains a clipping of a newspaper cartoon in which a doctor's receptionist asks an old lady, 'Why won't you tell me your age? It's just a number'. 'Mine is unlisted!' the old lady replies. Leslie may have been quite amused by the fact that she got away with the deception for so long.

Through the years, Leslie kept the same look, haircut, hair colour, makeup and figure. And her race times were remarkably consistent. After running her first sub-three-hour marathon in 1978, she ran sub-three every year until at least 1987. As Leslie entered her 20th year of road racing in 1994, it seemed that she would indeed get her wish and run forever. But it was not to be. By the middle of the year, cartilage and nerve damage in her knee brought her running career to a stop. In May she had competed in, and won, her last marathon, the notoriously hilly Isle of Wight Marathon, finishing in 3:00:59. It was her seventh win at the race. She had won more than 60 marathons and always told reporters that she had finished 206.

At 49, Leslie had lost the ability to take part in the activity which had been at the heart of her life, her friendships and relationships for more than 30 years. Coaching, officiating or managing a club were activities that held no appeal for her and they were not where her talents lay. Pragmatically, Leslie looked for another outlet for her competitive spirit. In powerlifting she found not only a way to excel in another sport, but also it led to a long-term relationship which lasted for the rest of her life.

Powerlifting is a competitive strength sport in which participants perform three lifts using barbells with weight plates: bench press, squat and deadlift. Leslie had always enjoyed going to the gym and had watched weightlifting on television. When she realised you could compete in powerlifting, she decided to give it a go. At her first competition in 1995, she lifted just the barbell without weights. After she'd finished her set, one of the referees, Budgie (Bernard) Mullan, approached her, offering to coach her and help improve her technique. Budgie began coaching Leslie at her gym three times a week. A few months later, a friend of Leslie's prompted him to ask Leslie out. Leslie and Budgie were soon in a relationship and eventually he moved in with her. Retaining her independence was important and Leslie made it clear that she did not want to marry.

Over the next 25 years, Leslie and Budgie travelled the world competing in powerlifting competitions as well as competing in the UK. Budgie's daughter Mandy remembers that it was Leslie who set her sights on world records and encouraged Budgie to compete. 'Inwardly, she had this drive just to do as well as she could.'[41] They both set many world records, but whereas Budgie competed in his age category, for most of her career Leslie refused to compete in a masters age category, preferring to enter the open category for her weight class.

Caroline remembers going to watch Leslie in a competition. She came on to her own walk-on music and bounced off the stage after completing her lift, all smiles, as the other competitors and spectators applauded her. She says, 'I think that kept her going. Being in competitions, she needed that.'

Leslie's last powerlifting competition was in March 2023 when she was 78. After a few years of declining health, she was taken seriously ill just before Christmas Day 2023 and died in hospital on New Year's Day 2024. At the height of the 1980s marathon boom, Leslie ran more marathons than any British man or woman. She represented Scotland and Great Britain. She pushed at and opened the doors of ultrarunning for women and set two ultradistance world records. Despite her high public profile in the 1980s, Leslie has received less recognition than her male contemporaries. When she died, there were few obituaries in the national press, although *Athletics Weekly*, *The Times* and Scottish Athletics marked her passing, but until December 2024, there was no Wikipedia entry for Leslie.

Every time she lined up at the front of a race with the fastest men, she claimed women's place on start lines, and every time she ran in road races, she asserted women's right to run. Although she didn't align herself to feminism, she embodied women's liberation, providing a role model for women, and through her media profile, her generous spirit and her presence at races, she had an impact on countless women, and men, as they began their running journeys.

9
THE MARATHON BOOM

'It was a very exciting time ... a wonderful time
to be racing and training.'
– Caroline Rodgers[1]

At 9 a.m. on Saturday 3 August, 1980, Jean Britton was among dozens of female runners who, along with their friends, well-wishers, journalists, TV crews and spectators, were milling about in Battersea Park in Southwest London waiting for the start of the Avon International Women's Marathon.

Jean couldn't quite believe she was there alongside some of the world's best marathoners. She was proudly wearing the red cotton Avon Running vest which all the entrants had been given. The cosmetics company had decided it would be good to have one of the thousands of British women who worked as their door-to-door sales reps running in the race and, with some trepidation, 38-year-old Jean had volunteered. The problem was that it had all happened only two months before the race and Jean wasn't a runner. Now she was nursing blisters from her brief period of intensive training. She'd managed to run 13 miles a few days ago, but who knew if she'd make it to the finish of the marathon. When she'd been interviewed by a journalist from the *Guardian* earlier in the week, she'd said her aim was to do at least 13 miles.[2] The journalist observed: 'Salt tablets and sheer grit will keep her going, and a loyalty to Avon.'

A buzz of friendly chat filled the air. The runners were in the shade of the trees, but the heat was already building. At 10 a.m. the starting pistol was fired and they set off for three laps of the park, cheered on by the small crowd of spectators who'd gathered for the start. The lead car had a cameraman on the roof, filming the race for the BBC, but Jean was nowhere near the front of the field of 181 women.

As Jean and the last few runners left the park, now about eight miles into the race, they felt the full heat of the sun. Jean stopped to drink at every water station. As the miles ticked slowly by, she began to see weary women who had dropped out. One or two were limping. Jean could sympathise as, despite putting plasters on her blisters, the familiar burning sensation was back. Chatting to another runner, an American, helped to pass the time and, as they were going at a similar pace, they decided to stick together. Encouragement from spectators lifted their mood, especially at the Tower of London where hundreds of people had gathered to see the runners coming the other way in the final miles of the race. Jean and her running partners ran round the Tower, heading east for a lap of the Isle of Dogs. With their pace slowing, this was a hard part of the race. There weren't many spectators and the volunteers at the water stations were getting ready to pack up. Jean began to wonder if they would make it to the finish within the four and half hour cut-off. They stopped to use the toilets at a pub and Jean put some new plasters on her feet.

Sheer grit was indeed required to get through the final painful miles. As they got close to the finish at the Guildhall in the City of London, Jean was delighted to find that there were still some people there to watch the last runners come in. 'You've done it!' they shouted as she and her American companion ran the last few yards hand in hand, finishing with 39 seconds to spare, in 4:29:21. Young men in red Avon t-shirts put medals featuring an image of Atalanta, the gifted runner from Greek mythology, around their necks.[3] Jean couldn't believe it was over and that she had endured 26.2 miles in the heat with blistered feet. Interestingly, Jean's 'slow' time would have placed her in the top half of the field at the 2025 London Marathon.

The race was the third in Avon's series of international women's marathons, after Atlanta in 1978 and Waldniel in 1979. As a multinational beauty company with a workforce of nearly a million female sales reps worldwide, Avon was keen to sponsor women's sports. In 1977, they recruited Kathrine Switzer to manage their new women's tennis circuit. In her memoir, *Marathon Woman*, Kathrine relates that, although the idea of a women's marathon in Atlanta had already been floated at Avon, it was her proposal, based on the compelling argument that women's running 'was going to become one of the biggest participatory sports in the world,' that led to the creation of the Avon International Running Circuit. This series of races for women, managed by Kathrine, was held in countries across the world where Avon had a presence.[4] Its first event was the Atlanta Avon International Women's Marathon in March 1978 and part of its purpose was to prove to the sport's international governing bodies that women from many countries were strong competitors over the marathon distance.

It was no coincidence that the 1980 London race took place just two days after the men's marathon had been held at the Moscow Olympic Games. At its July meeting the International Olympic

Committee (IOC) had agreed to add the women's 3000 metres to the 1984 Olympics but had postponed the decision about the marathon to its meeting in February 1981. For Kathrine, who was leading the Avon campaign for the women's Olympic marathon, the London race was 'the deal-breaker'. The number of countries in the race had exceeded the IOC threshold for considering new events. She wrote, 'Women's marathon running was an established global sport. London was the proof. They *can't* refuse us now, I thought, and we have six months to remind them.'

The race was a big deal. For those British women who had yet to compete abroad it was their first chance to test themselves against top women from other countries. It was the first time a marathon had been put on in the heart of London with roads closed by the police.[5] Primetime TV coverage by the BBC, NBC in the USA and continental channel Eurovision ensured a huge audience, providing inspiration to women around the world.

Joyce Smith was the favourite to win, but a bout of chicken pox had left her below par and she finished seventh in 2:41:42. Twenty-five-year-old Lorraine Moller from New Zealand was the surprise winner in 2:35:11, a national record and the world seventh best time. In fourth place was 23-year-old Joan Benoit, the USA record holder and second fastest marathoner of all time.

Several of our rulebreakers started the race. Leslie Watson finished in 53rd place in 3:11:15, Jean Lochhead was six places behind her in 3:17:28 and Avril Lewis was 73rd in 3:20:42. Avril remembers the heat: 'It was very hot and I did not understand enough about drinking liquids and suffered a lot near the end.'[6] The heat got the better of Miriam Rosen, who was forced to drop out at 18 miles: 'I got desperately hot. I've regretted it all my life. It's the only time I've dropped out of anything,' she told me.

Margaret Thompson and Lyn Billington also dropped out around the halfway point. However, it wasn't the heat that made Margaret stop: 'I had been given a new lightweight pair of shoes to wear and made the beginner's mistake of wearing them instead of my own well-used shoes, Tigers, and I was struggling with sore feet from the start. I had to drop out ... with shredded feet! I remember hobbling back to the finish.'[7]

Why did so many women runners suffer from blisters? Margaret was not alone: Dale Greig, Bridget Cushen, Christine Readdy and Leslie Watson all had problems with blisters. Wearing a new pair of shoes for a marathon, as Margaret did, could be a reason, and lightweight racing shoes tended to have thinner soles, increasing rubbing and sore spots, but fundamentally women were running in shoes designed for men (or boys if they had small feet). Nike introduced its first women's shoes in 1975 in the USA but as shoe lasts (the forms that determine the shape of shoe) are very expensive to manufacture Nike scaled down a men's last rather than creating a new women's last.[8] The result was a poor fit as anatomically women's feet are not the same as men's. Most women have a narrower heel relative to the forefoot and higher, more flexible arches than men, and their load distribution is different. Just making a narrower version of men's shoes wasn't going to work and women commonly found shoes didn't fit at the heel, causing them to slip. Some brands began to develop women-specific lasts in the late 1970s, improving the fit and comfort of their shoes, but in the UK in the early 1980s women's shoes were still not widely available. Today I can go into a running shop and choose from a wide range of shoes specifically designed for women and tailored to my running gait. Most of the women in this book just had to make the best of running in shoes that weren't designed for them.

Margaret Thompson says that she never considered herself to be a marathon runner: 'I don't think I had the resilience or temperament to reach a high level.' In the late 1970s and early 1980s, she was often injured, meaning she rarely managed to complete a full 12-week training block. And nerves meant that Margaret often went off too fast and then found it hard to keep running.[9]

The births of her three daughters, in 1977, 1979 and 1981, also took Margaret out of racing for extended periods. Shortly before the birth of her second daughter, Margaret was one of the four women featured in the 'Running a Family' article in the May 1979 issue of *Jogging*. She explained that, although she had run a 3000-metre race five months after having her first daughter, it had taken her eight months to get fully fit again. This time, she had decided to keep running later into the pregnancy. At seven months, she was jogging two or three miles every morning and hoped that this would make the return to training easier. The article was accompanied by a large photograph of Margaret jogging, in a short-sleeve sweatshirt, tracksuit bottoms and Nike trainers. It may well have been the first photograph of a heavily pregnant woman jogging to be published in the British press. Today, Margaret, in her early 70s, is still competing in races, as well as doing her local parkrun from time to time.

In 1980 the UK was in the midst of a road-running revolution. Just as the all-male road-racing world had been disrupted by the women rulebreakers and ghost runners, now many of the men and women who had taken up jogging wanted more than fun runs; they wanted road races. Whereas most of the women rulebreakers were super-fit club athletes who could hold their own against the hard men of the roads, joggers were focused on fun, fitness and community. In their eyes every runner deserved a medal, however long he or she took, not just those who could finish within a certain time.

Road races were created to meet this demand, many advertising that they were open to 'joggers' as well as 'runners'. The People's Marathon held in Solihull on Sunday 11 May, 1980, is a prime example of the transformation of the road-running landscape. Organised by Centurion Joggers, one of the new breed of clubs focused on inclusive jogging and road running, the marathon marked the end of the first National Jogging Week.[10] It was advertised as a race for novices and, in fact, runners who had completed a marathon in under 2:50 weren't allowed to enter – this meant men, of course, as at the end of 1979 only five British women had run that fast.

There was unprecedented interest in the race, which sold out in advance with hundreds of hopefuls unable to get one of the 750 places. Most of the 498 finishers were first-timers, the last finisher took 6:22:00, and all of them got a certificate and a commemorative medallion. The editor of *Athletics Weekly*, Mel Watman, took part himself and wrote presciently: 'In years to come, when marathon fields several thousand strong will be commonplace in Britain, it will be seen that the event which triggered off the mass long-distance running movement in this country was the inaugural People's Marathon.'[11]

The 'marathon boom' was well and truly underway. The People's Marathon was one of more than 50 marathons held in the UK that year. A decade before, in 1970, there had been about 15, most of them had fewer than a hundred finishers, and men usually didn't even think of running a marathon unless they could finish within three and a half hours.

When Chris Brasher and John Disley brought the first mass marathon to the streets of London on 29 March, 1981, they were seeking to emulate the New York City Marathon, which Brasher had excitedly described as 'the greatest folk festival the world has seen.' With over 7000 starters, London was soon being referred to as 'the people's marathon', demonstrating just how forward-thinking the organisers of the 1980 Solihull race had been when they named their race. It is no surprise that it followed part of the route used for the Avon London marathon as several of the same people were involved in the planning, including Lyn Billington's husband, Dave.

Margaret Lockley hadn't run the 1980 Avon marathon and had almost given up on racing, convinced that women's marathon running wasn't going to take off in the UK, because the governing bodies weren't investing in it. Hearing about the plan for the 1981 London Marathon changed everything. She says,

'I just didn't think they would be bothered to progress with it. And that's kind of why in '79 I just lost interest, until they said they were going to have a London Marathon. And I thought, "Well, that's a bit different. Got to run in London."' Margaret's renewed enthusiasm paid off as she finished 10th in 2:47:29, a personal best. Joyce Smith won in 2:29:57, breaking her own British record. At 43 she became the third woman in the world to run under two and a half hours. In 1984, 12 years after competing in the 1500 metres at the Munich Olympics, she would run in the first Olympic marathon, finishing 11th in 2:32:48.

Leslie Watson finished 11th in the London Marathon in 2:48:06 and Caroline Rodgers was 17th in 2:56:55. For Christine Readdy, who finished 28th in 3:02:53, it was her first marathon since her win at the Feltham Ladies Marathon in 1976 (her time was still in the top 20 best British performances). After Feltham, Christine didn't get invited to other marathons and at that point there wasn't even an English women's marathon championship, let alone any international championships, so she chose to run shorter races, winning several 'ladies' road races, as well as competing in mixed road races, finishing first woman in several 10-milers. When I interviewed Christine, she told me that the big training commitment that a marathon requires put her off, saying, 'It takes a lot out of you, and if it doesn't work out on the day, it can be depressing, because you put such a lot of time into it.' She preferred shorter distances, where if you didn't race well, you would be ready to have another go in a few days' time.[12] Two weeks before the London Marathon, Christine had returned to the Milford 21 cross-country race, which she first ran in unofficially in 1974. Seven years later, in 1981, women were finally allowed to enter officially. Seven women started the course, described in the *Athletics Weekly* race report as 'indisputably the toughest cross-country race in the land', and all seven finished. The winner, Jenny Pearson of Sheffield, was fast enough to place halfway up in the men's field. Christine finished fourth.[13]

Radio 2 listeners could follow the London Marathon action live. Sports journalist Cliff Morgan hosted a *Music and Marathon*

Special from 8.30 a.m. to midday, featuring live reporting from various points on the course and from the lead vehicle. BBC 1's *Grandstand* programme had previewed the race on the Saturday afternoon. On race day, BBC 1 showed a 50-minute programme of race footage at 4 p.m., before *Match of the Day*. Clips from the race also featured in the news bulletins. Nearly every household had a TV and with only three channels to watch, the race reached a big audience. In Roger Domeneghetti's book, *Everybody Wants to Rule the World: Britain, Sport and the 1980s*, Chris Brasher's son Hugh, who is the London Marathon Events CEO today, describes the impact of the television coverage: 'You can't underestimate the power of the BBC as a broadcast partner … It suddenly reached people that could never have been reached previously. They looked at the 6000 people out on a rainy day taking part and they said, "Well, they're no different to me. If they can do it, so can I." People watching it got inspired by the TV coverage to then enter the next one.'[14]

For the British marathon pioneers, road racing was really taking off and in the early 1980s new opportunities to represent Great Britain at international championships arose, opportunities that simply hadn't existed for women in the 1970s. The first European Athletics Championships women's marathon was to take place in Athens in 1982 (the men's marathon had been part of the championships since the inaugural event in 1934) and there would be a women's marathon at the inaugural World Athletics Championships in Helsinki in 1983. In the spring of 1981, the campaigning by Kathrine Switzer at Avon and the Nike-supported International Runners Committee led by Jacqueline Hansen finally paid off when the International Olympic Committee finally agreed to add the women's marathon to the 1984 Los Angeles Olympic Games.

The British women's marathon squad was relaunched in February 1982 with a boost from sponsorship – £30,000 over three years – by the mineral water brand Evian.[15] Athletes were selected for the squad based on their potential to win medals at international events, such as the forthcoming European Championships. The women had access to free running gear, training camps and coaching, along with as much Evian mineral water as they could drink. However, the strict amateur rules dictated that they couldn't be paid, nor could they accept appearance money or prize money. Being a full-time athlete wasn't an option and most of them were fitting in their training alongside jobs. The 1982 squad consisted of the six women who had topped the marathon rankings for 1981: Joyce Smith, the British record holder, Carol Gould, Gillian Adams, Suzan Hassan, Gillian Burley and Karen Goldhawk.

In 1983, the squad was expanded to 12 – the women who had put in the best performances in 1982. Joyce Smith, Carol Gould, Gillian Adams, now under her married name of Horovitz, and Gillian Burley remained in the squad. The eight women who joined included four who have already appeared in our story: Caroline Rodgers, Leslie Watson, Margaret Lockley and Jean Lochhead. Caroline, 33, who was the third British woman to break three hours at the Feltham Marathon in 1976 and was great friends with Leslie, had won the Gosport Marathon in April 1982 in a personal best time – 2:44:17. Leslie, 38, had also run a personal best at the New York City Marathon in October 1982 – 2:44:18. Margaret Lockley, 35, winner of the first national marathon championship in 1978 and 10th place finisher at London in 1981 had improved her personal best by two minutes in 1982 to 2:45:21. Jean Lochhead, 36, the Welsh cross-country international who ran an unofficial 10-mile world best when she crashed the Croxdale 10 in 1975, had finished sixth at the 1982 London Marathon in 2:46:04. This had earned her selection to represent Great Britain at the Berlin Marathon in September 1982, which she won in 2:47:05.

A team kit was created: pink tracksuits, t-shirts and vests with the Evian logo and matching shorts. Caroline was none too fond of the kit, describing the tracksuits as 'horrible'. An Evian promotional photograph shows the group of 12 wearing the vests and shorts, with the three women in the front row kneeling on the floor. Jean didn't particularly enjoy the photoshoot but accepted that it was part of being in the squad, commenting, when I interviewed her, that, 'By the time we'd been through makeup, we could barely recognise ourselves.' She also remembers how painful kneeling on the uncarpeted floor was.

The squad raised the profile of women's marathon running and encouraged other women to try to improve their performance to get into it. Being part of the squad gave women opportunities for travel abroad to marathons in countries which they might never otherwise have visited, often flying first class, and travelling together as a team with plane fares, accommodation and meals all provided. 'You didn't pay for anything,' Caroline remembers. And if you finished in the top three in a race, you were usually invited back the following year.

Jean Lochhead returned to the Berlin Marathon in 1983, finishing second and setting herself a personal best of 2:43:56. However, it was to be her last marathon. Jean, who was also a competitive fell runner at the time, turned her back on competitive road racing. When I interviewed her, she said, 'I never enjoyed [marathons] – much nicer to run over moorland.'[16] In the 1980s, orienteering became her main focus and today she competes in dozens of orienteering events a year in the 75 to 79 age category. She prefers urban orienteering on roads.

Aged 37, Margaret Lockley ran her all-time best, 2:36:06, in the 1984 London Marathon. As it was the sixth-fastest time by a British woman that year, it led to her being selected as one of the six women in the 1985 Evian national marathon squad and as one of the five British women for the inaugural World Marathon Cup in Hiroshima in 1985, where she was the second British finisher in 35th place. Margaret had intended to run the London Marathon in 1986 but back problems prevented her and eventually led to her giving up competitive running. After moving to the Isle of Man in the 1990s, Margaret became involved in fell running as a competitor, race organiser and official, and has been made a life member of her club, Manx Fell Runners, in recognition of her contribution to the sport. She coaches athletes and is involved in officiating at races. Her son Ollie Lockley (born 1993) represented the Isle of Man in the marathon at the 2022 Commonwealth Games in Birmingham.

In the early 1980s, the rules around amateurism became more relaxed as the international governing body, the IAAF, gradually gave in to pressure from athletes and commercial organisations. Although officially athletes still couldn't be paid, it was a bit of a grey area, particularly in the USA where race organisers often offered big cash prizes and some shoe brands paid athletes to wear their products. In the UK top runners could receive sponsorship, but this was usually in kind rather than money. Leslie Watson, Caroline Rodgers and Gillian Burley were among the athletes sponsored by Nike. Gillian recalls receiving a large box of shoes and the latest running kit from Nike twice a year. Although athletes weren't allowed to accept appearance money or prize money, this was sometimes circumvented by 'brown envelope' under-the-table payments. Caroline recalls that on one occasion competing in a marathon in the USA proved quite lucrative: 'I went there with hardly anything, to be honest, and I came back quite wealthy.'

Caroline started the decade ranked eighth in the UK for the marathon, thanks to her personal best time of 2:54:37 at the 1979 national marathon championship at Sandbach. It was in 1981 that Caroline's running career really took off. Within the space of six weeks, starting with the North Down Festival Marathon on 6 June, she won four marathons. A week after North Down she won the Polytechnic Marathon, on 4 July she won at Milton Keynes in a personal best of 2:49:22 and eight days later had a commanding victory in the Spanish Marathon Championship, crossing the finish line seven minutes ahead of her nearest rival, according to the report in *Athletics Weekly*.[17]

Over the next five years, more race wins followed and Caroline travelled to races in France, West Germany, Hungary, the USA, the Philippines, Singapore, Barbados and Trinidad. While she has fond memories of her trips abroad, she told me about two trips that stuck out for the wrong reasons.[18] In April 1985, Caroline, who is Black/mixed race, and Leslie were in Marseille for the marathon. They were in the habit of going for a run round the streets in the days before a race, combining a warm-up with sightseeing. One day someone repeatedly shouted a racial slur at Caroline. She was shocked, as was Leslie, and it is still a vivid memory.

Caroline had never experienced abuse when out running in the UK. There were well-known Black women athletes representing Britain in track and field, such as hurdler Sharon Colyear, heptathlete Judy Simpson, and javelin throwers Tessa Sanderson and Fatima Whitbread. However, there were very few women, or men, of colour running long distance. Suzan Hassan had been in the marathon squad in 1981 and 1982, and Julie Asgill, another woman of colour, would join the Evian squad in 1984, but Caroline was used to being the only person of colour at races.

An even more shocking incident occurred when Caroline was in West Berlin for the 1984 marathon. The race organisers had put her and other athletes up in a top hotel on West Berlin's most prestigious street, the Kurfürstendamm. On one of the days leading up to the race, Caroline got into the lift at the hotel. It was a small lift, full of people in suits. As it started moving, she was punched in the ribs. It was a deliberate act of violence, inflicting pain. As the lift was packed, she had no way of knowing who her assailant was. Caroline says that she might have said something if she had known who it was. If any of the other people noticed, none of them said anything. She was in no doubt it was a racist assault.

Caroline ran the marathon but was left feeling vulnerable. 'I was desperate to get out of there because it was awful, because you don't know who it is,' she recalls. She went to the race organisers after the race, told them about the attack and asked for a plane ticket back to the UK immediately, rather than staying on in Berlin for a couple of days as scheduled. The organisers were apologetic but said they couldn't change the arrangements.

Caroline was friends with Liz Sloan who, along with Ann Kramer, co-wrote *Running – The Women's Handbook*, published in 1985 by Pandora Press, a new feminist publisher. As well as featuring practical advice, the book looked at women's experience of running in a feminist context, including the experiences of older women and women with disabilities. The book featured a brief profile of Caroline and paid tribute to her as a rulebreaker who had run unofficially in men's 10-mile races in the 1970s: 'It is very much thanks to runners such as Caroline that women now have the opportunity to participate in these events; it hasn't always been as easy as it is today.'

The book's cover features a picture of Caroline and a friend, Lyn, running together along the towpath of the Regent's Canal. Caroline remembers, 'We had to keep running up and down, up and down, until they got the right picture.' Caroline enjoyed her running career and says: 'I'm so glad that we ran when we did … It was beginning of marathon running in this country and everybody was running … It was a very exciting time … a wonderful time to be racing and training.'[19] Caroline continued to compete in marathons and achieved many top-three finishes until the late 1980s when injury led to her retirement from racing. In 1989, she decided to study for a social sciences degree and then trained and worked as a social worker. She also qualified and worked as a personal trainer.

Did the marathon boom mean that road races were equally open to women as to men? Was rulebreaking really over and done with? Not really. A few of the athletics clubs that had been organising men's road races for decades had difficulty coming to terms with the idea of admitting women to their 'men's races'.

Morpeth to Newcastle was one of the classic British road races, always attracting a large field of top male club runners. It was also the UK's oldest race, having been established in 1904. In 1978, three years after Avril's unofficial run on New Year's Day 1975, women still weren't officially admitted. Undeterred, Norma Campbell ran unofficially, finishing the 13.6 miles in

1:36:30. Impressively, at 49 Norma was running fast enough to place in the top two thirds of the field of over 400 men. Her time was just outside the 1:35:00 required for a merit certificate.

However, the organisers remained intransigent. When Jen Neligan phoned to ask for an entry form for the 1979 race, she was told, 'We don't allow lasses to run in the race.'[20] Unperturbed, Jen planned to ghost-run in the race, but that year it was postponed due to roads blocked by snow and she wasn't able to make the rescheduled date. She ran the route on her own on another day. However, Gillian Burley from Gateshead Harriers was able to make the rescheduled date. She remembers starting off in full training gear, 'nylon trousers and jacket over Ron Hill tracksters and sweatshirt', only to find she was much too hot and having to take layers off and leave them with club supporters en route. Her unofficial time was 1:32:40.[21]

Mike Bateman, a committee member of Morpeth Harriers at the time, ascribes the continued exclusion of women from the race to 'the antediluvian attitudes' of the three Newcastle clubs that organised it: 'They wanted Morpeth to help with the event, but we said we wouldn't unless they allowed women to run.'[22] When Gillian got her 1980 Boston Marathon place, she told the *Newcastle Journal*, 'The people who organise races in the North-East are so sexist it is unbelievable. It's not the only reason I'm going to America for this run, but it's certainly one of them.'[23] She crashed two other races in the Northeast in 1979, a 10-miler and a half marathon.

Another two years passed. Still no official female competitors at Morpeth to Newcastle. In 1981, there was a record entry of 1080 men for the race, of whom over 700 finished. The *Newcastle Journal*, the race sponsor, noted in its report on the race that, 'Several women and girls competed unofficially – only men may enter – and completed the course. They included Helen Boyes, Philippa Harbottle, Alison McVey and Philippa Rushton.' Helen Boyes was a member of Morpeth Harriers and one of their best cross-country runners. In the face of this protest run, the organisers eventually gave in and at last permitted women to enter in 1982.

Jean Lochhead won the first official women's race with Gillian Burley, who had crashed the race in 1979, second.

Portsmouth AC, organisers of another classic men's road race, Chichester to Portsmouth, had refused to let Lyn Billington run in 1977. A month after the 1981 London Marathon, a letter appeared in *Athletics Weekly* from the race organiser and club secretary, Andy Gibb. He was disconcerted by the number of race entries he was receiving from people he categorised as 'fun runners', who had failed to get a place in the London Marathon.[24] He'd received a phone call from 'a very charming lady who informed me that she had put her entry in the post and hoped that it was not too late.' It transpired that the organisers of the London Marathon had sent out a list of alternative road races with the rejection letters, and that list included Chichester to Portsmouth, a race which did not admit women. Gibb emphatically stated that it was 'not, by any stretch of the imagination, a fun run.' There was a gulf between the inclusive spirit of the London Marathon and this traditional road race. Gibb concluded his letter with an exhortation to the London Marathon organisers: 'I'm all for giving encouragement to newcomers to the sport, but please, Mr Brasher, not 66-year-old ladies.'

Two weeks later, three letters appeared objecting to Gibb's comments. One was from Lyn. While she agreed that the 16-mile race was not suitable for fun runners, she took issue with the continued exclusion of women: 'After all these years, you are STILL not accepting LADIES. No doubt you would even have questioned a 43-year-old woman who had run a sub-2:30 marathon if she had rung up, but not a 66-year-old man. We are ALL in this sport to encourage, not to demoralise.'[25] Readers of Lyn's letter would have been well aware that the 43-year-old runner she was referring to was Joyce Smith, the winner of the London Marathon.

In his response, published two weeks later, Gibb pointed out some organisational difficulties associated with admitting women and slower runners: inadequate changing facilities for women at the start and the need for volunteers to stay out on the course for a much longer time. He also dug himself into a bit of hole, claiming not to be a 'male chauvinist pig', while simultaneously patronising the women who had written in: 'I'm sympathetic to their cause for women participating in men's road running events irrespective of their standard of performance.' Gibb finished by saying, 'Cheer up ladies, all is not lost' as one day there would, almost certainly, be a women's race.[26] This sounds to me a bit like saying 'over my dead body', but whatever Andy Gibb may have thought, the tide of opinion had turned and the 1982 race officially admitted women for the first time, with the women's race starting 30 minutes before the men's, and a time limit of 2:45 for men and 3:15 for women.

In the course of the 1980s, the organisation of road races changed. Following the formation of the Sports Council in 1972, local authorities had become more involved in sports provision. Some put on road races themselves or supported local organisations to put on races. TV coverage of the London Marathon highlighted the potential for fundraising, and charities and community organisations, such as Lions Clubs and Rotary Clubs, began to organise races. The Manchester Charity Marathon in October 1981 raised over £1 million for the Spastics Society.

This upheaval benefitted women because the organisers of the new races had positive reasons to include them. They wanted to attract as many runners as possible, men and women. Local authorities were delivering the national Sport for All programme; fundraising groups wanted to attract as many participants as possible. Companies were increasingly interested in race sponsorship as races provided media coverage and opportunities to market a wide range of products to the large new group of fitness runners. In most cases, they wanted to sponsor mixed races.

As road racing became more commercialised, more men's races admitted women and others were killed off by the competition. The new fitness runners were looking for what we might now call a different race experience. By the mid-1980s, women had plenty of races to enter and there was no need for rulebreaking and ghost running. However, a few traditional men-only races lingered on. The Finchley 20, where Margaret Lockley had got into so much trouble for ghost running in 1978, remained staunchly men-only until 1987, when Leslie Watson was the first female winner, in 2:07:12. Renamed the Hillingdon 20, the race is still going and is said to be 'the oldest continuously contested 20-mile road race in the world'.[27]

While women now had the right to run in most road races, there was another way in which they were treated very differently to men: prizes. In *Running – The Women's Handbook*, Liz Sloan was indignant about unequal prizes, saying that: 'In mixed races, women face various kinds of put-down. Prizes, for instance, are frequently only half the value of men's prizes.' She gave the example of a 10-mile race where Caroline Rodgers had won a prize. The first three men won sports kit and the first three women won: a bread bin, a brush and comb, and a plastic handbag. Another example was the 1983 Wakefield Half Marathon. The male winner 'earned himself a trip to New Zealand, while the winner of the women's event won herself a mini-break in the Dutch Bulb fields – well under half the value of the men's prize.' Liz herself had complained, successfully, about unequal prizes at a fun run in 1983, where the winning man's performance was seemingly worth 12 times the woman's. Liz came in first woman and was awarded a bottle of wine. The first man won a crate of wine. She said, 'I stood my ground, however, complained against discrimination (ungrateful woman I heard them whisper) and the wine was shared.'[28]

In the book's publication year, 1985, at the Nescafé Antrim Coast Road Marathon, the winning woman's prize wasn't even half the value of that given to the male winner. Both received Nike vouchers, but the main prize was a travel voucher: £1,500 for the man and £500 for the woman. Race organisers argued that the quantity of prizes, and their value, should be in proportion to the number of entrants. Because only a small number of women entered there did not need to be equal prizes.

The race sponsors often provided the prizes and if there were to be an equal number of prizes for men and women the organisers would have to persuade the sponsors to stump up more money or find additional sponsors. Most race organisers did not see it as their responsibility to encourage women to enter by offering equal-value prizes. Nothing was going to change unless women like Liz kicked up a fuss.

Sometimes organisers apparently forgot about the women altogether. Jean Lochhead remembers that at the Rowntree's 10-mile race in York one year there were no prizes for women. She complained and was sent a box of Black Magic and a note saying they didn't realise women would be running, which bemused her as she had entered in advance.

When I interviewed Jill Danskin, Leslie's friend and London Olympiades teammate, she remembered finishing first woman at a fun run and hearing the first male finishers being announced. The women weren't even announced. To rub it in, the men were given prizes and the women got nothing. At weekends in the 1980s, Jill would travel to road races in the Southeast as part of the London Olympiades team. With strong runners like Leslie Watson and Gillian Burley they would usually win the team prize. In November 1984, Jill, Leslie and Gillian were the first team in the inaugural Brighton Half Marathon, but when it came to the prizes they were in for a massive disappointment. The men's team got really good prizes. But when one of the women enquired about their prizes she was told it was ties – three men's ties bearing the name of the club that organised the race, Brighton & Hove AC. Jill recalls her reaction. 'I went bananas. I was absolutely outraged.' She refused on principle to accept the prize.[29]

Perhaps it was this experience that provoked Jill to write to *Athletics Weekly* about 'the all too frequent male bias in many mixed road races'.[30] She cited the example of a recent half marathon where the first three men's teams had received substantial prizes and shields, whereas the first team was the only women's team to receive an award and this was shields. There were no prizes. She proposed a different prize structure: 'While I concede that women's times are slower, the gap is narrowing at the top. I can also understand that prizes are presented on a percentage basis, but surely it would encourage women if the prizes were either a) equal or b) smaller and more numerous.'

Jill's letter prompted 42-year-old Janet Thompson to write in pointing out that most races didn't give prizes for masters (veteran) women 'whereas for veteran men there are usually many prizes and in age categories.'[31] While acknowledging that there were fewer women running, she urged race organisers to do their bit to encourage more women to run by providing prizes. Women runners, after all, had to be more dedicated than men, she said. 'Most of the veteran women running today have families and home commitments. How many men would run if they had a woman's commitments? When one is a veteran woman runner it means high organisation to train and race. Would there be as many veteran men running if they had to do the same as women? I don't think so.'

When they weren't being awarded men's ties, women's prizes were often highly gendered. It was not uncommon for the male race winner to be given a sports watch and the female winner to be presented with an iron or 'beauty' products. Jean, who won several road races in the early 1980s, recalls receiving heated rollers and a waxing kit as prizes. And she says: 'For one presentation picture I had to pose with a bouquet which was borrowed from the men's race and had to be given back, which came as a surprise to me!' Gillian Burley had a better experience at one race where she was presented with a beauty set as her prize but managed to swap with one of the men – he got the beauty set for his wife and Gillian got the power drill she really wanted.[32]

While the need for rulebreaking diminished in the early 1980s, women's participation in road races remained low. Disappointingly for an event that aimed to be inclusive, just 24 of the 498 finishers,

5%, at the 1980 People's Marathon were women. It was a similar picture at the 1981 London Marathon, where 4.25% of the 6418 finishers were women. For most of the decade, women's participation in mixed road races was around 5 to 15%. There may, of course, have been women who were choosing not to race, instead running for fitness. Social attitudes still linked competitiveness to masculinity and this may have put some women off.

Women's participation in running was also affected by safety, or the lack of it, on the streets, particularly at night. The Reclaim the Night movement had started in Leeds in 1977. Marches took place in many cities and towns demanding that women should be able to be outside at night without the fear of male violence. The experiences of two women who featured in *Running* magazine (formerly *Jogging*) in 1981 provide some insight into women's concerns about safety. One summer evening, Diana Cook from Richmond in Surrey was out running when a 'young thug' deliberately drove at her. When she got home, infuriated and frightened, she immediately wrote to the magazine. 'I think that men cannot realise the sort of sexual harassment women runners meet on the roads', she observed.[33] She contrasted this experience with running the London Marathon, where she had been 'warmed and encouraged by the terrific support given by both men and women spectators. It is ironic that those who were cheering may now be the ones jeering us.' She concluded that perhaps harassment could be 'the explanation for the shortage of women runners.' This prompted a letter from Margaret Dalton in Glasgow who said that she had had even more frightening experiences when she was training for the London Marathon, leading her to stop running on her own. She'd found two male friends who were willing to run seven miles with her twice a week.[34] She was convinced that the fact that she'd not been able to do long runs before the race had contributed to her not finishing the race, ending her letter: 'Paradise is a place where women can run 15 miles *unmolested*!' Frustratingly, nearly 50 years later, this sentiment still resonates with women runners' experiences today. Recent research into women runners in

Greater Manchester and Merseyside by the University of Manchester found that a majority had experienced some form of abusive behaviour when running and were worried about their personal safety.[35] Joining a club and going on group runs offered women more security, and women-only races and groups formed an important pathway into running for women in the 1980s. Women sometimes found themselves turned away from mixed clubs or felt that they didn't fit in if they couldn't run fast enough. Linda Rimmer from Liverpool wrote to *Running* about her experience: 'I am 27 and have been running for four years now and went along to Liverpool Harriers recently to find out about joining. They replied snootily that there wasn't much call for joggers at their club, but I could use their track with one of their one of their injured athletes if I liked. I left feeling like I'd had a boot up the backside when all I'd wanted was a little guidance on my standard of running and some advice on how to move into competitive races.'[36]

In the summer of 1981, *Running* appointed its first female sub-editor, Ali Turnbull, who later became assistant editor. The magazine was doing well, but the editorial team were always looking for ways to broaden its appeal. Aware that most of the magazine's readers were men, they came up with an idea for reaching more women.

In 1983 Ali led The Sisters Project in partnership with Avon, which sought to match experienced women runners, 'big sisters', with beginners, 'little sisters', with the goal of training together for the Avon Women's 10-mile race that autumn. Ali announced the project in the April issue, expecting to receive about 100 replies, and was astonished and delighted when more than 800 letters poured in. Around 500 women were matched and on 2 October, 1983, 235 of them completed the Avon 10-mile race at Copthall, North London, part of a record field of 795 women.[37] Interestingly, when the beginners were asked afterwards about the benefits of participating in the project they placed losing weight and looking better at the bottom of the list, with getting rid of stress, sleeping better and feeling fitter as the top three benefits.

It took the *Woman's Own* magazine's series of fun runs in 1984 to truly attract large numbers of women to road races and increase public awareness of women's running. Women's magazines were read by nearly 24 million women and *Woman's Own*, aimed at busy wives and mothers, was one of the leading titles. As historian Tracey Loughran points out, it was a big departure from the typical attitude of women's magazines where exercise was most often linked to losing weight: 'The idea that ordinary women might exercise to feel healthy rather than to look good simply did not feature. There was little sense that some women might even *enjoy* exercise. The assumption was that most women hated their bodies and just wanted to be thinner.'[38] With sponsorship from Nike, *Woman's Own* worked with race organisers to hold 32 women-only races on the first weekend in September 1984. Seventeen thousand women flocked to the races, either running or walking the 10 kilometres. Many had set up jogging groups to prepare for the event. Races were held in all four nations of the UK and in some places it was the first time a women-only race had ever taken place. The series continued for five years, until 1988. When marathon runner Fraser Clyne wrote an end-of-year review of Scottish road running in 1984, he credited the *Woman's Own* races in Aberdeen and Grangemouth with creating a 'women's running boom' in Scotland, observing that, 'Until 12 months ago only a handful of women were ever seen taking part in Scottish road races.'[39] Almost 1000 women had taken part, over 400 of them at Aberdeen, where there had never been a race with as many as 50 women.

Today the London Marathon is very proud of its elite men's and women's wheelchair races. In 2024 it announced 'a significant and historic moment for disability sport' when it became the first marathon in the world to award equal prize money to wheelchair and able-bodied athletes.[40] But in the early 1980s, it was a very different picture.

In 1981, ironically the United Nations International Year of Disabled Persons, Chris Brasher and John Disley were vehemently opposed to wheelchair racers taking part in the inaugural London Marathon. They insisted that it was a 'foot race' and said that it would be both impractical and unsafe to permit people in wheelchairs to participate. Despite a vociferous campaign by wheelchair athlete Tim Marshall, supported by the British Sports Association for the Disabled, Brasher and Disley dug their heels in for two years. In the end it was the Greater London Council's threat to withdraw its funding of the race that forced Brasher and Disley to reluctantly agree at the last minute to a wheelchair race at the 1983 marathon.[41] Even then, in a news clip from the press conference announcing the agreement, Brasher melodramatically asserted that including wheelchairs would be 'a formula for another accident, another person being disabled.'[42]

There was in fact plenty of evidence that this was not the case and the Great North Run, several marathons, and other road races had welcomed wheelchair racers. But as sports media historian Roger Domeneghetti points out: 'Brasher's attitude was not uncommon. Britain in the 1980s was an unwelcoming environment for disabled people.'[43] There was no anti-discrimination law relating to disability and few accommodations, such as dropped kerbs or accessible toilets, to make life easier for people using wheelchairs or with other disabilities.

In 1983, 17 wheelchair athletes finished the London Marathon. The first woman was 29-year-old Denise Smith in 4:29:03 and Joanne Roberts finished in 6:09:03. Tim Marshall recounts that Brasher, piqued at being forced to accept wheelchair competitors, pronounced that they weren't eligible to receive London Marathon medals as they weren't taking part in a foot race. Alternative medals were provided by the British Sports Association for the Disabled. In 1984, this was rectified when the Greater London Council organised a reception for the 1983 wheelchair competitors at which they were awarded the official medals for 1983. From 1984 onwards, wheelchair competitors were given the same medals as everyone else.

Denise was an accomplished sportswoman who had competed as a swimmer at the 1974 Commonwealth Paraplegic Games in New Zealand. She used running to improve her cardiovascular efficiency, alongside her swimming training. In the early 1980s, she became interested in road racing. She managed to fit in a demanding training programme alongside working full-time and was a member of Reading AC. In *Running – The Women's Handbook,* Denise described her training regime: 'I train between 30 to 50 miles a week, depending on the weather, and I also do flexibility work. I occasionally do weights to balance the other muscles, but I find that I do enough weight training lifting my own body weight around.' She was frustrated that wheelchair athletes were not treated as equals to able-bodied athletes, saying: 'Training is hard; it's not all downhill. We have the same ability to train and run.'[44]

After Denise's death in 2020, her sister Verna recalled how Denise had prepared for the first London marathon: 'She had done the Gloucester marathon as her first one, around six months before ... She punctured lots of tyres, because they didn't realise about sweeping the roads and stuff like that. We were dashing round the shops trying to get things like puncture repair kits and tyres – I remember Halfords were amazing.'[45] As there were no racing chairs available, Denise was using a four-wheel chair of the type used in wheelchair basketball. The June issue of *Marathon and Distance Runner* magazine had a photo of Gordon Perry, the first man to finish the London Marathon, being presented with a new lightweight training wheelchair, worth hundreds of pounds, by Ken Livingstone, the leader of the Greater London Council. There is no mention of Denise. I'd like to think that she, too, was presented with a top-notch wheelchair, but I suspect that she was not. However, Denise was not a woman to be put off by things like that.

Although 1983 was Denise's only win at the London Marathon, she finished in the top three every year from 1984 to 1987, with a fastest time of 3:21:19 in 1985.[46] In 1984, along with other athletes, she set up the first national wheelchair marathon.

It took place at the Gloucester Marathon in October and Denise finished second woman. She also took part in the Great North Run. An impressively versatile athlete, Denise competed at the 1984 Winter Paralympics in Innsbruck, winning three silver medals in ice sledge speed racing, and later took up disability waterskiing, becoming a world champion.

Thirteen-year-old Tanni Grey, watching the 1983 London Marathon on TV, was inspired: 'It was the first time that I saw international disabled athletes competing. It just showed disabled people doing sport and it wasn't patronising. I was already doing a bit of wheelchair racing, but the London Marathon definitely tipped the scales. It seemed quite exciting and fast. I thought, "I'm going to do the London Marathon one day; that's what I want to do."'[47]

Just eight years later, in 1991, Tanni would finish third in the race. The following year she won in 2:17:23, the first of her six wins between 1992 and 2002. She held the course record, 2:00:10 set in 1996, for nine years until it was broken by Francesca Porcellato of Italy, the first athlete to finish in under two hours, with 1:57:00, in 2005. Tanni also represented Britain at five Paralympic Games, from Seoul in 1988 to Athens in 2004, winning 16 medals on the track, and won medals at three World Championships.

By 1985, many thousands of British women had competed in races, done a fun run or gone out jogging. Running had become more acceptable for women and all, or nearly all, road races were open to them. There was an Olympic marathon for women, at last. And there were role models to inspire the runners of the future.

THE DEBT WE OWE

The women interviewed in this book were part of a revolution in road running. When they were taking their first steps as road runners, people thought running on the roads was eccentric and seeing a woman out running was even more of an oddity; it just wasn't feminine or appropriate. If they were bold enough to run on the roads, women had to put up with a lot.

While many thousands of women took up running between 1975 and 1985, women's participation in road running, and particularly in racing, was much lower than men's. And, despite the marathon boom, running wasn't anywhere near as popular as it is today. From around the year 2000, participation went up significantly in the UK and many of these new runners were women. Although there were still more men than women running, women's participation was increasing more quickly.

Today, Sport England research suggests that one in eight women in the UK is running regularly – more than 3 million women – and that women are 'driving the resurgence in running'.[1] Women can be confident that they can enter, compete in and finish any road race they choose. Although there is a significant variation across ethnic groups, with Black and Asian women less likely to run, women make up a much bigger proportion of the field in races than they did in the 1990s.

Of the 56,736 finishers in the 2025 London Marathon, 44% were female, more than 10 times the participation rate in 1981, 4.25%. When I did a brief survey of 10 road races held in 2024/25, from 5 kilometres to marathon distance, I found that on average 43% of race finishers were women. The most recent data published by parkrun, from 2019, shows a similar participation rate, 44%.[2] While women are still under-represented – they make up 51% of the UK population – if more women are starting to run that gap may narrow.

When our rulebreakers were running, women did not have control of their own narrative. Their running, their experiences and their words were reported, and interpreted, by the male-run media. Violet Piercy is an unusual exception; she was expert at working with the press, radio and cinema news to get her message across. The 10-minute radio talk she gave in 1926 allowed her to talk directly to the listeners. And her words haven't been lost. A hundred years later we can still read some of what she said.

Since the start of the century, blogs, social media and podcasts have increasingly given women a voice, a space, and the freedom to talk about running and the impact it has on their lives. In the past 10 years, women runners have successfully used these channels to start and to amplify campaigns around equal access to races. One example is the grassroots campaign RunEqual, started in 2017 by Maud Hodson, using social media and an online petition. The campaign aims to equalise the distances for men and women in cross-country races. At the World, European and Scottish championships, women and men both race 10 kilometres, yet in England most women running in cross-country races compete over shorter distances than men. At the English national championships, the women's race is 8 kilometres while the men's is 12. RunEqual encourages individuals to persuade their clubs to press for equal distances at local, county and regional cross-country events. Other women have used social media to build communities of runners. For example, in 2019, British-Jamaican runner Tasha Thompson founded Black Girls Do Run UK because she rarely saw other Black women at races and wanted to create both a London-based running club and a wider community where Black women could 'connect, motivate, and empower each other through the transformative experience of running.' She told me that at a grassroots level, social media is an accessible way of organising runs, sharing lived experiences, and building trust within underrepresented communities. And for Tasha, increasing the visibility of Black women on social media is an important part of challenging the misconception that black women do not run.[3]

The rulebreakers and ghost runners in this book were physical activists. Every time they turned up at a race, they were asserting themselves as distance runners through their bodily presence.[4] They defied the athletics authorities and broke social norms. And they persisted – for years after the rules had changed – in asserting the right of all women to race as far and as hard as men. They were the women who were denied opportunities but took them anyway.[5] They created new identities for themselves when there were no role models to follow.

And most of our rulebreakers had a much deeper and more extensive impact on the sport. On athletics committees and governing bodies, they advocated for women and girls, creating more opportunities for them to compete. As club women's captains and coaches, they supported new generations of athletes – several of them are still doing this today.

They were empowered, both by others and through their own actions, as they experienced the liberating effects of running and racing long distance. Their running was a challenge to patriarchal order and a way of expressing emotions that were not considered feminine: aggression, frustration, anger and competitiveness. And they, in turn, empowered others through their presence and by their example.

Women's stories have been marginalised because they don't fit with the dominant narrative of male sporting achievement. Sometimes, women have even been written out of the history of our sport, as if our races never happened. But each time we stand on a start line, like the rulebreakers, we are using our bodies to say, 'We are strong. We are powerful. We run long distance.'

ROLL OF HONOUR

Carolyn (Lyn) Billington: A British canoe international, Lyn discovered her talent for running while training with the squad. In 1968, aged 23, she joined an athletics club, shifting her focus to running. She later joined Feltham AC in Hounslow and married another club member, Dave Billington. Together they organised the 1976 Feltham Ladies Marathon as a showcase for British running talent. It was Lyn's first long-distance road race and she finished second in the second-fastest time by a British woman. In the 1970s and 80s she challenged the continued exclusion of women from many road races. In 1979, she was one of four women who unofficially ran the 54-mile London to Brighton race, opening up ultra distances to women.

Alison Blake: When she took up running in 1972, joining her local club, Plymouth AC, Alison was 23 and the mother of four children. She quickly made an impression in track and cross-country races, competed at 3000 metres in an international match and was selected for England in a cross-country home countries international. In March 1975 she was one of five rulebreaking women at the Tonbridge 10 run organised by Adele Brignall, finishing first in 58:24 and setting the unofficial British record. In July that year she also won the first official women's long-distance road race, the Reebok 6. In April 1976 she ran unofficially again in a men's 8-mile road race. After winning her first marathon, the Duchy of Cornwall in 1979, she won it again in 1980, placing her ninth in the UK all-time rankings for the marathon.

Adele Brignall: Having joined Tonbridge AC as a teenager in the 1960s, Adele was coached for 1500 metres and cross country, but in March 1975, aged 24 and frustrated at the restrictions on women's running, she organised an unofficial women's run at the Tonbridge 10 in March 1975. Later that year, she competed in the Masters and Maidens Marathon, an unofficial race, although she dropped out during the race, she returned and ran it under her married name Cross, in 1977.

Angela Briscoe: In July 1975 Angela finished second to Alison Blake in the first official women's long-distance road race, the Reebok 6. Having started athletics at 14, in her late teens she was one of Britain's best 1500-metre runners. In 1970, aged 18, she represented Great Britain at the European Junior Championships in Paris, finishing fourth in the 1500 metres. In the early 1970s she also represented Great Britain at international track and cross-country events. Angela crashed a few races in the mid-1970s, including the Wigan 6 and the Parbold Hill 6.25 miles cross-country race.

Gillian Burley: After joining Gateshead Harriers when she was a postgraduate student at Newcastle University, Gillian began road racing and in April 1979, aged 22, qualified for the 1980 Boston Marathon when she ran 2:58:09 at the Duchy of Cornwall Marathon. In 1979, she competed unofficially in three road races in the Northeast, starting with Morpeth to Newcastle on New Year's Day. One of the top British marathoners of the early 1980s, Gillian was selected to represent Great Britain at many races and at the inaugural World Cup Marathon for women in Hiroshima in 1985.

Bridget Cushen: Brought up in Ireland, Bridget became involved in athletics after moving to London for work in 1959. In 1966, she competed unofficially in a men's 3000 metres track race – the longest distance women could race on the track was the mile. Her action helped make the case for the 3000 metres to be added to the women's championships. In 1973, aged 33, she challenged the ban on women's long-distance racing by competing unofficially in the Harlow Marathon. From 1975, Bridget became part of the new masters athletics movement (for men 40+ and women 35+), competing in the UK and abroad, and leading the development of the movement by serving on many UK and international governing bodies for 50 years.

Jill Danskin: Having moved to London from Dundee aged 18 to study at university, Jill started running in her 20s. Her ambition was to do a marathon. In 1984, at a fun run in Regents Park, she met Leslie Watson who persuaded her to join London Olympiades Athletic Club. Jill travelled to many races with the club and became lifelong friends with Leslie.

Dale Greig (1937–2019): A Scottish pioneer who ran in the men's Isle of Wight Marathon in 1964, aged 27, today Dale's time of 3:27:25 is recognised by World Athletics as a world record. She competed in athletics from her teens and in 1959 set up her own women's club, Tannahill Harriers, because there was no club open to women in her home town, Paisley. A strong cross-country runner, she won the national title four times and was instrumental in reviving women's cross-country competition in Scotland in the 1960s. A tough endurance athlete, in the early 1970s, Dale ran the Isle of Man 40, the 53-mile London to Brighton race and the Ben Nevis fell race – all unofficially. From the mid-1970s she competed in masters championships, winning the first international masters marathon for women in 1974 and taking a leading role in the organisation in charge of international masters road running events.

Palm Gunstone: Brought up in a family associated with Dundee Hawkhill Harriers, Palm joined the club aged 13, in 1959. Her parents, who had both competed for the club, were athletics officials. A strong cross-country runner, Palm was selected to represent Scotland at three World Cross Country Championships, in Belgium in 1973, in Italy in 1974 and in Morocco in 1975.

Palm raced against Dale Greig in many cross-country races and they were lifelong friends from the late 1960s.

Dame Marea Hartman (1920–1994): Marea joined the committee of the Women's Amateur Athletic Association in 1950 and was its honorary secretary from 1960 to 1991. She held powerful and influential roles in athletics nationally and internationally, and, as chair of the women's commission of the athletics international governing body from 1968 to 1981, she successfully pushed for more events to be added to the women's programme, including the 1500 metres and 3000 metres.

Doreen King: Watching the 1960 Rome Olympic Games on TV got 15-year-old Doreen interested in athletics and she joined Bellahouston Harriers. From 1963 to 1965 she was in the Scottish top ten rankings for the mile and became a strong cross-country runner. Friends with Dale Greig, they were rivals in many races. In 1968, Doreen finished second behind Dale in the Scottish cross-country championship and they were both selected to represent Scotland at the international championship in Blackburn where Doreen was the first Scottish runner to finish. Inspired by Dale's example, she became a ghost runner herself in the men's Scottish Marathon in Glasgow.

Lydia Kirk: The first event Lydia won, after starting running as a 22-year-old student, was a 2-mile fun run in Newcastle in June 1978 and she ran in the inaugural *Sunday Times* Fun Run in October 1978. She ran her first marathon, the Isle of Wight Marathon, in May 1979. She then ran four more marathons that year, winning one of them, and improving her time by over 43 minutes to 3:00:40. In 1979 she was also one of four women who unofficially ran the 53-mile London to Brighton race, finishing second behind Leslie Watson.

Avril Lewis: On New Year's Day 1975, 20-year-old student and athletics club member Avril Jones unofficially ran in the 13.6-mile Morpeth to Newcastle road race and ended up on the front page of the local paper. Later that year, on 30 November, Avril, now under her married name Lewis, was one of six women starters at the first official marathon open to women, the Barnsley Marathon, where she finished fourth. She broke the rules again, running unofficially in the cross-country Offa's Dyke 15 in 1977 with a friend.

Jean Lochhead: From 1967 Jean competed for Wales in international cross-country championships and, aged 27, on the track at the 1974 Commonwealth Games in New Zealand. She ran unofficially at the Croxdale 10 in May 1975, running two seconds faster than Alison Blake's time at the Tonbridge 10 in March. One of the first women fell runners, she ran her first race in 1978. As a top British marathon runner at the start of the 1980s, she represented Great Britain at the Berlin Marathon twice, winning in 1982 and finishing second in 1983, her last marathon.

Margaret Lockley: Winner of the first English national marathon championship in 1978, aged 31, with a time that placed her second on the British all-time rankings, Margaret (née Ashcroft) had been running since her teens. In April 1975, shortly before the rules changed, she crashed the Chris Vose 10-mile race in Warrington. In April 1978, she found herself in hot water after running with a man's race number at the men-only Finchley 20. She was one of the top British marathon runners from 1978 to 1984, when she ran 2:36:06 at the London Marathon. In 1985, she competed for Great Britain at the inaugural World Cup Marathon race for women in Hiroshima.

Alice Milliat (1884–1957): A highly regarded, pioneering administrator of women's sport in France and internationally, Alice led a long campaign to get women's athletics included in the Olympic Games. Co-founder and first president of the International Women's Sports Federation which organised the Women's Olympic Games in 1922 and the Women's World Games in 1926, 1930 and 1934.

Violet Piercy (1889–1972): A vocal proponent of long-distance running for women at a time when it was unheard of, in the 1920s and 30s, Violet staged her own solo road runs. An expert self-publicist, she attracted press coverage and large crowds gathered to watch several of her runs. Her last marathon run, in June 1936, was timed over the Polytechnic Marathon course, starting ahead of the men's race. Today her time, 4:30:00, is recognised by World Athletics as a world record.

Christine Readdy: In the early 1970s, Christine, who had started running at 14, used local men's races in Staffordshire for training, joining in behind the main group of runners. In March 1974, aged 21, she attempted the Milford 21-mile cross-country race and then returned to the race the following year, still as an unofficial competitor, and finished it. In April 1976 she set the British record at the first women's marathon at Feltham in West London. Her time, 2:50:55, placed her ninth in the world rankings. She continued competing in road races, winning lots of 10-mile races, but didn't run another marathon until the inaugural London Marathon in 1981.

Caroline Rodgers: On her doctor's advice, as a way of improving her asthma, Caroline, who grew up in London, started athletics in her late teens. Her first official long-distance road race, when she was 26, was the Feltham Ladies Marathon, where she finished third, within the previous British record. Caroline became good friends with Leslie Watson, often trained with her, and they travelled to marathons abroad together in the 1980s. In 1983, they were both in the national marathon squad.

Miriam Rosen: In October 1975, under her maiden name Bescoby, Miriam competed in the unofficial Masters and Maidens Marathon. She got into running after starting orienteering at university in 1969, aged 20. After the Masters and Maidens Miriam joined Barnet Ladies AC and in October 1978 she participated in the inaugural *Sunday Times* Fun Run, the biggest mass event since the start of the 1970s jogging craze.

Vera Searle OBE (1901–1998): Between 1923 and 1925, under her maiden name Palmer, Vera set a world record at 250 metres and two at 440 yards. In 1926, she was one of a small contingent of British athletes who sailed to Sweden to compete in the second Women's World Games in Gothenburg. After retiring from athletics competition that year, she married Wilfred Searle, but remained very much involved in the administration of the sport. She served on the Women's Amateur Athletic Association (WAAA) Executive Committee for more than 60 years. From 1973 to 1981, she was the WAAA's first female chair and then served as president until 1991.

Joyce Smith: A top track and cross-country athlete in the early 1970s, Joyce set the 3000 metres world record in 1971, won the international cross-country championship in 1972, competed at 1500 metres at the 1972 Munich Olympic Games, was English cross-country champion in 1973 and won bronze at 3000 metres at the European Athletics Championships in Rome in 1974. She did long runs with the men at her club, Barnet AC, but got into trouble when she ran in a men's 5-mile road race unofficially. After retiring from track competition in 1978, she decided to run a marathon, breaking the British marathon record by over nine minutes in her debut race in June 1979, aged 41. She would break the record five more times. When she won the inaugural London Marathon in 1981, her time, 2:29:57, made her the first British woman to run under 2:30. She lowered the record to 2:29:43 the following year at the London Marathon, aged 44.

Margaret Thompson: In October 1975, Margaret set the British women's record, 3:07:47, at the Korso Marathon in Helsinki, Finland, taking nearly 20 minutes off Dale Greig's 1964 time. Growing up in Cumbria, she started athletics at school and joined a club aged 15. In 1972, aged 18, she moved to Southeast England to train as a teacher at Bedford College of PE, joining the local athletics club, Luton United AC. In the early 1970s she ran unofficially in a few local men's road races and once in a

7-mile men's cross-country league race as part of the club team. In 1978, she finished second behind Margaret Lockley in the first English national marathon championship.

Leslie Watson (1945–2024): One of the best-known runners of the 1980s thanks to press coverage, promotional work and television appearances, Leslie ran more marathons than anyone else at the time – she was reported to have run 206 in her 20-year career, winning more than 60 of them. Born in Glasgow, she joined an athletics club aged 10. After qualifying as a physiotherapist, she moved to London in 1970 and soon established her own practice. She joined the women's club London Olympiades Athletic Club and ran her first marathon distance at the unofficial Masters and Maidens Marathon in October 1975. In 1979, she was one of four women who unofficially ran the 53-mile London to Brighton, winning the race. The following year the race officially accepted women and she was once again the winner.

LIST OF IMAGES

REFERENCES

INTRODUCTION

1 'Pioneer Margaret steps out', the *Guardian*, 14 April, 1975
2 'No suffragettes in sport, please', Joe Lancaster, *Manchester Evening News*, 14 April, 1975
3 *The Complete Book of Running for Women*, Claire Kowalchik, Pocket Books, 1999
4 *Marathon Woman*, Kathrine Switzer, Da Capo Press, 2009
5 'Breaking into the marathon: Women's distance running as political activism', Jaime Schultz, *Frontiers: A Journal of Women Studies*, 40:2 (2019)
6 *A Long Time Coming: Running through the women's marathon revolution*, Jacqueline Hansen, self-published, 2013
7 *First Ladies of Running*, Amby Burfoot, Rodale, 2016
8 Starting Line 1928, a women's running oral history project, https://www.startingline1928.com/
9 Black female marathon history, https://tedcorbitt.com/black-female-marathon-history/
10 *'Tripping Daintily into the Arena': A Social History of English Women's Athletics 1921 to 1960*, Lynne Robinson, PhD thesis, University of Warwick, September 1996

CHAPTER 1 THE STARTING LINE

1 Sir William Arbuthnot Lane quoted in 'Women hurt in cross country race', *Westminster Gazette*, 14 February, 1927
2 Based on accounts in *They Run with Surprising Swiftness: The Women Athletes of Early Modern Britain*, Peter Radford, University of Virginia Press, 2023

3 *They Run with Surprising Swiftness: The Women Athletes of Early Modern Britain*, Peter Radford, University of Virginia Press, 2023

4 1927 race report, English National Cross Country Championships website, http://national.crosscountrychampionship.uk/html/reportCC19273L.htm; 'Women hurt in cross country race', *Westminster Gazette*, 14 February, 1927; 'First women's cross-country championship', *Daily Express*, 14 February, 1927

5 *Sport and the Physical Emancipation of English Women 1870–1914*, Kathleen E McCrone, Routledge, 1988

6 Quoted in *The Eternally Wounded Woman – Women, Doctors, and Exercise in the Late Nineteenth Century*, Patricia A Vertinsky, University of Illinois Press, 1994

7 The ideas of Dr T.S. Clouston described in *The Eternally Wounded Woman – Women, Doctors, and Exercise in the Late Nineteenth Century*, Patricia A Vertinsky, University of Illinois Press, 1994

8 *The Official Centenary History of the AAA*, Peter Lovesey, Guinness Superlatives Ltd, 1979

9 *Sporting Females – Critical Issues in the History and Sociology of Women's Sports*, Jennifer Hargreaves, Routledge, 1994

10 *Sport and the British: A Modern History*, Richard Holt, Oxford University Press, 2025

11 *Athletics of To-day for Women – History, Development and Training*, FAM Webster, Frederick Warne & Co Ltd, 1930

12 'The development of women's track and field in England. The role of the athletic club, 1920s–1950s', Lynne Duval, *Sports Historian*, 2001

13 'Champion lady runner of the world training in Ormskirk', *Ormskirk Advertiser*, 14 August, 1919

14 '90 years on … celebrating the formation of the Scottish Women's AAA', Arnold Black, Scottish Athletics website, https://www.scottishathletics.org.uk/about/history/arnolds-archive/58688-2/

15 *A Contemporary History of Women's Sport, Part One*, Jean Williams, Routledge, 2014

16 The FFSF – Fédération Féminine Sportive de France

17 *Alice Milliat – La Pasionara du Sport Féminin*, André Drevon, Vuibert, 2005

18 'Women's basketball: Net ball: An American game?', Keith Myerscough, Playing Pasts, https://www.playingpasts.co.uk/articles/gender-and-sport/womens-basketball-net-ball-an-american-game-part-6-of-7/

19 'Mascot keeps smiling', *London Evening News*, 21 March, 1921; 'From the classroom to the coast: The life of Julia Andrew, forgotten pioneer of women's fitness', paper given by Margaret Roberts, August 2025
20 The FSFI – Fédération Sportive Féminine Internationale
21 *The Official History of the Women's Amateur Athletic Association, 1922–2012*, Mel Watman, SportsBooks Ltd, 2012
22 *'Tripping Daintily into the Arena': A Social History of English Women's Athletics 1921–1960*, Lynne Robinson, PhD thesis, University of Warwick, 1996
23 Vera Searle quoted in *The Official History of the WAAA: 1922–2012*, Mel Watman, SportsBooks Limited, 2012
24 *'Tripping Daintily into the Arena': A Social History of English Women's Athletics 1921–1960*, Lynne Robinson, PhD thesis, University of Warwick, 1996
25 IAAF – International Amateur Athletic Federation
26 *A Contemporary History of Women's Sport, Part One*, Jean Williams, Routledge, 2014
27 *Better, Faster, Farther: How Running Changed Everything We Know About Women*, Maggie Mertens, Algonquin Books of Chapel Hill, 2024; 'Breaking into the marathon: Women's distance running as political activism', Jaime Schultz, *Frontier: A Journal of Women's Studies*, 40:2 (2019)
28 'A Japanese honour', *The Scotsman*, 3 August, 1928
29 *First Ladies of Running*, Amby Burfoot, Rodale, 2016

CHAPTER 2 VIOLET PIERCY – LONDON TO WINDSOR IN RECORD TIME (FOR A LADY)

1 Violet Piercy quoted in 'Up and up and round and round: Giddy limits', *Reynolds's Illustrated News*, 31 March, 1935
2 'First woman across', *Western Daily Press*, 7 August, 1926; 'Girl swimmer "spurted" by songs', *Yorkshire Evening Post*, 7 August, 1926; https://en.wikipedia.org/wiki/Gertrude_Ederle
3 'Girl conquers the Channel', British Pathé newsreel, 9 August, 1926
4 *A Contemporary History of Women's Sport, Part One*, Jean Williams, Routledge, 2014; 'Woman motor "ace"', *Western Mail*, 1 June, 1926; 'Thrilling events on the sands at Skegness', *Leicester Evening Mail*, 1 June, 1926

5 *Sporting Females – Critical Issues in the History and Sociology of Women's Sports*, Jennifer Hargreaves, Routledge, 1994

6 *Sporting Females – Critical Issues in the History and Sociology of Women's Sports*, Jennifer Hargreaves, Routledge, 1994, 2013

7 'The forgotten first lady: Rediscovering Violet Piercy, marathon pioneer', Peter Lovesey, PlayingPasts.co.uk, 2020, 2021

8 *The Guinness Book of the Marathon*, Roger Gynn, Guinness Superlatives Ltd, 1984

9 'The forgotten first lady: Rediscovering Violet Piercy, marathon pioneer', PlayingPasts.co.uk, 2020, 2021

10 *Ladies and Lords: A History of Women's Cricket in Britain*, Rafaelle Nicholson, Peter Lang, 2019

11 *Women in England 1870–1950*, Jane Lewis, Harvester Wheatsheaf, 1984

12 *Singled Out*, Virginia Nicholson, Penguin Books, 2008

13 *The Official History of Britain: Our story in numbers as told by the Office for National Statistics*, Boris Starling with David Bradbury, HarperCollins Publishers, London, 2022; '12 things you didn't know about women in the First World War', Imperial War Museums, https://www.iwm.org.uk/history/12-things-you-didnt-know-about-women-in-the-first-world-war

14 'Camera interview – the runner', British Pathé, 12 April, 1927

15 'Women in sport', *The Illustrated Sporting and Dramatic News*, 16 October, 1926

16 'Woman runs 20 miles'; 'The marathon girl', *Westminster Gazette*, 4 October, 1926

17 *All Sports Weekly*, 16 October, 1926, quoted in 'The forgotten first lady: Rediscovering Violet Piercy, marathon pioneer', Peter Lovesey, PlayingPasts.co.uk, 2020, 2021

18 'No road racing for women', *Daily Mirror*, 22 May, 1928

19 'Points from talks broadcast', *Essex Newsman*, 16 October, 1926

20 'Mary had a little lamb', British Pathé newsreel, 25 December 1930

21 'Camera interview – the runner', British Pathé newsreel, 12 April 1927

22 '"How to be slim" – woman runs 10 miles in 85 minutes', *Westminster Gazette*, 25 July, 1927

23 'Nice girls are best athletes', *Greenfield Daily Reporter*, Greenfield, Indiana, 13 July, 1928

24 *Progression of World Athletics Records*, World Athletics Heritage, 2024

25 'Up and up and round and round: Giddy limits', *Reynolds's Illustrated News*, 31 March, 1935
26 'First women's road relay', *News Chronicle*, 11 November, 1935
27 'Women athletes' problem', *Grimsby Evening Telegraph*, 25 October, 1934
28 'Athletic review 1947 – post-war running', Katie Holmes, June 2021, https://runyoung50.co.uk/athletic-review/
29 Interview with Liz Joyce, December 2020; 'How women's athletics has changed – Liz Joyce', Maggie Cooper, *The E=MC² of Running* podcast, 1 February, 2021

CHAPTER 3 DALE GREIG – MUCH MORE THAN A FOOTNOTE

1 Dale Greig quoted in 'Too cold for soccer – but not the girls', Sydney Hulls, *Daily Express*, 21 February, 1966
2 'Dale completes tough weekend', *Southern Evening Echo*, 12 March, 1963
3 'Geoff Winchester wins IOW marathon', Sam Ferris, *Athletics Weekly*, 6 June, 1964
4 Handwritten note of Dale's mile splits recorded by Bob Beggs, Dale Greig's collection; 'Dale–Marathon girl no 1', *Sunday Express*, 24 May, 1964
5 Headlines from *Daily Express*, *Western Daily Press* and *Bristol Evening Post*, 25 May, 1964
6 'Sportlight', John Bromley, *Daily Mirror*, 25 May 1964
7 'Dale's run has men in a spin', Harry Langton, *Daily Express*, 25 May 1964
8 'Secretary Dale Greig keeps up with the best of the men', *Paisley and Renfrewshire Gazette*, 26 June, 1964
9 'The sporting kind, Dale fights 4-mile limit', John Pirie, *Daily Record*, 8 August, 1964
10 'Dale the incredible', *Paisley Pictorial*, 28 May, 1964
11 '*The Neilsonian* – attractive centenary number', *Renfrewshire Gazette*, 19 July, 1952
12 'Women's Notes', Dale Greig, *The Scots Athlete*, June 1958
13 Ibid.
14 Interview with Malcolm Ross, 25th July 2020
15 'Dale Greig: The go-it-alone girl', Jim Logan, *Athletics Weekly*, 7 April, 1973

16 'Pat dreamed of a club for girl harriers – now it is a reality', *Greenock Telegraph*, 1 December, 1960
17 'Patricia A. McCluskey', 'Women's A-Z MacCallum to McQueen', Scottish Distance Running History website, http://www.scottishdistancerunninghistory.scot/womens-a-z-maccallum-mcqueen/
18 'Miss Greig retains her title', *The Scotsman*, 11 March, 1968
19 Letter from Dale Greig to Mrs J. G. Brown, Honorary Secretary, SWAAA, 28 March 1960, Dale Greig's collection
20 'Scottish Women's AAA – notes by Helen Wilkie (Hon. Secretary)', *The Scots Athlete*, May 1954
21 Minutes of the SWAAA Annual General Meeting held on 4 November, 1961, National Records of Scotland
22 'Too cold for soccer – but not the girls', Sydney Hulls, *Daily Express*, 21 February, 1966
23 '"Amazons" in the blizzard', Daily Record, 21 February, 1966
24 *First Ladies of Running*, Amby Burfoot, Rodale, 2016
25 'George and Margaret Lindsay', Scottish Distance Running History, 28 May, 2020, http://www.scottishdistancerunninghistory.scot/george-and-margaret-lindsay/
26 *Marathonlauf: Frauen – Geborene Marathonläuferinnen*, Karl Lennartz, Verlag Werbung UM Sport, 2007
27 *Ibid.*
28 *Ibid.*
29 'Athletics history by Scots girl', *The Scotsman*, 25 May, 1964
30 Interview with Doreen Stewart, 8 August, 2025
31 'Marathon competitor Dale in the running for the top honours', *Paisley Daily Express*, 5 July, 1971; 'Kinlochleven Games', *Inverness Courier*, 8 July, 1969
32 'Scots lass celebrates in style!', *Southern Evening Echo*, 17 May, 1971
33 'Dale Greig: Archive selection', Scottish Distance Running History website, http://www.scottishdistancerunninghistory.scot/dale-greig-archive-selection/
34 'Tough test for invicta', Ian Macmillan, *Maidstone Telegraph*, 3 September, 1971
35 *Voices from the Hills: Pioneering Women Fell and Mountain Runners*, Steve Chilton, Sandstone Press, 2023
36 '174 men – and one girl – in gruelling battle of the Ben', *Aberdeen Press and Journal*, 6 September, 1971

37 *Voices from the Hills: Pioneering Women Fell and Mountain Runners*, Steve Chilton, Sandstone Press, 2023
38 'Dale Greig: The go-it-alone girl', Jim Logan, *Athletics Weekly*, 7 April, 1973
39 'The London to Brighton Race', Bill Brown, Road Runners Club newsletter, January 1973
40 'Brighton run by woman', *Liverpool Daily Post*, 2 October, 1972
41 'Girls do 50 miles in sponsored run', *Greenock Telegraph*, 5 May, 1972
42 *Scottish Marathon Club Magazine*, August 1978
43 *Athletics in Scotland*, race report via Colin Youngson
44 Aileen Drummond, Scottish Distance Running History website, http://www.scottishdistancerunninghistory.scot/aileen-drummond/
45 IGÄL – Interessengemeinschaft Älterer Langstreckenläufer
46 'Scottish Veteran Harriers Club: From 1970–1992 – then celebrating 50 years in 2020', Scottish Distance Running History, http://www.scottishdistancerunninghistory.scot/scottish-veteran-harriers-club-from-1970-1992-then-celebrating-50-years-in-2020/
47 The World Association of Veteran Athletes newsletter, 2 December, 1980
48 'Aileen Drummond', Scottish Distance Running History website, http://www.scottishdistancerunninghistory.scot/aileen-drummond/
49 'McColgan's debt to a marathon pioneer', *The Herald*, 25 April, 1998
50 Interview with Rosemary Kidd and Niki Kidd, 7 July, 2023
51 'Dale Greig', Scottish Distance Running History website, http://www.scottishdistancerunninghistory.scot/dale-greig/
52 'Palm Gunstone', Scottish Distance Running History website, 28 May 2020, http://www.scottishdistancerunninghistory.scot/palm-gunstone/

CHAPTER 4 OUT ON THEIR OWN

1 Interview with Bridget Cushen, September 2022
2 Ibid.
3 Lauriston Runners Club website, https://www.lauristonrunners.club/history/
4 'Tokyo is full circle', Bridget Cushen, *Athletics Weekly*, 12 September, 2019

5 'Marathon chat', *Sunday Independent* (Dublin), 9 December, 1973
6 'A victory to inspire the rest', John Rodda, *Guardian*, 29 October, 1973
7 'Bridget runs 26 miles to keep up with men', Sydney Hulls, *Daily Express*, 29 October, 1973
8 'Bridget Cushen … wondering what all the fuss is about', Walter Bartleman, *Evening Standard*, 29 October, 1973
9 'Rulebreakers', Katie Holmes, *Women's Running*, December 2022
10 'Irish suffragette Maeve Kyle', *Athletics Weekly*, 5 August, 2016
11 'The federal government takes on physical fitness', John F Kennedy Library and Museum website, https://www.jfklibrary.org/learn/about-jfk/jfk-in-history/physical-fitness
12 'Marchers beat Kennedy limit', *Nottingham Guardian*, 25 February, 1963; 'Hundreds fall out on long, long walk', *Daily Herald*, 25 February, 1963
13 *A Century of Women*, Sheila Rowbotham, Penguin Books, 1997
14 *Ladies and Lords: A History of Women's Cricket in Britain*, Rafaelle Nicholson, Peter Lang Ltd, 2019
15 *Ladies and Lords: A History of Women's Cricket in Britain*, Rafaelle Nicholson, Peter Lang Ltd, 2019
16 'Credit card sexism: The woman who couldn't buy a moped', Claire Bates, 6 July, 2016, https://www.bbc.co.uk/news/magazine-36662872
17 'World stadia championships results and history', World Masters Athletics website, https://world-masters-athletics.org/world-championships-stadia-history/
18 *Veteran Athletics*, newspaper of the British Athletics Federation, October/November 1987; 'Tokyo is full circle', Bridget Cushen, *Athletics Weekly*, 12 September, 2019
19 'A "token gesture" in World Athletics Governance? The IAAF Women's Committee under Ilse Bechthold, 1990–2005', Michele Krech, Jörg Krieger and Lindsay Parks Pieper, *Sport in Society*, 26:5 (2023)
20 'Christine joins in', *Staffordshire Evening Sentinel*, 11 March, 1974; 'Two hours broken in Chase 21', *Athletics Weekly*, 30 March, 1974
21 *Staffordshire Evening Sentinel*, 25 March, 1974
22 Interview with Christine Kilkenny (née Readdy), November 2024

23 'Women are no strangers to the marathon', Cliff Temple, *Athletics Weekly*, 3 February, 1973
24 'We sometimes think we have problems', Dave Dilnott, *Athletic Review*, November 1977
25 Interview with Dr Joan Ullyot by Amy Begley, 2013, *Starting Line 1928* podcast, 16 January, 2025, https://www.startingline1928.com/pioneerstories/dr-joan-ullyot
26 Email correspondence with Margaret Thompson, October 2020
27 *British Marathon Running Legends of the 1980s*, Gabrielle Collison, self-published, 2012
28 *The American Marathon*, Pamela Cooper, Syracuse University Press, 1998
29 *Marathonlauf, Frauen – Geborene Marathonläuferinnen*, Karl Lennartz, Verlag Werbung UM Sport, 2007.
30 *Veteris*, January 1975
31 Race results, Deutsche Ultramarathon Vereinigung e.V., https://statistik.d-u-v.org/eventdetail.php?event=2008
32 Eva-Maria Westphal race results, Deutsche Ultramarathon Vereinigung e.V, https://statistik.d-u-v.org/getresultperson.php?runner=30200
33 'Two Bridges', Scottish Distance Running History, http://www.scottishdistancerunninghistory.scot/two-bridges/
34 'Charlie Trayer – 1980s ultrarunning legend', Ultrarunning History, https://ultrarunninghistory.com/charlie-trayer/
35 'The Two Bridges Race', Don Turner, Road Runners Club newsletter, January 1975

CHAPTER 5 MAKING IT OFFICIAL

1 'Marathon held no terrors for these women', *Huddersfield Daily Examiner*, 1 December, 1975
2 'Girl runner leads the way', *Newcastle Journal*, 2 January, 1975
3 Interview with Avril Lewis, November 2024
4 'Over 900 took part in tenth marathon walk', *Surrey Advertiser*, 15 July, 1968
5 'Four children - THEN Alison Blake took up athletics!', Brian Mitchell, *Athletics Weekly*, 10 May, 1975
6 Interview with Adele and David Cross, 21 July, 2022
7 'Women join race for equality', *Kent and Sussex Courier*, 14 March, 1975

8 'Let women run longer distances', Brian Mitchell, *Athletics Weekly*, 5 April, 1975

9 Interview with Jeanne Coker for the Metros Hall of Fame provided by Metros Running Club, April 2025

10 'Longwood pip Holmfirth for team prize', *Huddersfield Daily Examiner*, 21 April, 1975

11 *'Tripping Daintily into the Arena': A Social History of English Women's Athletics 1921 to 1960*, Lynne Robinson, PhD thesis, University of Warwick, September 1996

12 Quoted in 'Marea Hartman – wisdom on the track', Katie Holmes, https://runyoung50.co.uk/marea-hartman/

13 'Vera Searle', The Athletics Museum, https://theathleticsmuseum.org.uk/vera-searle-nee-palmer-obe-1901-1998/

14 'Distance running for women', Minutes of Executive Meeting held on 27 April 1975, Women's Cross Country and Race Walking Association

15 'Women's road running rules', RFJ Scruton, *Athletics Weekly*, 3 April, 1976

16 'Celebrating the anniversary of the first London Marathon', Alison Hamlett, London Marathon Events website, March 2025 https://www.londonmarathonevents.co.uk/london-marathon/article/celebrating-anniversary-first-london-marathon

17 'About SheRACES', https://www.sheraces.com/about

18 'Good wins for Kenyon and Blake', *Athletics Weekly*, 23 August, 1975

19 Interview with Angela Briscoe, 5 March, 2025

20 'Brought up as an athlete', Dave Cocksedge, *Athletics Weekly*, 13 February, 1971

21 'Childbearing for women born in different years, England and Wales: 2020', Office for National Statistics, 27 January, 2022

22 'Ward Keeps Road Crown', Fred Hill, *Western Daily Press*, 20 April, 1976

23 'News from Yorkshire', Granville Beckett, *Athletics Weekly*, 17 May, 1975

24 Interview with Christine Kilkenny (née Readdy), 14 November, 2024

25 'Tagg from Wright in Barnsley "6"', Keith Lodge, *Athletics Weekly*, 13 September, 1975

26 'Christine logs double first for City AC', Tom Spencer, *Staffordshire Evening Sentinel*, 16 August, 1975
27 'Chelmsford AC Women's seven mile road race', *Athletics Weekly*, 1 November, 1975
28 Masters and Maidens Marathon, souvenir programme and race report, 1975
29 Interview with Miriam and David Rosen, 28 January, 2025
30 'Ian Thompson', Vivien Thomas, *Marathon and Distance Runner*, July/August 1:3 (1982)
31 Email interview with Margaret Thompson, 30 October, 2020
32 'Magic or pure hell? What prompts Britain's top marathoners', *Stride Out*, 1, 1979
33 *The Observer*, 30 November, 1975
34 'The 1975 marathon that "opened it up for the ladies"', Simon Thake, BBC News, 28 December, 2025, https://www.bbc.co.uk/news/articles/czone92x8ggo
35 'Some vital statistics', *Barnsley Chronicle*, 5 December, 1975, quoted in Barnsley Marathon 1975, https://www.barnsleyac.co.uk/about-the-club/history/
36 'The 1975 marathon that "opened it up for the ladies"', Simon Thake, BBC News, 28 December, 2025
37 'Marathon first may bring top-level rap', Granville Beckett, *Huddersfield Daily Examiner*, 6 December, 1975
38 Interview with Christine Kilkenny, 14 November, 2024
39 'Protest likely after world best', *Huddersfield Daily Examiner*, 12 May, 1975
40 'Plain wins "Hogs Back"', *Athletics Weekly*, 17 January, 1976

CHAPTER 6 WOMEN GO THE DISTANCE

1 Interview with Margaret Lockley, November 2024
2 'Christine is a cracker!', *Daily Mirror*, 17 April, 1976
3 'Magic or pure hell? What prompts Britain's top marathoners', *Stride Out*, 1, 1979
4 'Muddy Milford 21', *Athletics Weekly*, 10 April, 1976
5 Interview with Christine Kilkenny (née Readdy), 14 November, 2024
6 'Marathon woman', Angela Cobbinah, 12 March, 2017, https://angelacobbinah.wordpress.com/2017/03/12/marathon-woman/

7 'Three British girls break three hours for marathon', David Billington, *Athletics Weekly*, 1 May, 1976; 'Feltham Athletic Club's ladies' marathon', Harold Lee, Road Runners Club newsletter, August 1976
8 'Christine is a cracker!', *Daily Mirror*, 17 April, 1976
9 'Magic or pure hell? What prompts Britain's top marathoners', *Stride Out*, 1, 1979
10 Information provided by Andy Cairns from an interview with Lyn Billington
11 *Athletics Weekly*, 28 February, 1976
12 'Talking shop: Let women run on equal terms with men', Lyn Billington, *Jogging*, August 1979
13 'Francis leads victory chase', *Western Daily Press*, 13 June, 1977
14 'Offa's Dyke 15', *RACE*, September 1978
15 'More incentive now for British girls', Cliff Temple, *Athletics Weekly*, 31 March, 1979
16 *Ibid.*
17 Road Runners Club newsletter, January 1979
18 'More incentive now for British girls', Cliff Temple, *Athletics Weekly*, 31 March, 1979
19 'Egg race still on the menu', letter from Ken Fiddler, *Athletics Weekly*, 26 March, 1977
20 *The Official History of the WAAA, 1922–2012*, Mel Watman, SportsBooks Limited, 2012
21 'Where are they now?: Dorothy Hyman', Jon Culley, *The Independent*, 23 August, 1994
22 'Margaret Lockley wins inaugural marathon title', Cliff Temple, *Athletics Weekly*, 3 June, 1978; author interview with Margaret Lockley
23 'More incentive now for British girls', Cliff Temple, *Athletics Weekly*, 31 March, 1979
24 'Woman fighting off the seconds', Lynne Edmunds, *Daily Telegraph*, 21 October, 1978
25 'More incentive now for British girls', Cliff Temple, *Athletics Weekly*, 31 March, 1979
26 'Don Shelley appointed as national marathon organiser', Vince Regan, *RACE*, February 1979.
27 Interviews with Margaret Lockley, 1 November, 2024, and Caroline Rodgers, 10 November, 2024

28 'Marathon moan for ace Lyn', *Sunday Mirror*, 4 March, 1979
29 'Talking shop: Let women run on equal terms with men', Lyn Billington, *Jogging*, August 1979
30 Road Runners Club newsletter, August 1978
31 AGM report, Road Runners Club newsletter, August 1980
32 *A Long Time Coming: Running through the women's marathon revolution*, Jacqueline Hansen, self-published, 2016
33 'Angela Briscoe keeps on running', *Athletic Review*, January 1978
34 Gillian Castka (née Burley), by email, January 2026
35 Interview on the *Marathon Talk* podcast, February 2014
36 *RACE*, January 1978
37 'More incentive now for British girls', Cliff Temple, *Athletics Weekly*, 31 March, 1979
38 'The Joyce Smith story (part 2)', Mel Watman, *Athletics Weekly*, 6 December, 1980
39 'Running a family', *Jogging*, May 1979
40 'The Joyce Smith story (part 3)', Mel Watman, *Athletics Weekly*, 13 December 1980
41 'Report of the Honorary Secretary, 1978–79', Women's Amateur Athletic Association archive
42 Rankings data from runbritainrankings.com website as of 4 October, 2025
43 Interview with Joyce Smith, *Marathon Talk* podcast, February 2014

CHAPTER 7 JOGGING HITS BRITAIN

1 Letter from Mrs E Blake, *Jogging*, September 1979
2 'Yes, it was fun', Mel Watman, *Athletics Weekly*, 14 October, 1978
3 Interview with Miriam and David Rosen, 28 January, 2025
4 'How I beat Foster and still came "last"', Charles Lambert, *Liverpool Echo*, 4 October 1978
5 'The history of a habit: Jogging as a palliative to sedentariness in 1960s America', Alan Latham, *Cultural Geographies*, 22:1 (2015)
6 *Running, Identity and Meaning, The Pursuit of Distinction Through Sport*, Neil Baxter, Emerald Publishing, 2021
7 *A Contemporary History of Women's sport, Part One, Sporting Women, 1850–1960*, Jean Williams, Routledge, 2014
8 'Jogging club at Stone', *Staffordshire Evening Sentinel*, 13 August, 1971

9 'Jogging along ... on the crest of a craze', Christopher Ward, *Daily Mirror*, 10 January, 1975

10 'Fit meets flab', *Newcastle Evening Chronicle*, 23 February, 1975

11 '600 turn out for fun run', *Gateshead Post*, 3 November, 1977

12 'Jog along with Big Bren in the "fun run"', *Gateshead Post*, 13 September, 1977

13 Articles mentioning 'jogging' in the online British Newspaper Archive: 637 in 1977 and 2060 in 1978, 2 April, 2025

14 'What I look for in a running shoe ...", *Jogging*, October 1979

15 Profile: Lydia Kirk, Andy Etchells, *Jogging*, September 1979

16 Interview with Lydia Gould (née Kirk), 23 January, 2025

17 *Jogging Your Way to Health and Fitness*, James Hewitt, 1978, quoted in 'Fun, running and the jogging boom in Britain, 1970s – 1980s', Alex Mold, *Sport in History*, 44:4 (2024)

18 Profile: Stone Jogging Club, *Jogging*, May 1979

19 'Shoe supplement', *RACE*, September 1978

20 'A brief history of the sports bra', Kelly Bastone, *Runner's World*, 30 August, 2017, https://www.runnersworld.com/runners-stories/a20860634/a-brief-history-of-the-sports-bra/

21 'Back to your bras', *Liverpool Echo*, 16 March, 1978

22 'Berlei pioneers a top-selling sports bra', Melanie Doel, *Gwent Gazette*, 30 August, 1979; 'Taking wobble out of jogging', Lesley Ebbetts and Ronald Bedford, *Daily Mirror*, 26 February, 1979

23 'Are you in the running?', *Jackie*, 12 May, 1979

24 *Jogging for Fitness and Pleasure*, Cliff Temple, World's Work Ltd in conjunction with the *Sunday Times*, 1977

25 *Women in Britain Since 1945*, Jane Lewis, Blackwell, 1992

26 'Action replay – looking at women in sport', Jennifer Hargreaves, in *Feminist Action*, edited by Joy Holland, Battle Axe Books, 1984

27 'A brief history of Britain's racist sitcoms', Angus Harrison, 2017, https://www.vice.com/en/article/all-your-favourite-old-british-sitcoms-are-racist-as-hell/

28 'Ready, steady, GO!', Rosalind Renshaw, *Reading Evening Post*, 3 April, 1978

29 'The socio-technical history of manual sport wheelchair devices', Samuel Brady, PhD thesis, University of Glasgow, 2024

30 *Wheelchairs, Perjury and the London Marathon*, Tim Marshall, Clink Street Publishing, 2017

CHAPTER 8 LESLIE WATSON – QUEEN OF THE ROADS

1 Interview with Jill Danskin, February 2025
2 'Questions and answers – Leslie Watson', *SMC Magazine*, July 1979
3 'A lovely way to travel', Christopher Brasher, *The Observer*, 14 December, 1980
4 It has not been possible to track down any of the letters Leslie received. Lawrence Brampton thought the letter was from Marea Hartman, Honorary Secretary of the WAAA, but it may have come from the Women's Cross Country and Race Walking Association, which was affiliated to the WAAA and was the women's governing body for road racing.
5 'Leslie's streets ahead', Sue Hercombe, *The Journal* (Newcastle), 13 December, 1982
6 'Smith "knocked up" – Scots doctor gets married at Gretna', *Edinburgh Evening News*, 18 September, 1937
7 'Who's who in British athletics – Leslie Watson', *Athletics Weekly*, 13 June, 1981
8 'A life in the day of Leslie Watson', Geoffrey Cannon, *The Times*, 9 May, 1982
9 'A lovely way to travel', Christopher Brasher, *The Observer*, 14 December, 1980
10 'Questions and answers – Leslie Watson', *SMC Magazine*, July 1979
11 'Who's who in British athletics – Leslie Watson', *Athletics Weekly*, 13 June, 1981
12 Interview with Jill Danksin, October 2024
13 'The lady is a 26-mile tramper', David Emery, *Daily Express*, 2 November, 1977
14 'Questions & Answers - Leslie Watson', *SMC Magazine*, July 1979
15 'Leslie Watson – queen of the roads', Katie Holmes, RunYoung50, 10 December 2022, https://runyoung50.co.uk/leslie-watson-queen-of-the-marathon/
16 *A Century of Women*, Sheila Rowbotham, 1997 (1977 figure)
17 Interview with Caroline Rodgers, November 2024
18 'Questions and answers – Leslie Watson', *SMC Magazine*, July 1979
19 'The longest running show on the road', Tony Barnes, *Jogging*, December 1979
20 AGM report, Road Runners Club Newsletter, August 1980

21 'Ruth Anderson - Pioneer Ultrarunner', Ultrarunning History website, 2 October 2019, https://ultrarunninghistory.com/ruth-anderson/
22 Race results, *RACE/Athletes World*, September 1979
23 International Runners' Committee, Newsletter 1, February 1980; 'Two leading ladies', Road Runners Club newsletter, January 1979
24 'Beauty on the Brighton Run', James Langton, *Shepherd's Bush Gazette and Post*, 4 October, 1979.
25 *Athletics Weekly*, 8 December 1979
26 'Ruth Anderson – pioneer ultrarunner', https://ultrarunninghistory.com/ruth-anderson
27 Email from Colin Youngson, August 2025
28 'Watson vs. Schwam: A look back', Nick Marshall, *Ultrarunning*, October 1981
29 'The RRC 50 mile track race Copthall', Keith Walker, Road Runners Club Newsletter, August 1983
30 'The Loch Rannoch Marathon', Ian Graves, *SMC Magazine*, October 1982
31 'The lady is a 26-mile tramper', David Emery, *Daily Express*, 2 November, 1977
32 Interview with Lawrence Brampton, June 2024
33 'Questions and Answers – Leslie Watson', *SMC Magazine*, July 1979
34 'A lovely way to travel', Christopher Brasher, *The Observer*, 14 December, 1980
35 'Bust-up over a racy vest', John Peacock, *Daily Record*, 1 March, 1982
36 'Lightning hits three women', *Daily Record*, 22 June, 1966
37 'Age of no concern to Watson', John Goodbody – an article in Leslie Watson's scrapbook, probably from *The Times* or *Sunday Times*
38 'Marathon held no terrors for these women', *Huddersfield Daily Examiner*, 1 December, 1975
39 'Who's who in British athletics – Leslie Watson', *Athletics Weekly*, 13 June, 1981
40 Vets Column, Sylvester Stein, *Running*, July 1985
41 Mandy Mullan, interview with Budgie Mullan and Mandy Mullan, November 2024

CHAPTER 9 THE MARATHON BOOM

1 Interview with Caroline Rodgers, November 2024
2 'When I'm running, said the long-distance cosmetics executive and philosopher, I feel I'm part of the leaves, the grass, the sun, and the sky', John Cunningham, the *Guardian*, 1 August, 1980
3 'The Avon International Marathon, a first-hand account', RunYoung50 website, https://runyoung50.co.uk/the-avon-international-london-marathon-a-first-hand-account/
4 *Marathon Woman*, Kathrine Switzer, Da Capo Press, 2009
5 'Avon Marathon points way to Olympic acceptance', Mel Watman, *Athletics Weekly*, 16 August, 1980
6 Interview with Avril Lewis, November 2024
7 Email from Margaret Thompson, October 2020
8 'The first appearance of women-specific running shoes', Retrieved from movinshoes.com website, 17 January 2026, link defunct, June 2026
9 Email from Margaret Thompson, October 2020
10 '1980 Fun Run Diary', *Jogging*, April 1980
11 'People's Marathon an important milestone', Mel Watman, *Athletics Weekly*, 31 May, 1980
12 Interview with Christine Kilkenny (née Readdy), November 2024
13 'John Wild smashes record in Milford 21', Lawrence Kilkenny, *Athletics Weekly*, 25 April, 1981
14 *Everybody Wants to Rule the World: Britain, Sport and the 1980s*, Roger Domeneghetti, Yellow Jersey, 2023
15 'Marathon girls to run on water?', *Athletics Weekly*, 27 February, 1982
16 Jean Lochhead, by email, August 2025
17 'Caroline in Spain', *Athletics Weekly*, 5 September, 1981
18 Interview with Caroline Rodgers, August 2025
19 Interview with Caroline Rodgers, November 2024
20 Information supplied by Alex Jackson, husband of the late Jen Neligan
21 Gillian Castka (née Burley), by email, January 2026
22 Mike Bateman, by email, August 2025
23 'Racing away from the men', *Newcastle Journal*, 25 February, 1980
24 'Not a fun run', Andy Gibb, *Athletics Weekly*, 25 April 1981

25 'An open letter to Andy Gibb', Lyn Billington, *Athletics Weekly*, 9 May, 1981
26 'Andy Gibb replies', Andy Gibb, *Athletics Weekly*, 23 May, 1981
27 Hillingdon AC website, https://hillingdonac.co.uk/hillingdon-20-2025/
28 *Running – The Women's Handbook*, Liz Sloan and Ann Kramer, Pandora Press, London, 1985
29 Interview with Jill Danskin, October 2024
30 'Be fair to women', Jill Danksin, *Athletics Weekly*, 8 December, 1984
31 'Prizes for women vets', Janet Thompson, *Athletics Weekly*, 12 January, 1985
32 Interview with Gillian Castka (née Burley), January 2026
33 'Sexist abuse', Diana Cook, *Running*, July/August 1981
34 Untitled letter, Margaret Dalton, *Running*, September/October 1981
35 'The abuse of women runners: Perceptions, fears and experiences – briefing report', Dr Caroline Miles, Professor Rose Broad, Meg Oldham, University of Manchester, March 2024
36 'Friendly runners, please', Linda Rimmer, *Running*, May/June 1981
37 Interview with Ali Turnbull, December 2024; 'The Sisters Project', *Running*, December 1983
38 *Women and Running in 1980s Britain*, Tracey Loughran, University of Essex, https://runbundle.com/articles/women-running-1980s-britain
39 'Hutton dominates in '84', Fraser Clyne, *Running Review*, March 1985
40 'Historic first at 2024 TCS London Marathon', https://www.londonmarathonevents.co.uk/london-marathon/article/historic-first-wheelchair-race-prize-fund
41 *Wheelchairs, Perjury and the London Marathon*, Tim Marshall, Clink Street Publishing, 2017
42 'Paralympics archive: The marathon debate (1983)', *Channel 4 News*, https://www.channel4.com/news/paralympics-archive-the-marathon-debate-1983
43 *Everybody Wants to Rule the World: Britain, Sport and the 1980s*, Roger Domeneghetti, Yellow Jersey, 2023
44 *Running – The Women's Handbook*, Liz Sloan and Ann Kramer, Pandora Press, London, 1985

45 'Denise Smith: The disability sport pioneer who fought back from polio and a car crash', Rebecca Myers, *The Times*, 29 November, 2020

46 Elite wheelchair London Marathon medallists, London Marathon website, https://www.londonmarathonevents.co.uk/london-marathon/elite-wheelchair-london-marathon-medallists

47 Quoted in *Everybody Wants to Rule the World: Britain, Sport and the 1980s*, Roger Domeneghetti, Yellow Jersey, 2023

THE DEBT WE OWE

1 Active Lives Adult Surveys, November 2023 to November 2024, Sport England, https://www.sportengland.org/research-and-data/data/active-lives/active-lives-data-tables#november-2023-24-38806

2 'Gender balance through the parkrun journey', parkrun website, 16 February, 2022, https://blog.parkrun.com/uk/2022/02/16/gender-balance-through-the-parkrun-journey/

3 'About us', Black Girls Do Run UK website, https://www.blackgirlsdorun.co.uk/about-black-girls-do-run; email from Tasha Thompson, February 2026

4 'Breaking into the marathon: Women's distance running as political activism', Jaime Schultz, *Frontiers: A Journal of Women Studies*, 40:2 (2019)

5 *Ultra Women, The Trailblazers Defying Sexism in Sport*, Lily Canter and Emma Wilkinson, Canbury Press, 2025. In their book on female ultra-endurance athletes Lily Canter and Emma Wilkinson describe them as 'The women who have been denied opportunities, but took them anyway.'

ACKNOWLEDGEMENTS

I carried the idea of this book around in my heart and my mind for a few years before it became a formal proposal. I had the title, I'd worked out what the chapters would be, written a short pitch and researched publishers, but I hesitated; I was unsure of myself. The spark that made the difference came when I caught up with Juliet McGrattan at the National Running Show in January 2024. We'd first met in 2018 at the Women in Sport conference, after connecting on social media, and the National Running Show has become an annual meet-up for us. Juliet's two health handbooks for active women had been published by Bloomsbury, one of the publishers on my list. After I told Juliet about my book and why I wanted to write it, she kindly offered to mention it to her editor, Charlotte Croft. Thank you, Juliet, for opening this door for me.

Charlotte expressed an interest in my book idea, and I embarked on a writing adventure which started with a formal proposal, followed by two draft chapters as she guided me through what Bloomsbury were looking for. Thank you, Charlotte, for your enthusiasm and encouragement in the pre-contract stage. I am grateful to Charlotte, Megan Jones and copy editor Lisa Hughes for helping to shape the manuscript in its final stages with many comments and suggestions. And to all the team at Bloomsbury Sport who have worked on the book.

Thank you to athletics photographer Mark Shearman for permission to use some of his pictures of the long-distance pioneers.

To all the runners I interviewed for the book, I thank you for generously giving me your time and sharing your stories with me. Every interview was a pleasure and I have learned so much from you. I salute you for challenging women's exclusion from long-distance running and opening it up for all the runners who have followed in your footsteps, including me.

Angela Briscoe (née Lovell)
Gillian Castka (née Burley)
Adele Cross (née Brignall)
Bridget Cushen
Jill Danskin
Lydia Gould (née Kirk)
Palm Gunstone (née Lindsay)
Liz Joyce (née Brade-Birks)
Christine Kilkenny (née Readdy)
Avril Lewis (née Jones)
Jean Lochhead
Margaret Lockley (née Ashcroft)
Caroline Rodgers
Miriam Rosen (née Bescoby)
Doreen Stewart (née King)
Margaret Thompson (née Tunstall)

Thank you also to two other pioneers, Sandra Brown and Kathy Crilley, who also shared their stories with me. Although I haven't been able to include them in the book, they have helped to shape its narrative.

To Dale Greig's relatives, Rosemary and Niki Kidd, thank you for sharing your memories of Dale and showing me her archive. And thank you to Malcolm Ross who, as a teenager, first got to know Dale when she ran on the Isle of Wight. Thank you to Lawrence Brampton, close friend of Leslie Watson, Bernard (Budgie) Mullan, partner of Leslie, and his daughter, Mandy for sharing their memories of her with me. Thank you, Andy Etchells and Ali Turnbull, for telling me about *Jogging* magazine (later *Running*).

Two organisations have played a part in encouraging me to see myself as a researcher and a historian. Receiving an Independent Researcher Fellowship grant from the Women's History Network in 2020 for my research into Dale Greig instilled a confidence in me that what I was doing was valued by others. Members of the British Society of Sports History welcomed me as an independent researcher when I attended the society's first post-pandemic conference in 2021. The society's supportive, collegiate approach has helped me to develop as a sports historian and given me the chance to present my work. At the 2021 conference, I met fellow independent researcher and women's football historian, Steve Bolton and we've given each other mutual support since. Thank you, Steve, for always being one of the first people to congratulate me on small successes. Thank you also to Raf Nicholson and Fiona Skillen for conversations about the books we are writing which have helped to clarify my thoughts and given me fresh insights. Writing a book can be a lonely pursuit. Attending the Mslexia and Women's History Network online write-ins helped me feel part of a supportive community of women writers.

Thank you to the people and organisations who made connections to runners for me including Steve Chilton, author of a book about pioneering women fell and mountain runners, *Voices from the Hills*, David Griffiths who provides coverage of Isle of Man athletics via the Facebook page manxathletics.com, Job King and the Road Runners Club, Midland Masters AC, Metros Running Club, Ryde Harriers and Tonbridge AC.

Colin Youngson, a contributor to the Scottish Distance Running History website, has helped me in more ways than I can list here, including introducing me to Rosemary and Niki Kidd, sharing his own knowledge of Scottish running, and even sending me athletics magazines when I was in the early stages of building my collection. Thank you, Colin. The Scottish Distance Running History is encyclopaedic in its scope and I am grateful to Brian McAusland, its creator, for recording athletics history which might otherwise have been lost. The work of Arnold Black, former historian at Scottish Athletics, has been another valuable resource.

There are so many people who have helped me that I am sure to miss some out of this list. I'm grateful to fellow authors writing books about running, Andy Cairns, James Renshaw and Jacqueline Hansen, for providing support and information. David Rosen for sending me programmes and results for the Masters and Maidens Marathon. Frances and Fred Mudway for the results of the Avon London International Women's Marathon. Members of the Facebook groups, I Was or Am a Runner and Old Running Results and Pictures, for answering my questions about running in the 1970s and 80s. Fellow Holme Pierrepont Running Club member and friend Bernard Jarvis for many chats about running history during our runs together. David Clark, Frank Hilton Brooks, and Fiona and Julia Butcher, the daughters of the late Ted Butcher, for donating significant collections of athletics and running magazines. Oscar Bem of the Marathon Shoe History website for help with researching women's shoes in the 1970s. Maud Hodson of RunEqual for an overview of the history of the campaign and Tasha Thompson and Sophie Power for their feedback. Thank you to you all.

The first reviewer of so much of my writing ever since I started my website in 2014, my sister Judith Sutherland – thank you for reading early versions of several of the chapters of this book and for all your loving support over the whole long process of researching and writing it.

To all the women I interviewed who read chapters and to my other reviewers, Andy Cairns, Lynne Duval (née Robinson), Linda Evans, Rosemary Kidd, Isabelle Paterson, Helen Sutherland, Peter Radford and Fiona Skillen.

A special thank you to my aunt, Elspeth Stewart, who has encouraged me throughout, always reminding me that this idea had to become a book she can hold in her hands.

This book is dedicated to my mum and dad who gave me enjoyment of walks in the hills, camping and time outdoors, an interest in history, art and reading and, most of all, love. Mum died shortly after I'd submitted my proposal to Bloomsbury. I miss her every day. Dad, you have always been a role model for keeping fit and active and I hope I will be fit enough to follow your example and climb a Scottish mountain on my 80th birthday.

And finally, to my partner Simon, who, for more than two years, has vicariously experienced the day-to-day ups and downs of writing a book while also managing our house move and all the tasks to get our new house the way we wanted it. Thank you, Simon, for your love, your patience and for the many ways in which you've supported me throughout.

INDEX